# CROSSOVERS

# CROSSOVERS

## ANTI-ZIONISM & ANTI-SEMITISM

## SHLOMO SHARAN
## DAVID BUKAY

Routledge
Taylor & Francis Group

LONDON AND NEW YORK

First published 2010 by Transaction Publishers

2 Park Square, Milton Park, Abingdon, Oxfordshire OX14 4RN
711 Third Avenue, New York, NY 10017

*Routledge is an imprint of the Taylor & Francis Group, an informa business*

First issued in paperback 2017

Library of Congress Catalog Number: 2010003977

Library of Congress Cataloging-in-Publication Data

Sharan, Shlomo, 1932-
    Anti-Zionism and Anti-Semitism / Shlomo Sharan and David Bukay.
       p. cm.
    ISBN 978-1-4128-1155-2 (alk. paper)
      1. Zionism. 2. Jewish nationalism. 3. Antisemitism. 4. Jews--Attitudes 5. Palestinians--Attitudes. I. Bukay, David. II. Title.

DS149.S49719 2010
  320.54095694--dc22

                                2010003977

ISBN 13: 978-1-4128-1155-2 (hbk)
ISBN 13: 978-1-138-50873-6 (pbk)

# Contents

# Introduction

In January 2009, Israel fought a three-week war in the Gaza Strip against Hamas terrorists in Operation Cast Lead. Hamas is a singularly violent group that, like Hezbollah and al-Qaeda, poses an enormous threat to Israel, Egypt, Jordan, and to the Western world. Its Iranian-supported counterpart to the north of Israel is the Hezbollah terrorist army whose goals are directed at killing Jews in Israel. These two terrorist organizations testify to the violent anti-Israel environment in which this nation must function and survive. The Palestinian Arabs border the southern part of Israel, while the Iranian terrorists operate from, and in, Lebanon on its northern border. The late Yehoshafat Harkavi called the nature of these terrorist organizations "politicide"—the application of genocide to the entire political entity of the State of Israel.

Operation Cast Lead was a classic military operation where Israel wins the battle but loses the war due to its failure to conduct proper negotiations. The failure of Israel's negotiation stems in part from international pressures directed at them instead of it being directed at Hamas or Iran who are responsible for this conflict. The political failure was due to internal pressure emanating from Israel's own communications networks. For years Israel did not provide protection for its citizens, as individuals or as a collective. Currently Israel has agreed to a kind of cease-fire that permits Hamas to continue to exist and, in fact although perhaps not in theory, to enjoy international recognition and legitimization. It is as if to say that "nothing more can be done."

Every nation has its own minority groups, whether they be national, religious, or ethnic groups. Large immigrant countries such as the United States, France, England, or Australia, emphasize the national identity and the unique national symbols. None of them have changed their national anthem, flag, institutions, values, or its Independence Day in the wake of the waves of immigrants who reached their shores. Not a single change was introduced by those countries to their laws relevant to individuals seeking American citizenship, or in the language to which they swear allegiance. On the flags of England, Switzerland, and most Scandinavian countries there is a cross, a religious symbol. Would those countries respond positively to a suggestion (let us say by an Oxford or Cambridge professor, or from the University of Uppsala, or by representatives of specific minority groups) to change the national flag?

The State of Israel is like a burning log that miraculously escaped the bonfires of the Nazis. There is one Jewish State in the world, and it may not conduct experiments with its existence in order to test if it can survive or not, when it confronts the terrible threats to its life. Those dangers have no parallel in world history. Israel's anti-Zionists have learned nothing from it.

Israel's leaders can be easily misled by these clichés. We must remind ourselves constantly of the intelligent insights gained by Barbara Tuchman, one of the best world historians, in her masterful book *The March of Folly*. The effect that stubborn and blind Folly, typically accompanied by many leaders' hermetically sealed minds, have led nations and states to national disaster. (Tuchman cited the case of French leaders before the onset of World War I, as well as other stark examples, such as Hindenburg and the Weimar Republic). We could also mention the Versailles peace treaty.

Tuchman pointed to three stages in the development of this disastrous condition: (1) a new policy is proposed as an all-encompassing strategy, as a breakthrough that was never tested in practice; (2) a defeat occurs and failures multiply. At that point, wise leaders must call a halt to the application of their policy, examine it and its implications very closely, and, if necessary, change it. Heraclitus said "everything flows" referring not only to the river (Nature) he employed as a metaphor, but in history and human affairs in general. Obviously, Tuchman pointed out that the mind-set of some leaders failed to recall what that ancient Greek taught the world. The events that occurred that demand a change in policy are often interpreted as merely minor occurrences by the frozen minds of leaders. Their mistaken policy could be altered for the better during the process of implementation (as all feed-back mechanisms permit) and thereby avoid the negative consequences toward which they are marching. (3) The last of the three stages comes about, which is the collapse of the nation and the rapid emergence of national tragedies.

Palestinian violence and terror should have served as a wake up call for Israel long ago. But, our anti-Zionists clung to their old ways and continued their March of Folly accompanied by all its classical mental symptoms described by Tuchman. They continue to seek the destruction of the Jewish-Zionist state. Tuchman cited the case of King Philip of Spain who was the most impenetrable monarch of them all and sent the great Spanish Armada in 1588 against the British-Dutch alliance. A storm off the Hebrides Islands decimated the fleet after it was defeated by the British Fleet in the English Channel. Up to the end, Tuchman wrote that Philip clung to the belief that "no defeat could change his unequivocal opinion that his nation was extraordinary."

Israel's leaders did not learn the language employed by the Palestinians for concluding agreements. The term *Takhris al-Ihtilal*, in regard to perpetuating conquests, means that no Palestinian leader will sign an agreement which is not a just peace with honor but means the destruction of Israel. Every Palestinian leader will seek to wipe out the shame of *Takhris al-'Eb*, groveling or surrendering to the dictates of the Israelis, not to accept normalization (*Tatbi*`) which is a recipe for national disaster and elimination of the Palestinian problem. Peace can be a temporary arrangement only and less than a condition of *Tahdi'ah*. At best, when it is supported by Israel's military power, it will be a situation of non-combatancy and a cessation of fire (*Hudnah*).

The religious-historical basis on which the Arab Palestinians are willing to sign some agreement with Israel is the Khudaybiyah Agreement signed by Muhammad with the residents of Mecca in 628. That agreement was intended to be valid for ten years, but Muhammad broke it after only twenty-two months. That led to his victory over the Meccans and to their conversion to Islam. The Jihad war in the name of Allah and the *Shuhadaa'*, the homicide bombers who testify to their faith in Allah, pave the way for war with Israel. The main point is perpetual struggle with Israel until its total elimination because it is a nation of infidels who conquered Muslim territory, and no Muslim territory may be relinquished.

Arafat spoke about that in his May 21, 1994 speech delivered in Johannesburg reported in all of the daily papers in Israel.

I don't see this agreement [with Israel] as more than the agreement signed by our prophet Muhammad with the tribe of the Quraysh. We accept the peace agreement only in order to continue on our way to Jerusalem. Jihad will continue to the destruction of Israel. Jerusalem not only belongs to the Palestinian People, but to the entire Islamic nation (*Ummah*).

That is the prevailing position of the Palestinians to this day, whether they belong to the secular wing called Fatah, or to the religious wing called Hamas. The messianic anti-Zionist Jews turned the Muslim ideas upside down so that Zionism, Judaism, national pride, sovereignty, and patriotism became distinctly negative terms in regard to Israel. On the other hand, those very concepts are just and important in the Palestinian context and deserve to be appreciated, respected, and cultivated. Simultaneously they inserted into their lexicon an entire series of concepts that allegedly express Israel's policies, namely: racism; fascism, war-crimes, slaughter, apartheid, and all other revolting evils known to the world. Poet and novelist Chaim Guri expressed that awareness eloquently when he stated:

> One of the things most difficult for me today is the understanding that the conflict with the Arabs will continue for generations and will be transmitted from father to son, to grandson, to great grandson, and so forth. We didn't understand that in the past … but it became more and more clear with time that we had lived a great mistake…. Oslo was an illusion … and all the other agreements…suddenly we returned to square one of the conflict (Guri, 2001).

Jewish history is an example of how the Jews typically ignored repeated threats and acts of violence against them. That characteristic of the Jews appears to reflect a Messianic belief that lacks a basis in history—that tomorrow will be a better day than today. That belief resisted change even in the face of threats that were obvious and endangered Jewish lives. The poet David Shimoni (Shimonovitz) quoted the Jews who led the Bolshevik Revolution, who were the first to be eliminated as soon as the revolution succeeded: "Never mind, Jewish blood will serve as oil for the wheels of the revolution" said the idealistic Jews.

That is precisely what happened at the end of the 1930s when the war seemed to be fast approaching. The leaders of the Jewish community said: "We number over one million people in Germany—what can they do to us?" In the early 1950s, when Stalin's horrendous crimes were uncovered, including the murder of tens of millions of people, political leaders as well as Communist Jews in kibbutzim and cities in Israel continued to support Stalin's memory as "the sun of the nations", the father of "Mother Russia," Those examples, like many others, illuminate the fact that Israel suffered from the same syndrome of irresponsible assertions and views.

That outlook is still represented today by our contemporary anti Zionists. The lesson to be learned from recent, as from earlier, Jewish history is that the Holocaust can happen again. Paradoxically, the Jewish-Zionist State of Israel contends in public that another Holocaust will not happen and is patently impossible. However, one need only to read the Palestinian National Covenant of the allegedly moderate PLO and the covenant of Hamas to appreciate the fact that another Holocaust is definitely possible if Israel will not be militarily and politically strong. A thorough analysis reveals that there is no difference between Hitler's *Mein Kampf* and the two Palestinian documents in terms of their perceptions of the Jews and their ultimate aims.

The establishment of Israel did not change anything in the minds of Jewish anti-Zionists. They learned nothing from history, not even from Jewish history. Two fundamental errors on their part still hover over Israel's head like a dark cloud. First, they still think that Israel's victory in the 1967 war constituted illegal conquest of the Palestinian territory, and that the settlements are a stumbling block to peace that is waiting just around the corner. Second, in their minds, it is close to certain, that Israel can achieve a territorial compromise with the Palestinians as if the conflict between Israel and the Arabs is over specific tracts of land.

Unfortunately, the conquests of 1967 are not the reason for the inhuman terrorism perpetrated by the Palestinians against Jews and Israel, and the termination of those conquests has nothing to do with the goal of Arab terrorism. The goal is to liquidate the State of Israel as a Jewish-Zionist entity. That is also the goal of the Jewish anti-Zionists. At that point precisely the full scope and depth of the co-ordination of goals between those two groups becomes visible to anyone willing to look.

In the present volume, the authors propose to examine Jewish anti-Zionism and Palestinian anti-Semitism. These phenomena will be examined politically and from a philosophical point of view. Our goal is to expose their unique cultural characteristics and to set them apart so they can be recognized for what they are, ideologically and practically. Some people might wish to argue that a "historical" view of current affairs is useless since history itself is not reproducible and not retrievable. Hence, they claim, nothing can be learned from history. Israel's current President, Shimon Peres, has repeated his disregard for "history" several times, sounding like someone who thinks that knowing about the past is a waste of time and energy. He certainly disagrees with all the great historians of the nineteenth and twentieth centuries who, Peres would say, created a bogeyman to frighten us into our present state of not being willing to make peace with the Arabs who have attacked Israel relentlessly for one hundred years.

This approach seemed to have ruled out the use of human thought in the desire to promote peace. Yet, strangely enough, countries make peace with other countries with which they had a conflict, not with those countries with which there has been no conflict. To distinguish between those countries with which peace must be concluded from those with which peace has prevailed for some time, one cannot escape the need for various kinds and degrees of historical knowledge. In fact, all human beings with intact natural intelligence who were not the victims of biological or social trauma have a historical memory of themselves, of the period of their lives, from some time in their early childhood and onward. That memory gives human beings their identity above and beyond their biological existence. Identity is a decisive factor of individual and social-cultural-national existence. Therefore, its active—or latent—functioning exerts a powerful, often determining influence on the course of personal and collective-national events.

The volume strives to delineate some features of Israel's condition that has emerged in recent years that cannot possibly comprehended without some knowledge if its history. That is about as far as the present authors can go at this time without engaging an entire Philosophy of History. Our approach here is the opposite of the one expressed in Alfred Lord Tennyson's poem "The Charge of the Light Brigade": Yours is not to question why / Yours is not to make reply / Yours is but to do or die.

By way of introduction to the entire study we wish to emphasize one idea that is being acknowledged widely but is not always understood as a matter of fact, to wit: In our world today anti-Semitism has taken on the visage of anti-Israelism. That point was made by Bernard Lewis more than twenty years ago (1986) and has been noted by other well known academic figures on various occasions. Professor Larry Summers made the same observation at a Harvard University lecture in 2002, along with his observation of the role of academics in disseminating anti-Semitism in universities. He said:

> Vicious anti-Israel views have been supported by the progressive intellectual community. Serious scholars promote activities with clear anti-Semitic consequences.... The anti-Semitism of the past was the property of the populist Right. The new anti-Semitism is the product of the progressive Left and is expressed through anti-Israelism and anti-Zionism.

Prof. Summers discovered quickly that his job as president of Harvard was most precarious in light of the fact that he was a Jewish Zionist, and he had to resign. Professor Alain Finkielkraut noted that

The anti-Semitism of the Left [purports to be] ... anti-racist. Since Israel is perceived as the only racist country in the world, to be anti-racist means to be anti-Zionist ... from the point of view of the Leftist intellectual, if you are not anti-Israel you are in essence a racist, which is the most horrible curse the Left can bestow on you.

This book treats the symbiotic relationship between the anti-Semitic Palestinian doctrines and those Jews who are anti-Zionists. Current research examines these phenomena separately and fails to note their similarity. Palestinian anti-Semitism and Jewish anti-Zionism, which in many ways correspond to one another, stem from different sources: The Palestinian views derive from religious Islamic as well as nationalist-Arab roots, whereas the views of the anti-Zionist Jews grew out of an ideological-Marxist-Trotskyite background. Nevertheless, the two share a common goal, namely the destruction of the Jewish-Zionist nation, and a common strategy, which is to achieve a bi-national State as a first stage in its march to the goal, although they differ in terms of tactics. The Palestinians operate through the medium of Jihad, anti-Israel propaganda, and the de-humanization of Israel on the international stage.

The anti-Zionist Jews strive to have Israel perceived as an apartheid nation similar to the racist doctrines of South Africa during the years of apartheid there, and by means of that concept to propagate the de-legiti-mization of Israel on the international stage. The Palestinian educational system is the main social-institutional channel through which these views are disseminated. In Israel, the chief instrument of pro-Palestinian anti-Zionist propaganda is Israel's own mass media as well as academic institutions and the cultural bohemia. In both the Arab and Jewish cases, the means to the end is through socialization and systematic indoctrination of the people in Israel's internal as well as international organizational systems.

The first chapter of this book examines the status of Jews in the Muslim tradition and the development of the Islamic doctrine toward the Jews (and Christians) as a People of the Book. At first, when Muhammad was weak, the Muslims adopted an attitude of imitation and admira-tion. Later when he became a war hero, their attitude turned to one of hostility coupled with a desire to annihilate the Jews. Arab society in general displays admiration for power and for heroes. When Mu-hammad left Mecca after twelve years of preaching his new religion, he had a total of seventy followers. Once he began to be victorious in the battles he fought in Medina, thousands joined the ranks of his followers. Those ancient events serve as a paradigm for contemporary behavior by Arabs who have adopted a distinctly violent-militaristic pattern of relating to non-Arab groups and nations as well as to other Arab/Muslim groups.

The Arabs/Muslims constitute a warrior-dominated society which places great emphasis on social values such as honor, discipline, self-sacrifice, and responsibility or, in a negative sense, on blind adherence to authority, ruthlessness, and competition. Militaristic violence was consistently displayed by Arafat, and by the victory of Hamas over Abu Mazen and the PLO. That set of events provides a foundation for comprehending the anti-Semitism prevalent among Muslims in general and Palestinians in particular. The combination of religion (Islam) and culture as a bridgehead of the Arab-Islamic campaign forms the theoretical and practical foundation for the Palestinian's struggle with Israel. Its primary expression is the unequivocal rejection of Israel as a Jewish-Zionist State as was formerly annunciated in the PLO and Hamas charters.

The second chapter of the present book examines Palestinian policy in regard to Israel. The Palestinians wish to supplant Israel and make it their own country. That, in a nutshell, is their policy. Jewish history, tradition, territory, culture must all disappear, or rather be eliminated. The authors analyze that policy in connection with the Arab claim to "The Right of Return" (decision 194 of the UN General Assembly) regarding refugees. Our analysis seeks to encompass a wife range of the political-historical conditions prevailing on the international stage during the twentieth century. Our aim is to show that the "refugee" problem was extraordinarily complex and widespread in the world. The problem of the Palestinian refugees was, and is, one of the relatively simple problems to be solved. It has not been solved heretofore due to political manipulations by the Muslim countries as well as by the Palestinian leadership aimed at maintaining their status to serve as a political weapon against Israel. As with other issues discussed in this book, the activities of Israel's Jewish anti-Zionists are woven into the fabric of anti-Israel propaganda that emphasizes the so-called "occupation" that allegedly perpetuates the Arab-Israel conflict.

Chapters 3 through 5 treat the ideological and practical features of the anti-Zionists in Israel, as well as their numerous pronouncements. Their doctrines, values, ideologies are discussed and are subjected to a psycho-behavioral analysis in an attempt to clarify the extent to which these people represent larger groups. The Jewish anti-Zionists address their comments, and aim their activities, at other Jews in Israel. Their goal is to undermine the national allegiance and views of the pro-Zionist population, and to dismantle the foundations that foster coherence in Israel Jewry's position regarding the Jewish character of this nation. Israel's educational system provides a convenient institutional medium for the dissemination of the anti-Zionists' ideology. A large portion of Chapter 5 is devoted to the latter topic as well as to the central role of the media in the spread of the anti-Zionist ideology. The latter two—education and the media—are discussed from a social-science point of view including a content analysis of the main figures' behavior.

Chapter 6 deals specifically with the status of Jerusalem that, in our view, is a reliable measure of Palestinian anti-Semitism. The Palestinians utterly reject Jewry's historical and religious ties to Jerusalem, making believe that Jewry's three-thousand-year tie to the city is actually testimony to their—and Islam's—ownership of the area. The Arabs' position on the subject of Jerusalem emphasizes their cultural characteristics in respect to their struggle to take possession of Israel. Since the time of Muhammad, Jerusalem for Muslims was very peripheral, occupying no place in Islamic history. Only in the twentieth century, apropos the Palestinians' opposition to the Jewry's claim to the territory the British (and now the Arabs) called Palestine, the infamous Mufti of Jerusalem, Haj Amin al-Husseini began the Muslim crusade to take possession of Jerusalem. It was Yasser Arafat who exploited that subject to its fullest. He made the Arab claim to Jerusalem a central topic in the struggle against "the Zionists," a symbol of civilization's war between Islam and Judaism regarding the question of the Land of Israel. In respect to this question as well, the propaganda disseminated by the Jewish anti-Zionists in Israel assists the Arabs. The former group denies any connection between the Jews and the Land of Israel prior to the Jewish colonial conquests in modern times.

# 1

# Jews in Islam—The Anti-Semitic Perception

*"Mohammedanism is a militant and proselytizing faith ... the civilization of modern Europe might fall, as fell the civilization of ancient Rome."*
—*Winston Churchill, 1899*

*"The Muslim threat. like the Nazi threat, is the incarnation of evil. Like Nazism, one must annihilate that evil while it is still being conceived. A national leader who fails to understand that is worse than a fool, he is a danger to his People."*
—*Josephe Palgieri*

From an Islamic vantage point, Islam is not parallel to, and it did not come after Judaism and Christianity. Rather, it is considered to be the prime religion, the greatest of all three and the most perfect. Jews and Christians perverted Allah's true teachings given to the prophets before Muhammad. The Torah is Moses' book and the Zabur is David's book. `Isa received his revelation of Islam from a book (*al-An`am*, 6 verse 90) called *Injil* (*al-Ma'idah*, 5 verse 46). The Torah and the Gospels are considered false versions of the Qur'an. The Qur'an fulfills and sets apart all previous revelations, which are incomplete, tampered with, or tainted. Muhammad established all previous revelations. He is the last and final prophet (*al-Nisaa'*, 4 verse 47). All biblical heroes, from Adam to Muhammad, were Muslim prophets.

Originally, Muhammad had no intention of establishing a new religion in Mecca. He offered the Arabs the Book of Moses written in Arabic. He said that since the Torah was given to the Children of Israel and the New Testament to the Christians, the Arabs therefore needed a Book.

Surat al-Jatiyah, 45 verse 16:
> "We gave the Children of Israel the Book, and the judgment and the prophet-hood, provided them with good things, and favored them over other people."

*Surat al-Ahqaf*, 46 verse 12:
> "There was the Book of Moses before this, a guide and a mercy.
> And there is this Book confirming it in lucid language...."

*Surat al-Ma'idah*, 5 verses 44, 46, 48:
> "We sent down the Torah, which contains guidance and light ...
> we sent Jesus, son of Mary, confirming the Torah, which had been
> sent down before him...."

In Mecca, Moses was Muhammad's favorite prophet, and in Medina it was Abraham, who was a monotheist (*Surat al-Baqarah*, 2 verse 135; *Surat al-'Imran*, 3 verses 64-69, 77). From the perspective of the Qur'an, the book that Moses received on Mount Sinai is the true one and it includes the truth of the Children of Israel, as the chosen people:

*Surat al-Dukhan*, 44 verses 32-3:
> "We have exalted them (*ikhtarnahum*) over other people know-
> ingly...."

Surat al-Baqarah, 2 verse 47:
> "Remember, O the Children of Israel, the favors I bestowed on
> you and made you exalted among the nations of the world."

This Book [the Qur'an] is based on prophetic revelations of the ancient religions. For this, it is recommended to consult the People of the Book:

*Surat Yunus*, 10 verse 94:
> "If you are in doubt of what we have sent down to you, then ask
> those who have been reading the Book for a long time before you."

Muhammad recognized the Jews' rights to the Holy Land, to the Land of Israel as their only legitimate territory: "the Holy Land" (*al-Ard al-Muqaddasah*); "the Blessed Land" (*al-Ard al-Mubarakah*), "Land of the Jews" (*Ard Bani-Isra'il*).

*Surat al-A'raf*, 7 verse 137:
> "We than made the people who were weak (and oppressed), suc-
> cessors of the land to the east and the west which we had blessed.
> Thus, the fair promise of your Lord to the Children of Israel was
> fulfilled."

Surat al-Ma'idah, 5 verse 21:
> "Enter then, my people, the Holy Land (*al-ard al-muqaddasah*)
> that Allah has ordained for you, and do not turn back or you suf-
> fer."

Surat Bani Isra'il, 17 verse 104:
"We told the Children of Israel: dwell in the land. When the
promise of the reckoning comes we shall bring you together from
a motley crowd."

However, the Jews rejected Muhammad as a prophet and denied his preaching as parallel to Moses' religion, being the last prophet (*Surat al-Nisaa'*, 4 verses 46-7, 50, 153; *Surat al-Baqarah*, 2 verses 91, 108, 170; *Surat al-An`am*, 6 verse 124; *Surat Bani Isra'il*, 17 verses 90-3; *Surat al-Ahzab*, 33 verse 40; al-Saff, 61 verse 6). As retribution and after Muhammad's military success, his reaction to the Jews became harsh and violent, and he now operated as a new religious leader. The result: Allah's book was distinguished from others—Islam is destined to rule the world.

From that time on, Muhammad accused the Jews of having forged their Scriptures and altering the words of Allah. The Jews did not believe in Allah's signs. They bartered them away and lied to Allah, being wicked and hard-hearted rebels. They were the killers of all the Prophets (*Surat al-Baqarah*, 2 verses 61, 88-91; *Surat al-`Imran*, 3 verses 21, 112, 181; *Surat al-Nisaa'* 4 verse 155; *Surat al-Ma'idah*, 5 verses 70, 77-82; *Surat al-An`am*, 6 verse 146; *Surat al-Zukhruf*, 43 verse 48; *Surat al-Mujadilah*, 58 verse 14; *Surat al-Saff*, 61 verse 5).

The Jews, having been cursed by the tongue of David and Jesus (*Surat al-Ma'idah*, 5 verse 47), were transformed into apes and pigs (*Surat al-Nisaa*, 4 verse 161). The orders to the Muslims are clear: to fight and to subdue them (*Surat al-Taubah*, 9 verse 29). The Jews are among the Devil's minions (*Surat al-Nisaa'*, 4 verse 60). They are the most vehement of mankind in hostility to the Muslims (*Surat al-Ma'idah*, 5 verse 82). They are cursed by Allah, and for that their faces will be obliterated (*Surat al-Nisaa'*, 4 verse 47; *Surat al-Ma'idah*, 5 verse 64). If they do not accept the true faith, on the Day of Judgment they will be turned into apes (*Surat al-Baqarah*, 2 verse 65; *Surat al-A`raf*, 7 verse 166) and burned in Hellfire (*Surat al-Nisaa'*, 4 verse 55). They are the vilest of creatures (*Surat al-Bayinah*, 98 verse 7), hence: "Slay the Kuffar wherever you find them ... persecution is worse than slaughter" (*Surat al-Baqarah*, 2 verse 191). They are transgressors and deviators, and thereby lost the status of chosen people (*Surat al`Imran*, 3 verse 19; *Surat al-Jathiyah*, 45 verse 17; *Surat al-Saff*, 61 verse 5). Twice they were punished by destruction of their Temple (*Surat Bani Isra'il*, 17 verses 2-8). For the violation of the Sabbath, and denying the miracle of the tablets, they were turned into apes and pigs and their fate is Hell (*Surat al-Baqarah*, 2 verse 65; *Surat al-Ma'idah*, 5 verses 13, 112-115; *Surat al-A`raf*, 7 verses 138-151, 161-7; *Surat al-Jumu`ah*, 62 verse 65).

Allah's curse is on the Jews since they are the most dangerous enemies of Islam. They deny the prophecy of Muhammad: the scriptures of the Jews have been changed to hide the fact that Islam is the true religion (*Surat al-Baqarah*, 2 verse 159), for which they were punished by Allah (Ibn Ishaq, pp. 364-367). They deserve the horrors of Hell. As descendants of monkeys and pigs, they must be destroyed (*Surat al*-Nisaa', 4 verses 52, 56; *Surat al-Ma'idah*, 5 verses 60, 78, 80, 82; *Surat al-Hajj*, 22 verses 17-9; *Surat al-Jumu`ah*, 62 verses 6-8).

The Muslims became the only chosen community of Allah to make them victors (*Surat al-Ma'idah*, 5 verses 3, 7, 11; *Surat al-Ahzab*, 33 verse 9). Following the description of the Jews as *Bani Isra'il*, *Yahud*, and *Ahl al-Kitab* there is a new description, *Ahl al-Dhimmah* (the people of protection). The Jews are the most dangerous enemies of Islam and must be destroyed.

*Surat al-Nisaa'*, 4 verses 52, 56:
> "They are the ones who were cursed by Allah … and those who don't believe our revelations shall be cast into Hell…."

*Surat al-Jumu'ah*, 62 verses 6-8:
> "Say: O you Jews, if you claim that you are the favorites of Allah apart from all men, then wish for death … death will surely come to you…."

The stages in which Muhammad treated the Jews are as follows:

a) After the Badr war in 624, Muhammad started the deportation of the Banu Qaynuqa` tribe. The reason was Muhammad's characteristic attitude: they did not support him and his community in their holy war against the infidels (*Surat al-`Imran*, 3 verses 118-120), and he called on them to acknowledge his prophecy, or they would end up like the defeated Meccans. The result was deportation, with the help of Ibn Ubay, the head of the Hazraj tribe, who was an important ally to Muhammad. Under Muhammad's orders their hands were tied behind their backs, and he said: "may Allah curse them and curse him who is with them." After their departure, their property was confiscated and transferred to Muhammad (*Surat al-Anfal*, 8 verses 57-58; Ibn Ishaq, pp. 545-547). Muhammad then received the verses: "Say to those who disbelieve, you will be defeated and gathered into Hell, what an evil resting place" (*Surat al-`Imran*, 3: 12-13). From that time on, the order was to kill any Jew who falls into Muslim hands (Ibn Ishaq, p. 554).

b)  After the Uhud Battle in 625, Muhammad did not hesitate to turn his defeat to his advantage by deporting the Jews of the Banu Nadir tribe. The excuse was that the Jews did not support him with money and equipment. They even rejoiced at his defeat. Contrary to what was acceptable in Arabia, Muhammad told his men that they could cut down trees, including the most precious of all, the palm trees (*Surat al-Hasr*, 59 verse 5). This was sanctified by the declaration in the Hadith: "Muhammad bin Maslamah was told to go to the Jews and say to them, Islam has wiped out the old covenants" (*Sahih Muslim*, vol. 19, no. 4364). The Jews of Banu Nadir departed to the oasis of Khaybar, and the Muslims took hold of the richest land in Medina, and they were no longer dependent on the hospitality of the Ansar.

c)  After the victory of the Trench War in 627, the first to pay the price were the Jews of Banu-Quraythah tribe. Without the patronage of an Arab tribe, their fate was sealed by a massacre of the males and enslaving of their women as concubines and their children and their property distributed (*Sahih al-Bukhari*, vol. 5 book 58, number 148; vol. 5 book 59 number 448). The excuse was again that they had betrayed the community of believers by not assisting them when they were at war (*Surat al-Ahzab*, 33 verses 29, 50; *Surat al-Hasr*, 59 verses 2-4). In the Hadith we find this explanation: Angel Gabriel ordered Muhammad, and pointed towards the tribe of Banu-Quraythah, and Muhammad went out to fight them (*Sahih al-Bukhari*, vol. 4, book 52, no. 68). They surrendered to Muhammad and the verdict was that the men will be executed; children and women will be taken as slaves (Ibn Ishaq, pp. 463-464). As a gesture Muhammad suggested they convert to Islam, but the seven hundred male Jews went to their execution by beheading.

In keeping with Arab culture, a revelation came down justifying the punishment of the Jews: *Surat al-Ahzab*, 33 verses 26-27: "Allah made those of the People of the Book who had helped descend from their forts and he filled their heart with terror, so that you killed some and made many captives. And he made you inherit their lands and mansions and wealth, and a country you had not traversed before."

It was customary for the victorious to take the women and children. However, this was the first time it was sanctioned by a religion pretending to be merciful. By the same token, rape of women was also legalized (*Surat al-Nisaa'*, 4 verse 24).

d)  After the Hudaybiyah Agreement with the Meccans in 628, which most believers saw as a political defeat and inappropriate behavior for Arabs (Ibn Ishaq, 502-505), Muhammad succeeded in diverting his and the Arabs' frustration towards the Jews of Khaybar, which was the richest and most fertile oasis in the Hijaz, where it was quite possible they would find booty (*Surat al-Fath*, 48 verse 19). This is the source of the contemporary Palestinian song: "*Khaybar Khaybar ya-Yahud, Sayf Muhammad sa-Ya`ud*" ("Khaybar Khaybar O Jews, the sword of Muhammad is back"). The Jews of Khaybar capitulated after their palm trees were burnt, and accepted Muhammad's authority (Ibn Ishaq, pp. 515-516). As was habitual, Muslims took many captives, the booty was collected, and Muhammad took Safiyah Bint Huway, the Banu-Nadir head's wife as his concubine (*Sahih al-Bukhari*, vol. 1 book 8, number 367; vol. 4, book 52, no. 196; vol. 5: book 59, nos. 510, 523; *Sahih Muslim*, book 10, nos. 3761-3762). Later, the Banu-Nadir were expelled by `Umar, the second caliph, claiming that there should be only one religion in Arabia, and infidels are not allowed to stay there (*Sahih al-Bukhari*, vol. 5, book 59, nos. 362, 392; *Sahih Muslim*, vol. 10, no. 3763).

From then on, the process was linear and steady (*Sahih Muslim*, book 041, no. 985; *Sahih al-Bukhari*, vol. 4, book 52, no. 176): "The hour of judgment shall not come until the Muslims fight the Jews and kill them, so that when the Jews hide behind trees and stones, and each tree and stone will say: 'Oh Muslim, oh servant of Allah, there is a Jew behind me, come and kill him.'"

Jews and Christians disappeared from Arabia and ceased to exist personally and collectively up to and including today in a racist process of ethnic cleansing. This state of affairs is demonstrated by the Ordinances of `Umar (*al-Shurut al-`Umariyah*) which presented Islam's policy towards non-Muslims. It specified the terms of capitulation of the Dhimmis and the limitations put on upon them. The main topic is that security (*Aman*) is given to them in exchange for total loyalty to Islamic polity and laws, and paying the poll-tax. Any inappropriate mentioning of Muhammad, or the Qur'an, or Islamic religion, is bound to result in the loss of security, and the ruler is authorized to kill them and to expropriate all their belongings. Thus, it is a contract: accept Islamic rule, behave nicely, be completely loyal, do not even try to speak negatively against Islam, and you will be protected by the Muslim ruler. However, as Bernard Lewis clearly proves, this was the exception (1986). The regular treatment was exemplified by al-Maghili, a medieval Moroccan theologian, who wrote: "Love of the Prophet requires hatred of the Jews," and by Sirhindi, a seventeenth-century Sufi theologian, who declared: "Whenever a Jew is killed, it is for the benefit of Islam."

The best account of this relationship is detailed by Bat Ye'or (2002). Dhimmitude is a comprehensive system that has permeated Islamic civilization and culture from its inception. For more than a millennium, this system had encompassed social customs and behavior, the legal system, economic life and political oppression in countries ruled by the Muslims. Dhimmitude is policy of basic violation of human rights and freedoms, deliberate humiliation, and execution in the wake of even minor violations. The infidel has no rights whatsoever, unless he is protected by Islamic law. The right to life was conceded on payment of the Jizyah, with humiliation and submission. Refusal to pay was considered treason, which automatically brought Jihad war. The machinery that enabled this kind of relationship was Jihad.

In the above manner, Islam developed a relentless and unequivocal hatred of Jews and of Christians, albeit to a somewhat lesser extent. Such hatred knows no bounds. It includes intolerance to the presence of Jews on the holy soil of Arabia, a policy implemented unswervingly by the Saudis today, even when Jewish soldiers in the American army were stationed in Arabia by the U.S. government. Unable to prevent the Jews' physical presence, the Saudis would not allow the Jews to celebrate Jewish holidays on its own soil. The U.S. government agreed to remove the soldiers to a naval vessel anchored offshore for the period of the holiday. The religious-historical antagonism of Islam for Jews makes possible a more realistic view of the Muslim rejection of Israel and Jews rather than the popular notions of Israel's territorial "occupation" as the focus of the century long conflict between Arabs and Jews in Palestine/Israel.

These historical observations were focused on the development of hatred toward Jews in early Islam and some of its continuing effects in our time. But hatred of the Jews does not purport to explain the Arabs' "attachment" to Judea and Samaria and parts of present day State of Israel. Given the overwhelming significance of Arabia in the history of Islam, plus early Islam's explicit recognition of Jewry's divine right to the Land of Israel, from whence comes the seeming importance of the Land of Israel for Arabs/ or Muslims?

## The Arabs/Muslims and the Land of Israel

The Palestinian objective is to transfer the historic rights of Jewish people to the Land of Israel accrued over four thousand years of existence to the Palestinians who have no history and who emerged only recently. The Palestinian Arabs are trying to implement a policy that aims to appropriate the identity and legitimacy of the Jews for themselves. They demand that the world recognize them as the sole legitimate owner of Palestine. However, it is clear from every point of view that this demand is totally spurious for which there is no evidence whatsoever.

Historically, "Palestine" was never a territorial-cultural and political unit, nor were the so-called "Palestinians." There never was a people or a nation in history by that name. Retaining the Roman name the English named the Land of Israel "Palestine" in English, "Filastin" in Arabic, and "Palestina (E.I.)" in Hebrew.. They just as well could have chosen the name "The Holy Land" or some other name. In that case, there would have been no country called "Palestine" and no People called "Palestinians."

The fact is that during the Mandatory period, Arab inhabitants of the Land of Israel actually resisted using the Arabic name Filastin. They called themselves "Arabs" and considered themselves to be living in the territory of Southern Syria. In 1945, the renowned Arab historian Philip Hitti vehemently claimed before the Anglo-American Committee of Inquiry that no Palestine had ever existed in history and that there was no Palestinian People. This was also the official position of the Palestinian and Arab representatives themselves to all international committees in the 1940s. During the 1950s, in all international conventions and the Arab leaders' declarations, there was no "Palestinian refugee" problem but Arab refugees. Even as late as the UN Resolution 242 of November 1967, it mentions only "Arab refugees," not "Palestinian refugees," or a "Palestinian People."

In short, there has never been a Palestinian history, no Palestinian country, no Palestinian nationalism, no ethnic group called Palestinian, nor is there a Palestinian language. Of course there is a distinct Palestinian national identity at this time, but it is relatively new since it was created during the last thirty to forty years. Palestinian identity has arisen because Israel was established a State and, more important, due to Israel's victory in the 1967 war. Before that, all through the twentieth century, "Palestinian" always referred to individuals living in the geographic area called Palestine that politically and territorially belonged to Syria. Indeed, for most of the first half of the twentieth century, "Palestinian" and "Palestine" almost always referred to the Jews of Palestine. The Jews were the only ones who accepted that title, while the Arabs totally rejected it.

The course of history is distorted by Palestinians as if their ancestors are the seven Peoples of Canaan and the Philistines. That assertion has no basis in genuine historical records. Even more important, amazingly, they have succeeded in transforming the Israeli-Palestinian conflict from an Arab expansionist ideology, from a war to eliminate a State and a People, into an issue of occupation and Colonialism. They have diverted world attention from Muslim terrorism, perhaps unprecedented in history, and have convinced the Western world that they are engaged in a legitimate struggle to achieve independence. By means of a clever tactic they recycled declarations of annihilation by Jihad, a holy war against the (Jewish and Christian infidels) into slogans of the struggle for freedom of an oppressed people.

Contemporary Palestinian politics displays two main strategies toward Israel The secular one known as the Phased Strategy of the PLO-Fatah; and the religious ideology of Hamas. Both approaches affirm the total obliteration of the State of Israel as a sovereign independent nation. Alas, both strategies include reducing the Jews to a status of Dhimmis (people "protected" by Islamic rule). Both wish to establish an Arab-Palestinian State on Palestine in its entirety from the Mediterranean Sea to the Jordan River; both resist any possibility of Jewish existence as a nation entitled to a state.

Israel is the only state in the world that is under existential threats of annihilation on a daily basis. The Arabs and Palestinians have lost many wars. If Israel loses even one, she may cease to exist. From an ideological perspective, the Palestinian objective is to transfer the historic rights of the Jewish people to the Land of Israel, accrued over four thousand years of existence, to the Palestinians who have no history but only a present. This policy aims to appropriate the identity and legitimacy of the Jews and transfer it— though in reality there is no such thing—to the Palestinians. They demand to be the sole legitimate owners of Palestine.

This entire scenario is an externalization of a religious fantasy or belief typical of Arab society that asserting a claim about some social-political phenomenon derives from doctrine not from reality. One can invent ancestors, previous empires, glorious military victories that were fought in people's minds, and that constitutes evidence for geographical sovereignty,

a) *The historical dimension.* Since the Palestinians are the descendants of the Canaanites and the Philistines, they preceded the Jews in their right to Palestine alone.

b) *The religious dimension.* For them, Jerusalem has no sanctity whatsoever for the Jews; the Jewish Temple was in Nablus and not in Jerusalem; and the Western Wall is part of the Wall of al-Aqsa Mosque, the place where Muhammad's horse, al-Buraq, was tied to. The whole area of Jerusalem exclusively belongs only to the Palestinians, and no stone in Jerusalem has connection to the Jews.

c) *The political dimension.* The Jews today have no connection to the Jews of the past who disappeared long ago. Contemporary Jews are religious groups of impostors who are not the real Jews, but rather part

of the Zionist plot to gain control of Palestine, which is wholly and
totally Islamic and Palestinian.

That ideology is accompanied by a sophisticated strategy to win over
Western public opinion. The Palestinians have initiated a highly successful campaign to penetrate European consciousness with the idea
that Israel is the last remnant of colonialism implanted in the Middle
East by European imperialism. That idea or belief is intended and indeed has in fact contributed to the intensification of Europe's sense of
guilt and remorse: (1) Israel occupies the land belonging solely to the
Palestinians; (2) Israel has uprooted the Palestinians as a nation, and
scattered them out of their land; (3) Israel continues to liquidate the
Palestinians' national and social heritage, by planting a phony foreign
culture in the region.

Those are the main points of the Palestinian propaganda. Its reality
is distinctly different:

a)    The Palestinian issue is not a problem regarding refugees. Only a
      small minority of the Arabs who left Israel live in camps, and their
      socioeconomic data and living standards show clearly that their situ-
      ation not only resembles hundreds of millions of inhabitants of Third
      World countries, but in many ways the Palestinian economy and social
      situation are much superior to people who the world calls refugees.
      There are no similarities between the Palestinians and the conditions
      of more than a billion people in the Third World. Still, the Palestin-
      ians continue to get billions of dollars at the expense of these poor and
      miserable people. The money is then redirected to finance terrorism
      and corruption.
b)    The Palestinian issue is not the problem of a People being uprooted
      from their land. Most of the people who call themselves Palestinians
      live in the territory of mandatory Palestine, between Israel and Jordan
      and within Israel itself. In that respect, the issue is not whether they are
      refugees (the vast majority of them are not) and not whether they were
      expelled from their land (there was no Palestine), but rather, what is it
      they want? Their objectives are clear: they are not uprooted, but they
      want to uproot a People; their country was not stolen, but they wish to
      steal a country that was never their own; they are not poor and miser-
      able people who live in wretchedness, but rather seek to wreak upon
      the authentic owners of the country a Jihad massacre and protracted
      conflict, all of which are widespread in Arab culture.
c)    The Palestinian issue is not a problem of a society that was forcibly
      extracted from its human environment and thrown out of its original
      culture and society, since almost all Palestinians live and reside in an
      Arabic speaking society and culture, and most of them in Palestinian

territory. Actually, the Palestinian's objectives are to push the Jews out of their country back to Europe and other places; to annihilate them, according to Muhammad's example; and to deny any connection of the Jews to the Land of Israel.

The Western nations, including of course the United States, have not internalized the goals of Islam (other than those expressed unequivocally by Iran) regarding Israel and the Jews. The West insists on viewing the matter in the context of a typical territorial conflict. Both dimensions of the current view preclude a realistic comprehension of the current conflict between Muslim/Arabs and the Jewish nation of Israel.

There are five basic misconceptions concerning the issues of the Israeli-Palestinian conflict:

> The first misconception is the number of fatalities. Since World War II, the Israeli-Palestinian conflict is the national conflict with the lowest number of victims, and at the same time, with the world's highest number of academic publications. Yet, the distorted and false attention given by the media to the number of Palestinians killed by Israel causes a flood of headlines and articles all over the world. The fact that Palestinians massacre and murder other Palestinians by the hundreds, as in Gaza during the recent war with Hamas, receives only a brief mention, if any, in the media. Moreover, if entire villages are destroyed in Sudan or in Algeria, or cities are erased in Syria, or hundreds are massacred in Iraq, in Afghanistan, in Pakistan every day, those events will get only scant attention if any on TV.

More than a billion people around the world suffer from real poverty, humiliation and starvation. Forty percent of world's population drinks polluted water. The health of half of them is harmed by that water. Twenty five wars are being fought around the world every moment—and nobody cares and nobody pays attention to them. Only the Palestinians receive exaggerated attention, 'humanitarian supply and care' and a huge amount of money—only to be wasted on terrorism and corruption.

How did it come about that there is no connection between the facts and numbers mentioned here, the demonic image of Israel and the "humanitarian plight" of the Palestinians? The answer lies in:

a)   The ethics of the international community are dictated by a television camera. CNN and BBC determine what is important and what is not, who is black and ugly and who is white and beautiful. In their distorted language, there are no Islamic/Palestinian terrorists, only militants; there is no Islamic terrorism, only gunmen or sometimes terrorists. Islam is not an extremist, fanatic and totalitarian religion, but peaceful and compassionate.

b)   Fifty-seven Arab and Muslim nations exert enormous pressure on the international community's institutions. Muslims number 1.4 billion

people, 20 percent of world's population. They represent the economic
interests of the huge petro-dollar companies. They act aggressively and
shamelessly in world politics to promote their interests without any
hint of goodwill and objectivity.

c)  The Palestinians succeeded in instilling in world public opinion and
political leaders the perception that their situation is like a gun barrel
that could explode and destroy the entire world. For the sake of world
peace, they say, this issue must be solved according to the interests and
wishes of the Palestinians, even at the price of Israel's disappearance.
If not we, the Arab Palestinians, aided by other Arabs and Muslims
from many countries, will destroy the West.

d)  The Muslim's violent political behavior frightens and paralyzes the
Western world. In the words of the head of the British Cartoon Union:
"we are not afraid of the Jews ... the Jews do not issue Fatwahs." That
is the reason why Israel is isolated, denounced, and condemned in the
international arena.

There is also another and more dramatic statistic: The total number of
casualties of the Arab-Israeli conflict *from 1882 to 2006* was 65,000, 85
percent of whom were from Arab states, half of them Egyptians. Only
9,000 were Palestinians, most of them caused during the two Intifadas
(1,800 and 3,700 respectively). Not millions, not hundreds of thousands,
and not tens of thousands. Compare that number to the twenty to thirty
thousand Palestinians killed by King Hussein of Jordan in the single
month of September 1970; or to the 8,000 Palestinians killed by the Syrian President, Assad, in Lebanon in November-December 1983; or to the
6,000 Palestinians killed by their own brothers in the "Arab Revolt" of
1936 to 1939; or to the hundreds killed in Gaza during the last months of
2008 and the beginning of 2009 in the war between Hamas and Fatah.

The second misconception is related to the meaning of the term occupation. When Palestinians say "Israeli occupation," it is not the 1967
occupation, but the 1948 occupation, and it is not the 1967 borders but
the 1947 borders. When they murder and massacre Israelis by inhuman
terrorism, it is not because of the "occupation," and not because of the
"settlements," but because Israel is a Jewish Zionist state that exists on
the land of "Palestine."

The Arab/Palestinian-Israeli conflict has nothing to do with territory,
any territory. That claim is the most sophisticated strategy employed by
the Palestinians intended to mislead and to deceive world public opinion.
It is a murderous ideology aimed at destroying Israel and annihilating the
Jewish People. The so-called "occupied territories" have no relevance
to the termination of the Israeli-Palestinian conflict. It is just another

problem in a large set of complex issues which, first and foremost, must focus on the recognition of Israel as a state and the Jews as a nation. Note the formal Palestinian ideology toward Israel that clearly exposes what they mean by "occupation." The term clearly has no relevance whatsoever to any conflict over territory. The Palestinian National Covenant declares that armed struggle is the only way to liberate Palestine. That is the Palestinians' overall strategy, not merely a tactical phase. The Palestinians assert their absolute determination and firm resolve to continue their armed struggle for the total liberation of Palestine (**Article 9)**. The liberation of Palestine means to repel Zionist-imperialist aggression, and aims at the elimination of Zionism from Palestine in its entirety (**Article 15)**. The partition of Palestine in 1947 and the establishment of the state of Israel in 1948 were entirely illegal (**Article 19)**. The Balfour Declaration [1917], the Mandate for Palestine [1919], and everything that has been based upon them, are deemed null and void. Claims of historical or religious ties of the Jews with Palestine are incompatible with the facts of history. Judaism is only a religion, not a nationality. Nor do Jews constitute a single nation with an identity of its own. They are only citizens of the countries to which they belong (**Article 20)**. The Palestinian People, expressing itself by armed revolution, rejects all solutions which are substitutes for the total liberation of Palestine (**Article 21)**. The liberation of Palestine will destroy the Zionist presence and will contribute to the establishment of peace (Article 22).

Lastly, how can one amend or abolish this Charter? It is stated in article 33:

> This Charter shall not be amended save by [a vote of] a majority of two-thirds of the total membership of the National assembly of the PLO [taken] at a special session convened for that purpose (**Article 33)**.

### The Hamas Charter declares its goals directly:

> Israel will exist until Islam will obliterate it ... [Hamas] strives to raise the banner of Allah over every inch of Palestine (Article 6). The Islamic Resistance Movement is one of the links in the chain of the struggle against the Zionist invaders. It goes back to 1930s, and it includes the struggle of the Muslim Brotherhood in the 1948 war and all Jihad operations.... The Day of Judgment will not come about until Muslims fight the and kill the Jews, and when the Jew will hide behind stones and trees, the stones and trees will say O Muslims, O the servants of Allah, there is a Jew hiding behind me, come and kill him (Article 7). The land of Palestine is an Islamic Waqf (endowment) until Judgment Day. It, or any part of it, should not be squandered: it, or any part of it, should not be given up. Neither a single Arab country nor all Arab countries, neither any king or president, nor all the kings and presidents, neither any organization nor all of them, be they Palestinian or Arab, possess the right to deny that. Palestine in its entirety belongs only to the Palestinians. This is the law

governing the Islamic Shari`ah (Article 11). Nothing is more significant or deeper than Jihad against the Zionist enemy. Resisting and quelling the enemy become the individual duty of every Muslim, male or female. Neglecting any part of Palestine is tantamount to neglecting part of the religion [which means death]. There is no solution for the Palestinian question except through Jihad to eliminate the Zionist invasion. Initiatives, proposals and international conferences are all a waste of time and vain endeavors (Article 13). It is absolutely necessary to instill the spirit of Jihad in the heart of the Muslim nation (Article 15).... Jihad is the path, and death for the sake of Allah is the loftiest of all wishes....

These charters express Arab ideology. There is no mention of the occupation, of 1967 borders or of peace with Israel with any borders. The town of Sderot is not in the territory occupied in 1967, nor is the town of Ashkelon or all the villages and Kibbutzim around Gaza. But they were shelled and bombed on a daily basis. Kiryat Shmonah and all northern Israel are not located in the 1967 occupied territories, but they have been bombed by Arab or Arab-aligned groups (or nations) for years. If the problem is 1967 borders, why do they continue bombing Israeli cities inside the 1948 border? If they are sincere in their demand to free only the 1967 occupied territories, why do they terrorize and shell the territory included in Israel since 1948? If they want to liberate the 1967 territories, why do they use homicide bombers against Israeli citizens inside the 1948 borders? If the issue is 1967 borders, why do they dig tunnels into Israeli area to hit villages in the 1948 borders? If the issue is the territories occupied in 1967, why do they want to "solve the refugee" problem inside Israel of the 1948 borders?

An unambiguous response to this question is found in Gaza. Israel retreated totally from Gaza a year ago. Not a single soldier or even one centimeter remained. There is no occupation of any territory in Gaza. And what happened? Hamas won the elections; the extremists took over the streets; Gaza became Hamastan Hizballahstan and Qa`idahstan by infiltration of arms, ammunition and terrorists. Iranian officers, Hizballah personnel and al-Qa`idah groups are operating in Gaza even after the Gaza war (January, 2009). What is the relevance of the 'occupied territories' to the war conducted by Hamas against Israel?

Indeed, on June 20, 2007, Islamist websites posted a 13-minute video, titled: "A message from Jaysh al-Islam to 'Izz Al-Din al-Qassam Brigades," congratulating the establishment of an Islamic Emirate (*al-Khilafah al-Islamiyah*) in Gaza. On June 25, 2007, al-Qaeda deputy, Ayman al-Zawahiri, called on Hamas to enforce the *Shari'ah* in Gaza and to become a front-line base of World Jihad. Muhammad Nazzal, a Hamas leader, has declared: "if al-Qaeda wants to come to Palestine, they are welcome." Domestically, there is chaos and anarchy in Gaza. Hamas "soldiers" murder and butcher each other; they kill injured people in ambulances and in hospitals; they burn down mosques and shell universities; they target women and children, they massacre each other by shooting, executing, and decapitating each other. All those atrocious and hideous acts are done openly and broadcast on television.

The same circumstances prevail in Lebanon. For all intents and purposes, Israel's retreat in May 2000 brought about the prominence of Hezbollah in Lebanon. Syria threatens to return to Lebanon and has targeted (i.e., assassinated) Lebanese who resist her presence, like Rafik al-Hariri. Iran has increased her influence on domestic Lebanese politics, and its embassy in Beirut is the base of terrorist activity in the whole region, to signal the rapid process of Iranization of Lebanon; and Israel is shelled frequently, whenever Hezbollah feels so inclined, along with direct military clashes. Even from Hezbollah's vantage point, the 'liberation of Jerusalem is no less important than the liberation of Beirut.

Indeed the problem is not, and has never been, the 1967 occupation. More importantly, its termination will not affect or end the conflict, as can be learned without doubt from the example of Gaza. If anything, further withdrawals by Israel will only exacerbate the struggle with the Arabs. Arab and Palestinian leaders continue to sell the fraudulent mantra that the Israel-Palestinian conflict is "the heart of the problem and the cause of hostility and violence in the Middle East." They know full well that there is not a grain of truth in that statement. There are many foci of violence in the Middle East, and the Israeli-Palestinian conflict is only one of them, and definitely not the most problematic one. The Arab and Palestinian leadership rides on this wave, in order to hide the collective Arab shame over the lack of unity and the hostility rampant among them. That claim also serves their goal of threatening Western interests in the Middle East as a way of gaining its support.

The third misconception is education to hate. Europe and the United States believe that Palestinians are ready and willing to reach a historic compromise with Israel. Even a superficial examination of the printed and electronic media emerging from the Palestinian Authority reveals an entirely different picture. Educational institutions incessantly express messages characterized by unequivocal incitement to violence and terror whose sole purpose is to destroy Israel. Sermons in mosques say the same. The leaders' declarations and their political and social agenda are anti-Semitic in the extreme. Declarations thundered in the streets are frightening. The Arab media picture a demonic Israel. All of these sources uncover an atrocious picture of Palestinian hostility toward Israel.

How can Europe and the U.S. really believe that Israel could conclude a peace agreement with nations that have been subject to the kind of socialization and indoctrination to despise Israel unequivocally, permanently and "to the death?" To change that current vicious cycle, Arab Palestinian education would have to undergo a fundamental transformation of its entire religious-historical-national foundations. The vicious cycle of indoctrination to death and *Shahadah* must be discontinued completely. Undoubtedly, that is a long term project. Given the prevailing atmosphere, the history of this perspective and the vast number of personnel involved in its implementation, that process could require decades or longer, even with the most determined will on the part of educators.

It is unreasonable to anticipate a change in the Palestinian or Islamic behavior towards Israel and the free modern world at large unless their educational systems decide to change their policies, methods, textbooks and verbal messages. Education for the hatred of Jews and Israel lies at the root of the issues that must be resolved positively. The Japanese analogy is instructive. As long as militarism was the basis of Japanese society and education, Japan could not enter the modern democratic world. The U.S. imposed a radical change on Japanese society and politics after the Second World War. Japan was forced to abandon its ancient tradition of nationalistic militarism and to embrace an open system of democracy. Only then was Japan able to transform itself into a modern democratic and technologically advanced nation.

### Palestinian School Books

Can any signs be discerned that the Arab Palestinians want to make peace with Israel? For example, what attitude toward Israel is reflected in Palestinian school books? The Palestinian educational system places major stress on their alleged identity stemming from antiquity and located on the territory that is now Israel. That is a fantasy the Palestinian Arabs continue to cultivate although it is a total fabrication and, consequently, lacks any basis in history. In order to accept that view, the Arabs would have to accept the historical record documented by scholars while simultaneously rejecting the views circulated by political propagandists and revisionists. The latter need no proof of any kind beyond the assertions made by their own spokesmen. They are their own court of law, and serve as their own judge and jury. The judge is Allah, the jury is made up of the Mullahs, and the audience in the court is constituted by the Muslims. Of course the Law was written by Muhammad.

The educational system and the PA media, mainly TV, repeat its anti-Israel claims by showing a map of the Middle East in which Israel does not exist and is entirely replaced by a country called Palestine.[1] A map entitled "Map of Palestine Before and After the 1967 War" defines the area of the State of Israel as the Arab lands conquered before 1967, while the West Bank and the Gaza Strip are defined as the Arab lands conquered in 1967. None of the textbooks used in the Palestinian Authority indicate Israel. A map which accompanies a compulsory lesson called "Palestine our Homeland" encompasses the entire State of Israel and specifies Israeli cities and villages as Arab even though most of them date from biblical times: Safed, Acre, Haifa, Tiberias, Nazareth, Beit She'an, Jaffa, Jerusalem and Beersheba. PA television shows the same map, many times each day, at the beginning and end of every news report. This substitution of Palestine for anything Israeli encompasses all of Israel's technological and scientific achievements which are identified as being of Palestinian origin. The PA consistently instills into the minds of its children, from early childhood, the necessity for, and inevitability of, a prolonged Jihad to liberate all of Palestine. That message also demands that the children should be prepared to fight and die to achieve that dream. Rejection of Israel, Zionists and Jews, based on moral, political, national as well as religious considerations, is total.

The nature of the Palestinians' views of Jews and Judaism, as reflected in their schoolbooks, were also examined by Sharan (1999 in Hebrew, and 2001 in English). The historical structure invented and fabricated by the Palestinians exposes the fundamental goal of Arab-Islamic culture to instill into the minds of children the need to hate and kill the infidels as an irrefutable truth for which there is no need for evidence of any kind other than their own beliefs. In so doing, they omit, refute, and deny others' heritage and existence. There is no mention of the Jews or acceptance of their historical claims. Unfortunately, Western ignorance on this subject is pervasive. Westerners also assume that there is some truth on both sides of every issue.

The Free World yields to these accusations and blames Israel. The Zionist ideology which nurtures the Jewish State is pointed to as the paradigm of racism, apartheid, imperialism, and ethnic cleansing, and doomed to failure. Jewry's national and individual characteristics are notorious, "well known" for centuries in Europe, namely: treachery, disloyalty and corruption.

The hatred instilled in every Palestinian child is sufficient to explain why Israel set up the road barriers. Yair Lapid, an Israeli leftist journalist and a novelist, addressed this issue with an uncharacteristic degree of candor:

> You are right—the most humanitarian act is to remove the roadblocks. But, in that case I will die, and I really do not want to die. The only thing that interests me is that the bus my daughter rides in will not be blown up by a so-called freedom fighter. She only wants to live. Promise me this, and you will see all the road-blocks vanish. Promise me that the terrorists will not use innocent people—small kids and old ladies, or other means- to transfer weaponry and explosive devices for murdering Jews in Israel, and you will not see barriers. Promise me to stop the vicious unprecedented phenomenon of the homicide bombers and you will not find barriers. All I ask is for you to understand that I do not want to die. And please don't tell me that the problem is the occupation. Palestinian terrorism was perpetrated in the 1920s and 1930s, much before Israel was established. The occupation should be removed, but terrorism and homicide bombers must be stopped much before. I want to live and so does my family. That is my first priority. And that is why the barriers are so important.

Suppose you suddenly experience a divine revelation. You become aware of what will happen to your own family. You are given the power to prevent any act against them before it happens.

a)    What will be your reaction if your revelation instructs you to put up a road barrier in order to prevent a man from murdering your own family? Would you do it?

b)    Assume for a moment that you have a gun and can kill the murderer before the murders your wife and children—would you do it?

c)    Suppose this divine knowledge instructs you to search a pregnant woman who smuggles a bomb that threatens to kill your own family. Would you stop her with the means needed?

d)    Suppose the revelation instructs you to search a baby carriage pushed by an old woman. Under the baby there is a bomb intended to blow up your own family. Would you carry out the search? Would you stop it by full search and arrest?

e)    Suppose too that the revelation instructs you to stop a journalist's TV car, or a vehicle that belongs to the UN car, that carries terrorists to murder your family: Would you do it, even if you know their supposed-neutrality?

All of the above scenarios actually occurred, and very often: The pregnant woman, the baby carriage, the old lady, the small kids, the ambulances, and the TV and UN vehicles. Over the last six years more than 200 terrorist acts and 100 suicide bombers were detected and prevented from entering Israel at the roadblocks. For example, in June 2006 two female homicide bombers were arrested at a barrier: One was a thirty-nine-year-old pregnant woman with eight children, and the other, a thirty-year-old woman with four children. The pregnant woman said that she wanted her yet unborn baby to be a *shahid* too, and that she knows that her act is sanctified and justified by her religion. She wants all her family to enjoy the pleasures of Paradise. Now, what would you, the readers of this book, do to prevent terrorism and homicide bombers directed at your families?

The fourth misconception is related to the religious variable. Unfortunately we must conclude that in the Middle East, for the time being, religion is not a constructive factor that can bring about peace and harmony. Let's look at the balance sheet:

*In Mandatory Palestine* the Christian plight is extremely harsh and persecutions are frequent. In 1948 Christians comprised close to 18 percent of the overall population. Now they number less than 3 percent, and the countdown continues. In 1948, the Bethlehem area was 80 percent Christian. In 1990, it had dropped to 60 percent, and in 2005 it was less than 15 percent. Joseph Farah, a Christian Arab, presented the details:

They (i.e. the Christians) are being driven out. They are being murdered. They are being systematically persecuted. This is a massive display of ethnic cleansing and population movement which is covered up by the international media. But the worst is that the perpetrators of these crimes successfully blame Israel for committing them.

*In Sudan.* Since 1983, an estimated 1.5 million Christians died from "war against humanity" crimes, and about two million have become refugees. Sudan's genocidal campaign of massacre, torture, rape and starvation makes it the single most terrifying country area in the world today. Sudanese massacred hundreds of thousands black Muslims in Darfur, and created 2.5 million new refugees, only because they are not Arabs. This is the greatest holocaust perpetrated on a People since World War II. The man who revealed that atrocious massacre in Darfur is Brian Steidel, a volunteer in the Peace Force. You can watch his horrifying film *The Devil on Horseback*. He could be assassinated like Theo van Gogh for his impudence in exposing reality. It is worth mentioning that Sudan is an honorable member of the UN Human Rights Committee. In Sudan there is a holocaust about which no one says anything, let alone actually do something to stop the genocide.

*In Iraq.* The Christians were 5 percent of the population in 1930, and now they number less than a few thousand, annihilated by the Muslims. To this story of genocide one can add the persecution of hundreds of thousands of Kurds. Furthermore, since 2003, another front has been opened: the massacre of Muslim Shiites by Muslim Sunnis in terrorist acts, by tens of thousands. `Umran Salman, a Bahraini journalist, expressed his assessment of the situation:

> Not since the Nazi era has there been anything like the declaration of war on the Shiites in Iraq. The Sunnis persecute the Shiites and declare them infidels. al-Qa`idah is waging a war of collective extermination against the Shiites in Iraq.

*In Egypt.* There is constant harassment and persecution of Coptic Christians. The Egyptian reformist, Tarik Heggy details:

> the Copts are surrounded by deep religious intolerance, hateful fanaticism and mortal persecution.

*In Algeria*, the government embarked on a campaign of forced Arabization of the non-Arab Berber Muslim population, including social and economic harassment. From 1992 an internal civil war has been raging between Muslims and the military regime, with more than 180,000 fatalities.

*In Lebanon*, the Christians comprised 86 percent of the population in 1920, and now they are less than 25 percent. Majid Aziza, a liberal scholar analyzes the plight of the Christians:

> They are massacred and tortured, their communities destroyed, and acts of coercion, discrimination, and collective expulsion have caused the near disappearance of Christians from the Middle East.

The Gaza Strip is the site of a horrifying civil war. The Watch Organization accused both sides of perpetuating war crimes against civilians. In 2008 one could hear for the first time in history new songs such as: Fath accuses Hamas of perpetuating Nazi means and of being blood suckers. Abu Mazen himself declared: "Hamas are the sons of evil … the worst enemies of the Palestinians … they deserve death… Hamas have brought Hizballah and Iran…. This is a struggle against the Emirate of Darkness and Backwardness. Gaza will turn into a Taliban-style Islamic emirate with Iranian and Syrian support."

Even in the Arab world there is fear from the consequences of a Hamas victory for regional and internal stability. That is the main reason for the summit convened in Sharm al-Sheikh in June 2007. The Egyptian press has expressed fears that the Muslim Brotherhood may seize power in Egypt, and said that lessons should be learned from the Palestinian experience. The same fears now prevail in Jordan. Muhammad Hasanayn Heikal, the most important and influential journalist in his day expressed his view that what happened in Gaza is "the end of the

Palestinian issue." The problem is that some see this state of affairs as an improvement, envisioning a secularist Fatah-run state living peacefully alongside Israel and a radical Gaza hemmed in by Israeli troops. However, Professor Fuad Ajami, of John's Hopkins University (*NYT*, June 19, 2007) pointed out:

> ... this is s sheer fantasy. An accommodation with Israel is imperative, but the Palestinian leaders still demanding to have it all 'from the river to the sea.' The Arab states have compounded Palestinian radicalism, granted them everything and nothing at the same time, and there was thus no need for Palestinian moderation and realism. The Palestinians should know better. No Arabs wait for Palestine anymore, and aside from a handful of the most romantic messianic Israelis, there is a recognition that the Palestinians must come to terms with reason and live in peace with Israel, or drop out of history.

The fifth misconception is related to a Palestinian State. At the present time the question is just where will another Arab nation be located within Israel's 1967 borders? What will be the nature of this new country and how will it relate to its neighbors? Will the Palestinians become more moderate and more tolerant of Israel's existence after they have their own country, or will they become more extreme and demanding? The UN and the West assume that a Palestinian state will be located within the territorial boundaries set up by Israel after the 1967 war and will not be a pariah state that employs terrorism and violence against its neighbors. The West also assumes that Israel and Jordan will continue to exist in their own borders.

Of the two possible forms of the projected Arab-Palestinian state, the PLO secular state will demand that Israel permit the return of 4.5 million refugees to territory within the 1948 borders of Israel. The Hamas form of the religious Palestinian state will immediately function as a radical Islamic nation that cooperates with Iran and Hezbollah as well as maintaining ties with the Jihadist elements in the world of Islam. A Hamas nation will spell the end of Israel and will also endanger the entire set of so-called moderate Arab or Moslem states of Egypt, Saudi Arabia and Jordan. It will also become part of the Islamic apocalypse of the Sunnah against the *Shi'ah*.

No additional evidence is necessary to show that the Palestinians, and particularly the Hamas organization, have not matured politically to the point where they can function as a moderate state. There is, of course, the option of creating an international trusteeship to be administered by representative of different countries, including Arab nations. Such a trusteeship could be inspected by the UN with the goal of cultivating

Palestinian responsibility for national sovereignty as quickly as possible. That trusteeship will attend to creating an educational system that will not teach violence or suicidal terrorism, and to allow the emergence of political elite that will lead the Palestinians to achieve a set of reasonable and limited aspirations. That kind of nation will not disrupt or threaten neighboring states, to wit—Israel and Jordan. However, we must remind readers that the UN is dominated by a large number of Muslim countries that are antagonistic to Israel, so that the suggestion of a UN inspected trusteeship is highly problematic.

Another fact that should be recalled at this juncture is the presence in the world of many national minorities that seek national independence and have yet to find it. John Minahan researched this question. He found that there are more than 200 such nationalities without statehood (Minahan, 1996), and no one is calling for the realization of those groups' right to self-determination. There is no discussion on the international stage about the need for the Kurds to be allowed self-determination and secede from Turkey and Iraq, even with the Turkish military actions against the Kurds in Iraqi territory. Nor is there any move to grant the Christians of southern Sudan self-determination despite their being subject to mass slaughter.

Why hasn't there been any reaction to the recent de facto takeover of Lebanon by the Iranian-supported terrorist organization Hezbollah whose financial and military needs are supplied via Syria? Is it because the Shiites comprise 40 percent of Lebanon's population? After all, it is widely acknowledged that a Shiite nation is a threat to the entire region. And what about a Palestinian state to be located on Israel's eastern border? Wouldn't that constitute a danger to the very existence of the Jewish state and of Jordan? If we may answer that question on the basis of Palestinian declarations—the answer is clearly positive.

Some argue that an international force should be sent to separate the countries from one another and supervise their activities regarding one another. Mahmoud Abbas (Abu Mazen) made that suggestion during recent visits in Europe. Yet, we have ample experience with international forces and their effectiveness, or lack of it, in the Middle East and elsewhere. That notion is next to impossible to implement, and, even if such a thing came into being, the forecast regarding the fulfillment of their task is gloomy, to say the least. Hamas announced, immediately following Abu Mazen's announcement of his suggestion, that it would kill the soldiers of any international force stationed in Gaza. No European country will send troops to join an international force exposed to

Hamas' murderous threats. Spain withdrew its troops from Iraq after the terrorist explosion in Madrid on March 11, 2005, and will do the same in southern Lebanon if any of its troops experience another terrorist act. In the bombing that occurred in Lebanon, three Spanish soldiers were killed and more wounded. That act was directed specifically at the Spanish troops in order to get Spain to withdraw its soldiers from Lebanon, thereby undermining the international force.

There is also the question of whether the so-called moderate Palestinians do indeed support a two-state solution? However, the "two-state solution" also calls for the implementation of "the right of return" of the Palestinian refugees into Israel's territory as delineated in the 1948 agreement. It should be obvious to anyone who does not share the "Palestinian" vision of destroying Israel that the "return of Arab-Palestinian refugees" to Israel's territory would in fact result in the elimination of the Jewish State. The Palestinians demand that Israel retreat to the 1967 borders. Following such a retreat, Israel would then be required to solve the refugee problem by allowing the so-called refugees to enter, and reside in, Israel. That means establishing an Arab-Palestinian state in Judea and Samaria, and a bi-national state in the territory now called Israel instead of the Jewish State of Israel. In the course of a few years it means there will be just one big Palestinian state from the Mediterranean Sea to the Jordan River. It is also highly probable that the Arab proposal implies the end of Jordan, being a part of historic Palestine where Arabs from Palestine constitute 70 percent of its population. The two-state solution is only a euphemism for the destruction of Israel.

Liberal Qatari commentator, Abd al-Hamid al-Ansari, published three articles in April and May of 2007 in which he criticized the Arab world for denying that terrorism and fanaticism stem from Arab culture and religion.

They have reached that level of madness and barbarism for three reasons: (a) the constant denial that Muslims perpetrate terror, and the habit of accusing their enemies of being responsible for all the evil in the world; (b) defensiveness as the reaction of choice to the manifestations of Muslim terrorism as if it is a virus that will soon dissipate and is basically alien to the Arab world and to Islam; (c) repeated justification of terrorism by claiming that it is the result of repression, poverty and wretchedness induced by Western injustices and its blind bias for, and preferential treatment of Israel.

Al-Ansari declared that all three reasons constitute absolute nonsense and are no more than cheap excuses. Terrorism stems from a culture of hatred and extremism rampant in the educational systems of Muslim countries. That culture is emphasized in Friday sermons in mosques, in the media and in politics. He called on the Arabs to abandon the culture of hatred and fanaticism.

We hope the Palestinians will, in fact, heed Al-Ansari's call and change their attitudes and behavior. When Sadat came to Israel with a realistic peace plan he was met with open arms and with Israel's agreement for his ideas. The same happened between Israel and Jordan. The very same will happen if and when Syria comes to the negotiating table with clean hands instead of nuclear reactors. Palestinians must set aside their ambitions to take over the entire area of the Land of Israel with no Jewish state there. They will also find a willing partner in Israel when they too come forward with a realistic plan. Once they drop their plans to eliminate Israel and recognize Israel as a Jewish-Zionist state, peace and tolerance will reign in the region.

### What Say the anti-Zionist Jews?

Israel's relationship with the Arabs and with the Arabs in Gaza, Judea and Samaria in particular, is the primary focus of the criticism leveled against Israel as a nation by many Jewish academics in Israel (except for the very few who finally left Israel). The litany of Israel's, and Jewry's, crimes as asserted by the anti-Zionist academics would fill a book that cannot be summarized easily here. With this drawback in mind, here is a condensed presentation of their views:

> "Israel insists on clinging to its Judaic origins. It must shrug off its moral, religious, historical connection to Judaism and early Zionism. The Jewish State "did not overcome the religious substance of Jewish nationalism and thus create a liberal, secular and open society at peace with itself and its neighbors."

"Israel has maneuvered itself into the position of standing squarely on the front line of fire between the Muslim world and the U.S. It must extricate itself from that dangerous condition. We must change our policies toward the Arab-Muslim nations and desist from provoking them. That can be accomplished by dismantling the "settlements" including the Golan Heights. The failed Second Lebanese War, the Yom Kippur War, the Intifada, the Scud missiles, terrorism, Kassam and Katyusha rockets have all proven that the price of military solutions leads nowhere ... now more than ever the time has come for an about face...in respect to the Muslim world..."(Ezrachi, 2007).

"Israel causes more damage to the Palestinians than they have caused us. The courts in Israel cover up claims of violence toward Arabs and of damage caused to their property. Consequently, such acts are performed with impunity. In other words, the courts in Israel support Jewish military hegemony. The media in Israel are denounced for not objecting to Israel's retaliation against the shooting of rockets on Sderot and nearby parts of the Negev" (Aviad Kleinberg).

"Israel Jewry refuses to accept responsibility for the catastrophe (Naqbah) caused by the Jews to the Arabs of Palestine by establishing Israel in 1948. Arab refugees from that cataclysmic event must be allowed to return to Israel from whence they were evicted. Israel belongs to Arab and Jews alike. The catastrophe for the Arabs is similar to the Holocaust. Yad va-Shem looks out on Dir Yassin where the Jews slaughtered the Arabs. To justify this violence Israel clings to the image of the besieged Jews who are always being attacked by external foes."

Support is expressed for Jews like Norman Finkelstein in the United States who denies that the Holocaust occurred. Alan Dershowitz, professor of law at Harvard University, should be denounced because he is an ardent defender of Israel and sharply criticizes anti-Zionists Norman Finkelstein and Neve Gordon.

In the months following the outbreak of the terrorist war against Israel led by Yasser Arafat, at the end of September, 2000, (the late) Professor Baruch Kimmerling of the Hebrew University of Jerusalem, set forth in public his world-view regarding the elimination of Israel as a Jewish-Zionist entity. His position included changing the national anthem, since he decided that its vocabulary was anachronistic and did not represent the views of Israel's citizens. We wonder if he ever heard the words of the British, French or US national anthems, the latter containing the words "…the bombs bursting in air … we saw through the night that our flag was still there … oh say does that Star Spangled banner still wave, o're the land of the free and the home of the brave?"

Kimmerling advocated changing Israel's flag since it derived from religious sources such as the prayer shawl (*Talit*) that reflects theocratic inclinations; to change Independence Day to a "State Day"; to change the Law of Return, whereby any Jew who arrived in Israel from another country is granted immediate citizenship, because Israel should be a bi-national state for "all its citizens" not a Jewish nation. Kimmerling proclaimed that "Israel as a Jewish-Zionist state will not survive for more than one generation." Clearly he formulated succinctly the entire theory of the post-Zionist outlook that seeks to eliminate Israel. The Palestinians and Muslims need not worry. The Jews will destroy their own country—if it survives the wars—just as "small foxes destroy vineyards" (Song of

Songs, chapter 2, verse 15) by chewing slowly but surely. The Arabs will only have to reap the harvest of anti-Zionist Jewry's self destruction.

The opinions of the anti-Zionist academics seem to exist in a near vacuum. Events in the international domain as well as the behavior of the Arabs, whether they call themselves Palestinians or by the names of the different Arab nations of the Middle East, (Iraq, Syria, Jordan, Saudi Arabia, and so forth) are almost completely ignored, creeping in now and then inadvertently. Israel's academic anti-Zionists assert that what the Jews, in or outside of Israel, say and do erupts out of the depths of their own prejudice and hatred, not in reaction to acts or statements made by the Arabs. The reader of publications written by members of this group is amazed at their disregard of any possible explanation of Israel Jewry's behavior toward the Arabs as a reaction to events transpiring in the environment. In that kind of world Jews are not defending themselves or their country but are perpetrating pogroms on an innocent and helpless Arab population. All "laws" of action and reaction are suspended by the anti-Zionists in favor of the "psychological" sources of prejudice deep in the historically or even genetically determined psyche of the Jews. Indeed it was suggested (Hammerman) that Jewish aggression against the Arab Palestinians stems from ingrained persecution beginning with Biblical times.

Given that the acts of aggression against Israel and Jews perpetrated by Arab groups and nations remain beyond the ken of the anti-Zionists except as resistance to Jewish/Israel aggression against the Arabs, there is no palpable explanation for Israel's behavior other than as some bizarre acting out of biological impulses. If one excludes the panorama of historical events (and not just the behavior of one group in a given location) as the primary arena and motivator of human behavior, one inevitably must have recourse to biology, genetics and inherited psychological characteristics. It is more than obvious that the anti-Zionists have cultivated an unmistakably racist view of Jews, Israel, and Zionism even as they denounce Israel as racist.

Just why the persecution is ingrained rather than originating in the environment, as described very clearly in the Book of Esther, is not discussed. Indeed, from the perspective of the authors, one of the amazing and distressing characteristics of the Jews is that, in the face of endless persecution through the ages, we inexplicably trusted and continue to trust, our non-Jewish hosts in many countries during our long sojourn in the Exile. That characterization includes the Jews of Germany in the first half of the twentieth century (Volkov, 2002). Equally amazing is that

Israel's Jewish leaders trusted agreements with the Arabs time and time again. One betrayal after the other did not imprint on their minds the folly of their ways. The very same condition prevails to this day; forty years of terrorism and Holocaust denial by Mahmoud Abbas, (Abbas, 1984) as Arafat's close associate; the murder of thousands of Jews, betrayal, cunning deception and publicly paraded corruption, has left almost no mark on the Jewish-Zionist leaders of this country. To what "ingrained" hatred of the Arab Palestinians do the anti-Zionists refer?

The use of the term "hate" by members of Israel's anti-Zionist academics highlights once again their imperviousness to events in the Muslim world. Do the anti-Zionists read books? What about Brigitte Gabriel's recent volume *Because They Hate: A Survivor of Islamic Terror Warns America* (2006), or Dore Gold's *Hatred's Kingdom* (2003) about Saudi Arabia's culture of Wahhabi fanaticism and support of worldwide terrorism against the West? Many US congressmen and senators objected to the American initiative (July 30, 2007) to give Saudi Arabia twenty or so billion dollars for the purchase of new weaponry precisely because that country is the financier of worldwide anti-Semitism and terrorism. At this writing (February, 2009) it seems that Arabian wealth decidedly outstrips that of the United States.

The anti-Zionists do indeed present matters in reverse of reality (Plaut, 2007). Psychoanalysts such as Anna Freud (1936) would call this phenomenon "reaction formation" in which a person defends him/herself against his own thoughts or impulses by transforming their meaning into their opposite. Because the original intent is laden with intolerable feelings, such as aggressive impulses against someone or something, the need is to direct this aggression elsewhere. The anti-Zionists cannot publically acknowledge Arab hatred toward Jews and Israel. Hence, they invest enormous time and energy, and money, in the effort to convince the world that global terrorism and Islamic fanaticism financed by Saudi Arabia are not real, only a figment of our imagination. Therefore, Arab hatred is altered from "them to us," so that "our hatred for them" is attributed to Israel Jewry by the Jewish anti-Zionist academics here.

This phenomenon is undoubtedly unique or at least extraordinarily unusual: A significant portion of a democratic nation's intellectuals asserts that the relentless hatred publicly expressed and disseminated by the Arab nations—including Egypt whose publication of anti-Israel and anti-Semitic material (such as the *Protocols of the Elders of Zion*) is unmatched anywhere in the world—actually is a reaction to Israel's or Jewry's hatred for them. How reality can be so egregiously distorted and transformed into one huge lie remains an enigma, regardless of how we might seek psychological/psychiatric explanations. Indeed, no nation would tolerate such behavior on the part of any of its citizens in times of war. Who in the United States claims that Americans hate Iraqis? Not even the most extreme detractors of George Bush made such a claim, and certainly not as an explanation of why Iraqis attack American or British soldiers in Iraq. The anti-Zionists, for their own reasons, have adopted Arab propaganda hook, line and sinker. That brings them in line with the Arabs nations on the one hand, and with the European nations on the other, against their own country. Perhaps that gives them a sense of protection from the threats directed against Israel from those countries.

## Note

1.    For example: Palestinian National Education for Second Grade, #519, p. 21; Modern Arab History and Contemporary Problems, Part II, for Tenth Grade, #613, p. 66; Social and National Education for Fifth Grade, #549, pp. 81, 84, 88, 89, 103, 107, 109, 110, 120, 124; Geography of the Arab Homeland for Sixth Grade, #557, pp. 12, 20, 23, 36, 48, 50, 53, 55, 61, 66, 72, 73, 75, 80, 81, 88, 90, 115, 124; Geography of Arab Lands for Twelfth Grade, #650, pp. 49, 55; Modern Arab History and Contemporary Problems Part II, for Tenth Grade, # 613, pp. 70, 91, 95. Modern Arab History and Contemporary Problems Part II, for Tenth Grade, # 613, pp. 70, 91, 72, 73, 75, 80, 81, 88, 90, 115, 124; Geography of Arab Lands for Twelfth Grade, #650, pp. 49, 55; Geography of the Arab Homeland for Sixth Grade, #557, pp. 12, 20, 23, 36, 48, 50, 53, 55, 61, 66, National Education for Fifth Grade, #549, pp. 81, 84, 88, 89, 103, 107, 109, 110, 120, 124; Arab History and Contemporary Problems, Part II, for Tenth Grade, #613, p. 66; Social and

# 2

# The Arab "Refugees:" A Historical View, Not a Narrative

Before discussing the subject of Arab refugees, it is important to examine the historical facts rather than accept the legends—the fraudulent declarations that have long since replaced those facts. Moreover, historical facts can only be properly understood when examined in their own historical context. Legends abound regarding the conditions under which the "refugee problem" emerged in 1948. What follows is a documented historical account of the subject. It is our intention to present that historical account unburdened by legends, narratives, or descriptions intended to achieve transparently political goals. We hope that the text achieves what we set out to do.

## The Broad Statistical Picture

1. There were 79 million world refugees during the period of 1933 to 1945. Of them, 15 million were Hindus, 8.5 million Sikhs, and 6.5 million Muslims who were displaced, in 1947, when India and Pakistan were created.
2. Two million refugees were created as a consequence of the population exchange following the 1919-22 Greco-Turkish War. That fact was codified by the 1923 Treaty of Lausanne.
3. Millions became refugees in Vietnam, Laos, and Cambodia as a result of the ruthless regimes that came to power following the U.S. withdrawal of its forces from those countries.
4. A population transfer of millions occurred between the former Soviet Union and Hungary, Poland, Czechoslovakia, Bulgaria, and Romania. The same situation also occurred in Germany and Korea.

5.    Millions of people moved from one country to the next inside Africa in the wake of the delineation of borders implemented by European imperialist nations. By comparison, the total number of 1948 Palestinian refugees was 640,000, exactly one half of 1 percent of world's refugees in the twentieth century.

Of particular interest is the question of why the Arabs fled Israel when the Jewish States was proclaimed, or about to be established?

## The Causes of the Arab Refugee Problem

The backbone of Palestinian English-language propaganda is the myth that Israel expelled hundreds of thousands of Arabs and created the Arab refugee issue. However, it has become more and more evident, even in the Palestinian Authority media, that the Arabs who became refugees in 1948 were not expelled by Israel but left on their own to facilitate the destruction of Israel. This plan was initiated by the Arab states fighting Israel, who promised the people they would be able to return to their homes in a few days once Israel was defeated.

Although there were some Palestinian Arabs that were evacuated from their own homes by the Israeli forces, it was only a small minority. There was never any mass expulsion of the Arab population as a whole from any part of Israel in 1948. There was no "ethnic cleansing" of Arabs. Otherwise, it would be impossible to explain how 400,000 were left behind, and how 1.2 million Arabs live in Israel territory today, comprising 20 percent of Israel's present-day population.

The cities of Ramlah, Lod, Akko, Haifa, and Ashkelon in Israel were small villages before 1948. According to Arab accounts, Israel's soldiers expelled a large portion of the Arabs residing in those cities at the time of the War of Independence. Yet, there are more Arabs residing in those cities today than there were before the Arabs were allegedly expelled from them. Small villages, such as Umm-el-Fahm, Nazareth, Sakhnin, Tirah, Taybeh, and many others have grown-up into large all-Arab cities over the past sixty years (Neuwirth, 2008).

There is a widely heard claim that the Arabs in Israel live in dire and frightful circumstances. In fact they enjoy the highest standard of living compared to the socio-economic condition of the populations in most Arab countries, and they are the only ones in the Arab world that have genuine civil rights and freedoms.

As for the ridiculous charges of massacre and slaughter, the figures are clear: the Palestinian population is somewhere between 3.6 and 4.2

million people in Western Eretz-Israel, about three times the total Arab population of this territory just prior to the War of Independence, and seven to ten times the Arab population in 1891. The overwhelming preponderance of the evidence strongly indicates that it was Arab, not Israeli, actions that were the primary cause of the displacement of Palestinian Arabs during the war. The most important fact that many people naively ignore or deliberately forget is that the war was begun by the Arab states' aggressive invasion of Israel immediately upon its formal recognition by the United Nations. The Arabs declared without hesitation their aim to annihilate the Jews and demolish their state. If any massacres and/or ethnic cleansing took place, they were performed by the Arabs only.

The supreme Palestinian Arab leader, the mufti of Jerusalem, Hajj Amin al-Husseini, exhorted his followers over Radio Cairo: "I declare a holy war, my Muslim brothers! Murder the Jews! Murder them all." Other Palestinian leaders and Arab leaders made similar pronouncements. As for the objectives of the Arab states' invasion, they were expressed clearly by the secretary general of the League of Arab States:

> On the day that Israel declared its independence, Azzam Pasha, Secretary General of the Arab League, at Cairo press conference declared "jihad," a holy war. He said that the Arab states rejected partition and would set up a "United State of Palestine." Pasha added: "this will be a war of extermination and a momentous massacre which will be spoken of like the Mongolian massacres and the Crusades." (*NYT*, May 16, 1948)

The Palestinian and other Arab leaders were quite frank about having begun the war. Jamal al-Husseini, the acting chairman of the Arab Higher Committee for Palestine, told the United Nations Security Council on April 16, 1948:

> The representative of the Jewish Agency told us yesterday that they were not the attackers, that the Arabs had begun the fighting. We did not deny this. We told the whole world that we were going to fight.

On April 23, Jamal al-Husseini admitted in a speech to the UN Security Council:

> The Arabs did not want to submit to a truce. They rather preferred to abandon their homes, their belongings and everything they possessed in the world and leave the town.

In fact that is what they did. Isma`il Safwat, one of the commanders of the Palestinian army, stated in March, 1948:

> "The Jews did not attack any Arab village, unless attacked first."

Kenneth O. Bilby, the correspondent in Palestine for the New York Herald Tribune during the War of Independence, wrote:

The Arab exodus, initially at least, was encouraged by many Arab leaders, such as Haj Amin al-Husseini, the exiled pro-Nazi Mufti of Jerusalem, and by the Arab Higher Committee for Palestine. They viewed the first wave of Arab setbacks as merely transitory. Let the Palestine Arabs flee into neighboring countries. It would serve to arouse the other Arab peoples to greater effort, and when the Arab invasion struck, the Palestinians could return to their homes and be compensated with the property of Jews driven into the sea. (Bilby, 1950)

In June 1949, only six months after the conclusion of hostilities, Sir John Troutbeck, head of the British Middle East office in Cairo and no friend to Israel or the Jews, made a fact-finding visit to Gaza and interviewed some of the Arab refugees there. Troutbeck reported that he had learned from these interviews that the

refugees...express no bitterness against the Jews (or for that matter against the Americans or ourselves) but they speak with the utmost bitterness of the Egyptians and other Arab states. "We know who our enemies are," they will say, and they are referring to their Arab brothers who, they declare, persuaded them unnecessarily to leave their home.... I even heard it said that many of the refugees would give a welcome to the Israelis if they were to come in and take the district over.

The Palestinian Arab newspaper *Filastin*, reported on February 19, 1949, that the Arab states which had encouraged the Palestinian Arabs to leave their homes temporarily in order to be out of the way of the Arab invasion armies, failed to keep their promise to help these refugees.

Take Haifa for example. The British news magazine, the *Economist*, no friend of Israel or the Zionist movement, reported on October 2, 1948:

Of the 62,000 Arabs who formerly lived in Haifa not more than 5,000 or 6,000 remained. Various factors influenced their decision to seek safety in flight. There is but little doubt that the most potent of the factors were the announcements made on the air by the Higher Arab Executive, urging the Arabs to quit. It was clearly intimated that those Arabs who remained in Haifa and accepted Jewish protection would be regarded as renegades.

On May 3, 1948, the American news magazine, *Time*, reported:

The mass evacuation, prompted partly by fear, partly by order of Arab leaders, left the Arab quarter of Haifa a ghost city. By withdrawing Arab workers their leaders hoped to paralyze Haifa.

Alan Cunningham, the last high commissioner for the British administration of Palestine, which was in the process of withdrawing from the country while the fighting raged, wrote to the Colonial Office in London on February 22, 1948, and again on April 28, 1948, that the British authorities in Haifa have formed the impression that total evacuation is being urged on the Haifa Arabs from higher Arab quarters.

> The American consulate in Haifa had telegraphed Washington on April 25 that local Mufti-dominated Arab leaders urge all Arabs to leave Haifa and large numbers are going. Three days later the consulate followed up this communication with another that said, "reportedly Arab Higher Committee ordering all Arabs to leave."

On April 27, 1950, only two years after the Arab evacuation of Haifa, the Arab National Committee of Haifa asserted in a memorandum submitted to the governments of the Arab states that the removal of the Arab inhabitants

> …was voluntary and was carried out at our request…. The Arab delegation proudly asked for the evacuation of the Arabs and their removal to the neighboring Arab countries…. We are very glad to state that the Arabs guarded their honor and traditions with pride and greatness…. When the Arab delegation entered the conference room it proudly refused to sign the truce and asked that the evacuation of the Arab population and their transfer to neighboring Arab countries be facilitated.

These conclusions do not date from the time of the events themselves but only much later. The evidence is available in declarations made by Arab spokesmen on the Palestinian Authority media:

> When the first war between Arabs and Israel had started, the "Arab Salvation Army" came and told the Palestinians: "We have come to you in order to liquidate the Zionists and their state. Leave your houses and villages, you will return to them in a few days safely"…it was too late to realize that the support of the Arab states was a big illusion (al-Ayyam, May 13, 2008).
>
> The leaders and the elites promised us at the beginning of the Naqbah in 1948, that the exile will not last more than a few days, and afterwards the refugees will return to their homes, which most of them did not leave only until they put their trust in those promises made by the leaders and the political elites. Afterwards, days passed, months, years and decades, and the promises were lost. They told us: the Jews attacked our region and it is better to evacuate the village and return after the battle is over. And indeed there were among us those who left a fire burning under the pot, those who left their flock of sheep…based on the assumption that we would return after a few hours. (al-Ayyam, May 16, 2006)
>
> My father and grandfather told me that during the "Naqbah," our district officer issued an order that whoever stays in Palestine and in Majdal is a traitor, he is a traitor. (PA TV, April 30, 1999)
>
> The Arab Muslim Kings and Presidents said that poverty is killing us … like the armies of your predecessors in the year of 1948, who forced us to leave, on the pretext of clearing the battlefields of civilians. (al-Hayah al-Jadidah, March 19, 2001)

### The UN and the Arab Refugees

The UN High Commission for Refugees (UNHCR) handles all refugees in the world, except the Palestinians. UNRWA, the largest UN agency (25,000 employees, most of them Palestinians), deals exclusively with Palestinian refugees. Unlike refugees in other parts of the world, Palestinian refugees are defined as any Arab who was in Palestine two years before the 1948 war. Unlike UNHCR, UNRWA covers all descendants, without any generational limitation, inflating their number to enormous legendary figures. Unlike UNHCR, UNRWA perpetuates the refugee problem and does not resettle the Palestinian refugees. Unlike all other refugees in the world, only the Palestinians get food regularly, and permanently, on a monthly basis. Unlike more than one billion poor, miserable, wretched and humiliated people around world who live in severe and inhuman conditions, the Palestinians receive many billions of dollars annually. These funds have supported the Palestinians' deep involvement in terrorism and corruption, worldwide.

Amazingly enough, 300,000 Palestinians were expelled from Kuwait and Saudi-Arabia, due to PLO's collaboration with the 1990 Iraqi invasion of Kuwait—without any social rights; without any ability to change their fate; without any complaint whatsoever; without any protest or rejection of the Arab world and the international community. Amazingly, they were allowed to enter the Palestinian areas by Israel. That kind of treatment was accepted as typical of Arab culture. As the Arabs perceived the situation, the Palestinian Arabs were invited by an Arab tribe to work in Kuwait and Saudi Arabia, and the tribe (now two Arab nations), has the right to expel them, as their presence in those countries was no longer needed. (Avneri, 1980; Peters, 1984)

However, the Jewish anti-Zionists in Israel asserted that their country discriminates against Arabs. The anti-Zionists draw a distinction between democracy and the Jewish domination of Israel. Israel—in the eyes of the anti-Zionists—is an ethnocracy not a democracy. Jewish democracy is an illusion, and Israel practices apartheid in a manner worse than South Africa before the fall of the Afrikaner or white domination there. The demolition of Arab homes by Israel, some 250 to 300 per year since 1948, should be discontinued and those homes should be rebuilt. Indeed, the outspoken and radical anti-Zionist, Jeff Halper, professor emeritus of anthropology at Ben Gurion University has devoted himself to raising funds for the reconstruction of "Arab homes demolished by the Israel army." At this time, Halper's "organization," of which he is the sole member, is being funded by the EU.

According to Halper and company, the world should boycott Israel in every possible sphere, particularly in the areas of military and financial support, as well as in the academic and professional sphere. Classroom instruction should be devoted to exposing the victimization of the Arab Palestinians and the clandestine connection between the universities and Israel's security forces. Another leftist sympathizer, Ilan Pappe, devoted much effort to encouraging the British boycott of Israel in all domains, economic, cultural, academic, and others. His campaign gained momentum in 2007 as many British labor, business and academic organizations approached the date when they were to vote on whether to undertake a massive boycott of Israel. The initiative petered out, although we cannot be sure that the last word on the subject has been spoken. Pappe now lives in England where he will most certainly attempt to continue his anti-Israel campaign.

Moreover, anti-Zionists claim that Israel's actions affecting defenseless Arabs and Palestinians are worse than those perpetrated by Hamas, Hezbollah, or other Arab groups against Jews and Israel, that Israel constitutes a danger to world stability. The British Medical Association should be invited to conduct a study of the extent to which Arab Palestinians are traumatized at checkpoints as they enter Israel from Judea and Samaria, or return to their homes there after a day's or week's work. The BMA should be invited to investigate the extent to which Arab Palestinians suffer from curfews imposed by the Israeli army on parts of the Arab population. Since Israel, in the anti-Zionist view, conducts state supported terror against the Arabs, their acts of terror against the Jews are justified. Neve Gordon of BGU (Political Science), acted as a human shield to protect Yasser Arafat in Ramallah from being arrested.

Thus, Israel is evil, racist, and oppressive and Zionism an colonialist movement. In the words of Benjamin Beit ha-Lachmi, a psychology professor at Haifa University, Israel is fighting against every liberation movement in the Third World:

> From Manila in the Philippines...in Honduras...in Namibia, Israel emissaries have been involved in a continuous war, which is truly a world war. And what enemy is Israel fighting? It is the population of the Third World which cannot be allowed to win its revolution. (cited by Isaac, Rael, and Erich, 1993, p. 139)

In their minds, it is widely "known and accepted," that no less than three and a half million Arabs have lived behind fences, wire, and concrete for the past forty years (compared to the huge Jewish population in Israel at the time of less than half that number). The way to end the reign of terror against the Arabs is to take up an armed struggle against Israel and prevent her from perpetrating more torture and murder of Arabs. Only one nation deserves to stand on the soil now occupied by Israel and that is an Arab nation. There can be no two-state solution to the conflict between Israel and the Arabs, only a one-state solution—an Arab state. Clearly Israel has to be de-Nazified: "Israel's Nazification needs no dictatorship since plenty of sturdy little Hitlers seems to be securely ensconced in ...many...hearts" (Neve Gordon).[9]

Adoption of relativity in one's historical-social perspective and in the study of historical and social affairs has introduced the fundamental assumption that each individual, group or nation possesses its own perspective on past events. Hence, its view of these events, that may constitute its own past and historical identity, are more in the nature of a narrative, i.e., their way of viewing matters, than of "objective" truth. To some, the Jewish-Zionist narrative of why and how Israel emerged is no more legitimate than the Arab narrative which claims that the establishment of Israel brought a catastrophe (*Naqbah*) on the Arabs, regardless of what it meant to the Jews. The anti-Zionist academics adopt the Arab "narrative" as their own or as the only justifiable one in their eyes. It follows that acts of self-defense on the part of Israel deepen the catastrophe for the Arabs. The use of the term narrative to avoid confronting the facts of history was held up to ridicule in the press (Glick, 2007) but anti-Zionists cling to their articles of faith before, during and after wars between Israel and its terrorist neighbors.

### Israel: A Catastrophe for the Arabs?

Just what, one might ask, is the catastrophe? Or, what about the establishment of Israel is a catastrophe as far as the anti-Zionists are concerned? They certainly do not view the matter through the eyes of the Muslim world for whom the catastrophe is, to no small degree, the mere fact that Jews occupy territory that was once Arab land ever since it was conquered in the seventh century by 'Umar (638-640 CE), and hence must remain Arab in perpetuity, according to Islamic doctrine. Spain, called Andalusia by the Arabs, must also return one day to the fold of Islam. Curiously, the present leftist prime minister of Spain, Zapatero, doesn't seem to agree with that view.

For the anti-Zionist Jews, the catastrophe does not stem from a grasp of the Islamic view of history but from the manner in which they comprehend their Jewish identity. The Arabs may object to Israel by employing concepts derived from Islam, but the anti-Zionist Jews think in terms of concepts derived from the social sciences and Marxist dogma that deride religion and particularistic nationality. In short, the concepts employed by the academic anti-Zionists in Israel are primarily based on an ideology that is traditionally anti-Semitic. They are not based on a rational approach to understanding history, but on Marx's twisted anti-Semitic conceptions.

It is hair-raising to grasp that the Jewish anti-Zionists in Israel live in a historical bubble of their own making. They cannot see out into the world as it is or was. For example, Ilan Pappe claims in his book *The Ethnic Cleansing of Palestine* that the Haganah planned to evict the Arabs from major cities. He never asks about the Arabs' plans for the Jews.

During the five months between the UN Partition plan on November 29, 1947, and May 1948 when Israel was established, massacres of Jews by Arabs were common. In fact, 1,256 Jews were slaughtered in Arab attacks during those five months alone. Commanders of the Jewish groups like the Haganah and Irgun had every reason to regard Arab villages as hostile and to proceed accordingly. Any other approach would have been suicidal. But the worst was yet to come.

Ilan Pappe and Neve Gordon along with others in the anti-Zionist group, rewrite history in their own image and carefully avoid any clash with reality so that the Jews figure as devils and Arab attacks and murder of Jews can be framed as reactions of desperation. Never mind that the entire approach is blatant one-sidedness that "tells" what the Jews did and systematically omits any reference to what the Arabs were doing. That creates not merely a totally distorted picture but, more important, a nefariously tendentious reconstruction of events that cannot be understood conceivably in any rational manner. The anti-Zionist literature leads directly to the conclusion that the Jews were driven by a biological urge to kill Arabs unrelated to events in the environment. That urge led to unrestrained hostility toward peaceful Arabs who were provoked into armed resistance. That is the historical picture the anti-Zionists would like us to believe. Precisely the same approach was repeated again and again in the work of other anti-Zionist authors.

In 1948 a coalition of Arab nations attacked the nascent state of Israel with every intention of eliminating all the Jews (which is what they said they intended to do). Israel came into being only three years after World War II and the Holocaust (the reality of which Abu Mazen has denied vehemently). The Arabs had been close allies of the Nazis all through the war. The Mufti of Jerusalem, Haj Amin al-Husseini, was a devoted follower of Hitler. Husseini pointed out to him that he, Hitler, had one purpose in common and that was to eradicate the Jews. The Arab League, as well as the so-called moderate Arab leader Ragheb al-Nashashibill made extreme genocidal comments regarding the Jews. If, as Kimmerling wrote, Hitler had completed his massacre of the Jews, Kimmerling (a Romanian Jew) would not have lived to express his hatred for Israel regardless of whether he was to be found in Romania or in Israel.

The anti-Zionist academics substitute the record of Israel's wars with the Arab nations with their own "narrative." Their version disregards the catastrophe planned by the Arabs for Israel's Jews, and adopts the Arab narrative to the effect that the establishment of Israel was a catastrophe for the Arabs. Ironically, even a cursory reading of events surrounding the Israel's War of Independence demonstrates that hundreds of thousands of Arabs remained in Israel after Israel was established despite the fact that Arab armies attacked Israel and threatened its very existence. Israel did not expel the Arabs within its borders as any other country would have done to a potentially irredentist population after the defeat of their home countries in war. After the defeat of Germany in 1945, the German nationals residing in many European countries, who took no active part in the war itself, were evicted and returned to Germany, particularly from the Soviet Union, France, Poland, Czechoslovakia, and more. Approximately 13 million Germans were transferred out of European countries and sent back to Germany even if they had resided in those countries for several generations. When Roosevelt, Churchill, and Stalin met in February 1945 at the Yalta Conference, the transfer of millions of Germans from parts of Germany that were to be annexed to western Poland, and sent to that part of Germany that was to remain intact after conclusion of the war, was seriously considered by all of the three Allied leaders (Wheeler-Bennett and Nicholls, 1974).

The Arabs now living in Israel are the offspring of Arabs from the countries whose armies attacked Israel several times, not just once in 1948, but in 1967 and 1973 as well, and were defeated. Had Israel evicted all of the Arabs from Judea and Samaria as well as from the Galilee and the Negev after the defeat of the combined Arab armies in 1948, and certainly in 1967, that step would have been accepted by other countries as the legitimate policy of the victor in order to avoid certain conflict in the future. In our day, conflict between the Arab and Jewish populations in Israel is considered to be a distinct possibility, even a threat, by experts on Israel-Arab affairs (Israeli, 2002), especially if and when Israel completes its plan for permitting the establishment of an additional Arab state in Judea and Samaria.

The annexation of Judea and Samaria by Jordan in December 1949, affirmed in April 1950, was recognized by two countries only, namely Britain and Pakistan, but by no one else, not even by the other Arab nations, not to speak of the United States and the European nations. The League of Nations, followed later by the United Nations, explicitly designated the territory of Judea and Samaria as part of the Jewish homeland. Arab propaganda convinced European nations, the United States and many Jews in Israel, that Israel's retention of Judea and Samaria after the Six-Day War constitutes "occupation" of the enemy's territory by an act of aggression which is inadmissible under the Geneva Convention.

That assertion and position has absolutely no basis in international law or in the resolution of the United Nations immediately upon its establishment in 1945 when it upheld the declarations and commitments of the League of Nations.

It is worthy to note clearly: the West Bank was annexed by Jordan, and Gaza was occupied by Egypt, imposing there a military regime, with a steady, fixed night curfew until 1967. However, Egypt and Jordan were never called occupiers. Nor were there any so-called Palestinians on the scene, not as a people, not as a nation, and not as a political identity. Of course the Arabs were there all the time, but, as noted, no one characterized the Egyptians as occupiers. Hence the people, who today are called Palestinians, were not "occupied" but liberated when they were in fact occupied by Arab occupiers. It is no less important to recall that the issue that appears to dominate the Palestinian Israeli conflict was never that of occupation, of rivalry over territory. Rather, the conflict was, and remains, due to the Islamic religious principle of denying Israel's existence as a state and as a nation.

Yet, contrary to all historical precedent and the decisions of the United Nations prior to its transformation into an Arab-Islamic dominated organization, leftist establishment adopted and implanted into Israel's accepted vocabulary the term "occupation." For Jews, that term refers to Judea and Samaria, but, for our Arab "peace partners," it refers to all of Israel (Epstein, p. 127). Indeed, the Arab-Palestinian in charge of "Palestinian" foreign affairs said that the Arab-Palestinians do not want a state in Judea and Samaria, they want all of Israel. Actually, the latter statement is not true either. The Arabs want the conversion to Islam, or the death, of the infidels, Christians and Jews. Since it is tactically inadvisable to include the Christians at this time, the Arab-Palestinians can be satisfied by naming the Jews as their sworn enemies and as the sworn enemy of the entire world, as Ahmadinejad made clear during his September 2008 visit to the United Nations and New York.

## Israel as an Ethnic Nation: Multiculturalism

The social sciences, especially sociology and political science (which is politics with no science) are heavily influenced by Marxist notions.

They focus on social class membership, social domination, government structure, the proletariat or the lower classes, and so forth. For many people in these fields of endeavor, the notion of an ethnic nation is either unknown or unacceptable. The "liberal" view emphasizes a multicultural rather than a national (or the term they prefer—"nationalistic') perspective.

Nationalism is a world-wide phenomenon. Its primary meaning is expressed through the particular identity of each nation's population. That identity forms the basis for each ethnic-national group to assert its sovereignty or control over its territory. The identity of Western nations consists of two dimensions: cultural—the traditions of its civilization, and political—the principles of competition, democracy and equality before the law (of all citizens including their elected leaders). These two dimensions are presently under attack from a variety of intellectuals whose position stresses the concepts of multiculturalism, relativism, and post-nationalism.

Post-nationalism is a variation on the theme of postmodernism. In effect it is a secular eschatological, proto-Messianic approach to the "religious" belief in universal Redemption. This perspective aims at a deconstruction of the ethnic nation-state. In our view, the attempt to transform the nation-state into a multicultural society is not merely naïve, it is patently foolish, suffused with animus and destruction. Dismantling of the nation-state as known today inevitably will lead to the emergence of relatively small nation-states. Such relatively small nations will be acutely unstable and will engender multiple inter-nation conflicts. The potential result of such a situation would be the existence of politically torn nations, a multi-civilization social-political reality that in fact does not identify with any civilization at all. History has shown that national-political units of that kind are incapable of maintaining a coherent society.

Multiculturalism seeks to exchange the fundamental privileges and rights of the individual with those defined in terms of ethnicity. That approach, of course, leads directly to the downfall of Western liberal democracy. Whatever is aligned with the West as a cultural phenomenon will collapse and disappear. The multicultural regimes of the Soviet Union and Yugoslavia have made their tumultuous exit, their constituent nations having all declared their independence. At this time, the anarchists seek to replay that scenario in the West under the guise of a false intellectualism sustained by political boorishness and patently reprehensible deeds.

But the problem is far worse than that. Just as the concept of the multicultural nation-state is gradually dying in Europe, where, ironically, Belgium and Holland are leading that process while England is the last in line, the old-fashioned idea is receiving support in Israel. In Germany, Angela Merkel announced that the notion of multiculturalism has disintegrated. "Whoever arrives in Germany to live, must respect our constitution and our Christian-cultural-Western roots" she said. Holland, which once preached absolute multiculturalism, has awakened after the assassination in February 2002 of Theo van Gogh, the artist and leader of the nationalist movement. Today Holland emphasizes the transmission of national values (although Holland is presently—January 2009—bringing a lawsuit for incitement against the head of its nationalist political part Geert Wilders because he pointed out the dangerous ideology of Islam). A new immigration law stresses, much like the Danish law, clear values. By contrast, Israel has undergone a change from the prevailing notion of the "melting pot" to the concept of "A nation of all its citizens." The latter is a sure recipe for the ultimate eradication of the Jewish Zionist state. The intention of those behind that approach is to transform Israel into a multicultural and multinational state. The true essence of that utterly confused idea is the establishment of an Arab Palestinian state from the Sea to the Desert at the expense of Jews as a People and a nation.

The multicultural idea flourishes in Israel. Professor Amnon Ruben-stein (professor of law) is correct when he said that the multicultural idea is a malignant disease that negates the existence of the Jewish People, of the Jewish nation and of the Jewish state. Zionism and the right of Jewish self-determination would disappear in a multicultural society (Rubenstein, 2005). That, in short, is the anti-Semitic doctrine of the self-hating Jews who despise their own people. Their goal is, no more and no less, to negate the Jewish state's right to exist and that of the Jews as a political entity entitled to its own homeland.

Even Europe is beginning to understand the nature of the connection between anti-Semitism on the one hand and anti-Zionism/anti-Israelism on the other hand. The connection means the denial of the Jewish people's right to define itself, and opposition to the existence of the State of Israel, all of which constitutes an essentially racist effort. Remarkably, it is in Israel itself that the anti-Zionist leftists seek the elimination of their own people and nation, and it is they who proposed the formula "A state of all its citizens." Europe has begun to comprehend that it must limit or even terminate immigration, whereas in Israel, under existential threat from its neighbors, the anti-Zionist and anti-Semitic left, seek to open immigration to those who wish to annihilate Israel and murder its Jewish citizens, the brethren of the leftists. So-called phony "liberals" in Israel operate with foolhardy blindness or with an opaque stupidity, and pay heed to the left. These forces accuse Israel of causing all of the troubles confronting this world. They want to delegitimize Israel using South Africa during the period of apartheid as a precedent. Some American Jews accuse Israel of practicing apartheid precisely because it reminds them of white South Africans and the blacks, and the Arabs in Israel are equated with the blacks.. Is that the mental background of Jeff Halper, Ben Gurion University's infamous Israel basher who is enamored of the term apartheid, which is an Afrikaner not an English word? (That word is also favored by Desmond Tutu who applied it to Israel ever since he became friends with the now-deceased Arafat).

Profound prejudice, sometimes the embodiment of anti-Semitism, is the only basis for the analogy between Israel and apartheid in South Africa. The blacks in Africa did not undertake a war against the South African whites, and the blacks were segregated for racial reasons. There was never any segregation by ethnicity or race in Israel. Arabs were, and are, free to choose where they wished to live or travel. Arabs choose to send their children to Arab, largely Muslim, schools where instruction emphasizes study of the Koran. They also segregate children from different Arab tribes so as to avoid inter-tribal conflict. Arabs do reside in separate communities in Israel, but there are large Arab populations in Haifa, Jerusalem, Jaffa-Tel Aviv, and Akko, again in given neighborhoods, all on the basis of their own choice, just as there are Jewish, black and Latino neighborhoods in American and European cities, such as Paris and London. It is rather commonplace to observe that people want to live with others who are most like them, who have a common origin, culture, religion, and so forth. The term apartheid serves anti-Zionists purposes because code words of that kind trigger a fallacious comparison between Israel and South Africa. In the United States the term segregation is used to refer to the restriction by law in a given society or location as to where people of a specified minority group may reside or go to school. Jeff Halper knows that no one will buy the idea that there is segregation in Israel so he and colleagues prefer the Afrikaner term whose exact meaning is vague for many people.

Geographically Israel is much closer to Europe than it is to the United States, Canada, or Australia. The latter three nations are what may be called multi-ethnic/national nations. None of them was ever an ethnic group since their ancestors immigrated to the United States from a number of north-European countries including the United Kingdom. However, like France and the United States, their political national identity is very clear: there is a French and an American nation, each with its national symbols and institutions, and all social groups in the nation must accept those symbols and institutions and abide by them—if they wish to remain or become citizens. One cannot argue with the national flag or the national identity of the state if one wishes to be a loyal citizen. Unfortunately, that is precisely the case in Israel.

Israel is similar to many ethnic nations in Europe and the Far East, such as the Czech Republic, Slovakia, Finland, Sweden, Norway, Holland, some Germany states, Poland, Latvia, Lithuania, Estonia, Romania, Hungary, Croatia, Serbia, Georgia, Thailand, South Korea, Taiwan, Turkey, the republics formed after the collapse of the Soviet Union, as well as Japan, the Philippines, and others. Moreover, many ethnic nations have minority populations among their inhabitants. That is the norm not an exceptional phenomenon.

Almost all of the countries named above are democracies, in one form or another, and are, simultaneously, ethnic nations. Some of the ethnic nations just mentioned will not grant citizenship to persons of different ethnic origin, Japan being the most notable instance of that policy. Yet, the world does not question Japan's democratic character. Israel does grant citizenship to non-Jews who apply for it. The anti-Zionists' denunciation of Israel as an "ethnocracy" whose Jewish majority wields hegemony over the Arabs, accuse Israel of maintaining an ethnic-cultural-religious Jewish society. Such hegemony is widely practiced and accepted in the world. But, a Jewish ethnic nation is considered by Israel's anti-Zionists as a racist endeavor even though self-determination was Woodrow Wilson's fundamental principle upon which Lord Balfour based his Declaration granting Palestine to the Jews as their national home (Fromkin, 1989). These views of anti-Zionist academics in Israel unequivocally indict them as Jewish anti-Semites.

A leading authority in Israel on anti-Semitism, Manfred Gerstenfeld (2007) noted:

> Anti-Zionism today has become very similar to anti-Semitism. Anti-Zionists accept the right of other peoples to national feelings and a defensible state. But they reject the right of the Jewish people to have its national consciousness expressed in the State of Israel and make that state secure. They are not judging Israel with the values used to judge other countries. Such discrimination against Jews is called anti-Semitism.

Raya Epstein (2003, p. 119) observed, with her usual illuminating insight:

> The new church [of European secular liberalism] inherited from its predecessor [Marxism/Soviet Communism] the moral identification with the PLO murderers and adopted the same anti-Semitism behind the mask of anti-Israelism. It is the very same anti-Semitism championed by the former communist church.

In our experience, many people in the United States are not aware of the fact that there are ethnic nations in contrast to the multi-ethnic society of their own country, and that there is a fairly large number of such nations. For the average American, the United States is the archetypal nation. Of interest is the recent development in Australia where the influx of Muslims prompted the government to clarify the limits of the multi-nation principle and emphasize the English speaking and patriotic nature of Australian culture and society. In Europe, however, "...anti-Semitism is revealed in the European-Muslim alliance that seeks to eliminate the Jewish character of the State of Israel" (Epstein, 2003, p. 125; see Bat Ye'or, 2002, 2004).

This does not prevent anti-Zionist Jews from continuously preaching violence against Israel. Professor Nurit Elhanan-Peled is one of the most openly pro-Palestinian faculty members at the Hebrew University. She may be best known for blaming Israel when her own daughter was murdered by a Palestinian homicide bomber. In a public statement, she stated the following:

> These words are dedicated to the heroes of Gaza, the mothers and fathers and children, the teachers and doctors and nurses who are proving every day and every hour that no fortified wall can imprison the free spirit of humanity and no form of violence can subdue life. The pogrom being carried out by the thugs of the Occupation army against the residents of the Gaza Strip is known to everyone.

For these and other anti-Semitic declarations, Ben Dror Yemini, one of the very few honest and responsible journalists in the Israeli press, denounced Elhanan-Peled in his *Ma'ariv* column on Dec 26, 2008, and explicitly called her an anti-Semite and a traitor. Elhanan-Peled uses the word "thugs," a favorite term for Jews used by anti-Semites, to describe the Jewish bullies who are in secret control of the world. The use of the term is not naïve and innocent, and erases the distinction between anti-Zionists and anti-Semites. She refers to the Hamas murderers as "freedom fighters," and to "Nazi Israel." She paints the Jews as the "threat to world tranquility."

According to our anti-Zionist academic, Israel is sunk up to its neck in the blood of innocent Palestinian babies and every breath that we take shoots out red bubbles of blood into the air of the Holy Land. She intentionally—and viciously—misuses the famous poem by Bialik about the Kishinev pogrom, "On the Massacre," and declares that "the child in question (mentioned in the poem—authors) is a Palestinian from Gaza, and his butchers are Jewish soldiers." That accusation is no different than the medieval blood libel for which so many Jews were massacred. The anti-Zionist Jews in Israel seem to be unaware of the potential "pogrom against the Jews" to which they are contributing. Perhaps they are willing to sacrifice their lives as long as the Jewish State will be destroyed along with them. Perhaps that is what constitutes the post-modern hero.

### Edward Said and Columbia University

There is of course the anti-Zionist and fanatic anti-Western spokesman Edward Said, the late Columbia University professor of English. With his very influential and egregiously twisted volume *Orientalism* (1978), he played a very important role in spreading hostility to Israel in the academic world. Said was an ideologue and mouthpiece for leftist anti-American, anti-Western and anti-Zionist ideas in the United States, who linked Israel with colonialism and racism. The Middle East was turned into many Arab/Muslim countries by the League of Nations in the 1920s and placed under the Mandatory rule of England or France, so that Palestine was in fact a British "colony." Leftist groups were, of course, opposed to "colonialism" so that such a link ipso facto turns Israel into an "enemy of the people" as "capitalistic imperialists" were called by socialists/liberals at that time (and maybe still called that by contemporary communist Jews in Israel's academia and other places).

Said can be credited with invigorating, if not inventing, and granting intellectual status to, the Arab-Islamic rage against Israel in the twentieth century. This intellectual status invested Arab-Moslem hatred toward the West with legitimacy and created the myth of the Arabs and of Islam as victims. A well-known view in psychopathology, and to the late Yasser Arafat, is that one must learn how to play the part of victim. Once having aroused the sympathy of people in Western countries, who in any case harbor negative feelings toward the Jews and are exposed relentlessly to the anti-American propaganda coming from Muslim and European countries, the perpetrators of this crime can easily identified as colonialism, imperialism, and Zionism. Said's *Orientalism* achieved great popularity among the self-hating (Jewish and non-Jewish) academics and liberals. In keeping with Arab-Islamic practice, Said projected all the guilt onto the West and the Zionists. Their Arab/Muslim "victims" were not responsible for any aggressive behavior they may have displayed. Rather, they were perceived as having justifiable grievances.

For Said—who enjoyed a huge salary from one of the largest and most well-known American universities—the West practiced racism, imperialism, and ethnocentrism. A European, by definition, is necessarily a racist, perhaps precisely because he is human. The West subordinated the Arabs and Muslims to the United States, politically, culturally, and intellectually. The study of the Middle East conducted by Western universities is only an expression of Western propaganda intended to falsify our view of the Arab world and to humiliate it. Only Westerners wrote the history of the Middle East so that it serves the purposes of the agents of imperialism. The Western historians do not even know Arabic, and the few Westerners who know Arabic do not know its history.

The Christian historians of the early twentieth century, particularly those who came from Germany, were accused by Said of being missionaries. Their aim was to undermine Islam and ultimately eradicate it so that Christianity could supplant it. Philip Hitti, an Arab researcher and stout defender of Islamic glory, is accused by Said of having been an enemy of Islam whose book is suffused with vitriolic attacks on Islam and ridicules Muhammad. As the reader could expect, Said lambasted the Jewish historians who allegedly dominated Middle Eastern studies in America's universities and who, subsequently, determined the direction of research in the field and distorted the Arab past and the nature of Arab society in the present.

Bernard Lewis, the British-born, Jewish professor (emeritus) of Oriental Studies at Princeton University, acknowledged by the Western academic world as the dean of Middle Eastern scholars, commented on Said's *Orientalism*. Lewis pointed out that Said always viewed the Orient as uniform and unchanging, and Orientalists were depicted as racists who provided a false picture of Islam. They were necessarily imperialists and ethnocentric. Actually, Said's work, said Lewis, is ahistorical, biased and unfit to be called research and is actually a reductionist absurdity. Said is arbitrary, full of contradictions. He refers to only a small part of the Arab world, certainly not to the Orient which is a huge part of the globe far greater than the Middle East. Said completely excludes Turkey and Iran from his book, as well as Semitic Studies. He disregarded the historical and linguistic context of Arab studies, so that his approach is a total falsification of reality, a display of a distressing degree of ignorance. In his imagination the West robbed, kidnapped, ravaged, and raped the Middle East by force and left behind an impoverished, uneducated, and unscientific Middle East. He interprets various authors' statements in a manner that bears no relationship to the obvious meaning of their texts. He simply ridicules modern research.

The Muslims ruled over large parts of southern Europe, and in Spain for 781 years, in Greece for 381 years and in the Balkans. It is not the case that Western countries ruled Muslim countries for long periods of time. The Ottomans were masters of Egypt for 365 years starting in 1517. It was a British protectorate for sixty-seven years. Iraq was a

British protectorate for fifteen years and Syria was a French protector-ate for fifteen years. Saudi Arabia was never under Western control, and Byzantium (Turkey) is still ruled by Muslims. Since the time or Ataturk, Turkey tried to be a secular nation, although at this time under the rule of Prime Minister Erdogan (January 2009) its Muslim identity and al-legiances are coming to the fore.

Said's assertions are not a function of plain ignorance but the product of his intentional reordering of history to generate evidence for his trumped up theory. Said did not even know Arabic and was totally unable to read any book or document that had not been translated into a language he knew, primarily English, so testified Bernard Lewis. His entire denuncia-tion of Orientalists stemmed from his political agenda and had no basis whatever in any form of genuine scholarship. It follows that he had no inkling of what the Arabs themselves had written about Middle Eastern studies. Rarely has there been a more egregious example of intellectual perfidy than that embodied in the book by Edward Said.

Ironically, Said's view of the Arab Middle East was far more negative than that expressed by European scholars, including those whom he se-lected for special mention as imperialists (Said, 322-323). The Egyptian philosopher Fu'ad Zakaria, is quoted by Bernard Lewis to the effect that oriental studies are not without blemish but the greater danger is that Arabs and Muslims deny their faults. The challenge is to take the bull by the horns and engage in self-criticism. But scholars like Lewis cannot avoid relating to the scholarly merits of Said's book. His judgment was that the book is worthless.

Ibn Warraq claimed that Said's book taught an entire generation of Arabs the art of self-pity, the politics of victimhood, and how Islamic fanatics should silence criticism of Islam. The aggressive tone of *Orien-talism* exudes "intellectual terrorism" since instead of logical arguments it disseminates denunciations of scholars as racists and so forth (Wind-schuttle, 1999). Said perpetrated errors in many topics that he mentions, but two invite comment here.

1.  The Muslims/Arabs are the only people who have revolted against the West with fanatical terrorism. Other nations do not.
2.  In Asia countries have succeeded in entering the modern world of progressiveness and technological advance.

Yet, countries in Africa are struggling to survive despite severe so-cial-economic-religious conditions. Most of Western aid does not reach Africa because it goes to the Arab Palestinians, despite their proximity to other Muslim countries that are weighted down with revenues from oil. The Middle Eastern Muslims are deeply involved in reactionary violence and terror. Their ideology is not a function of some post-colonial reaction but of Islamic fanaticism that cultivates dreams of restoring the Caliphate through domination of the territory in Europe once conquered by the Muslims.

Researchers in the field of Islamic Studies have been aware of the negative impact Said's book had on their discipline. Some scholars contracted a fear of asking potentially embarrassing questions that might upset Muslims. Montgomery Watt noted that Said was ignorant of Islam and attributed dubious motives to scholars and statesmen (Watt, 1991).

Humphreys observed that "Said's analysis of Orientalism is overdrawn and misleading … it is…seriously flawed…." (Humphreys, 1997). Said's style was termed "Stalinist" by Maxime Rodinson, himself no friend of Zionism (2001). An entire host of scholars, in addition to those cited above, condemned Said's book from multiple perspectives, as well as noting its terrible influence on the Arabs themselves who derived a false sense of satisfaction from his unfounded ramblings (Kramer, 2001; Makiya, 1993).

How did it come about that Said's book was so widely cited? Why was it reprinted so often? In our view, the answer to those questions is that Said's book embodies the "death wish" of the Left in the Western world. It reveals the "Anglo-Saxon flaw"—a masochistic yearning for self-flagellation and the motif of attributing guilt to oneself so typical of Judaism and Christianity, in contrast with the knee-jerk attribution of guilt to the "other" found in Arab-Moslem culture. Bernard Lewis (1993) attributed the success of Said's book to the hostility it expresses to the liberal democratic West. That view corresponds to the claim made by anti-Westerners in the West itself, to the effect that the United States is the source of all evil in the world. The Arab world's terrible economic problems stem from the West.

The latter statements impinge on Israel as well, and not only on the United States. The anti-Zionist left assisted Yasser Arafat to disseminate his ideas. They were based on the well-known accusations leveled against the United States and Israel namely: Occupation, imperialism and colonialism. The Arabs prefer to forget the terrible wound sustained, as they see it, when Arab countries were occupied by Western armies. Israel must be wiped off the face of the earth to completely eliminate the memory of those times. Indeed, Edward Said does constitute one of the intellectual foundations of the bizarre ideas preached by Israel's anti-Zionist Jewish Left.

# 3

# Anti-Zionist Ridicule and Jewish Patriotism in Israel

*"When the best are accused of being the worst, you have to look at the accusers."*
—*Alan Dershowitz*

*"We have a natural inclination —all too human and understandable:*
*To deceive ourselves and think that peace will appear one day as a crack in the wall*
*and will reach our tortured region."*
—*Ezer Weizman, former president of Israel*

Daniel Bar-Tal (2007) has made a career of writing about Jews' negative stereotypes regarding Arabs, especially those Jewish children have internalized from what they get in their schoolbooks. One must look hard to find any research in his publications about Arab children's hateful stereotypes of Jews/Israelis and how profound and pervasive is the hatred of Israel and Jews as preached in Arab/Palestinian schools and schoolbooks (Sharan, 1999). Recently the international media presented to the public the contents and images of Arab video games whose explicit purpose is to cultivate hatred of Israel and of Jews among Arabic-speaking children. Thousands of these games are sold every day in different Arab countries including Lebanon where they are produced by Hezbollah. These video games turn the entire topic of negative stereotypes in Israel's schoolbooks into a sick joke. No subtle verbal description impacts the minds of schoolchildren than the power of moving pictures on videos. This entire phenomenon, and the behavior of the Arab world in general toward the Jews and Israel, goes completely unmentioned in Bar-Tal's work.

Bar-Tal and Teichman (2005) studied Arab representation drawing as created by Israeli children. They made no effort to compare the Israeli's drawings to those of Arab children's representations of Israeli Jews.

There is no "0" point, as found on a thermometer, against which Bar-tal or any psychologist can compare someone's behavior and determine whether it is deviant, i.e. above or below "normal." A set of norms must be established to serve as the comparison against which given behavior can be assessed. If the behavior of Arabs toward Jews, or Arab textbooks' presentation of Jews/Israelis, is not measured or considered, what baseline data or criterion can be employed with which to compare the representation of Arabs by Jewish children? That comparison is required by all tenets of basic psychological research, otherwise the results lack validity. Also, we should be curious to learn how Israeli Arab children depict Jewish Israelis before and after the introduction into Arab Israeli textbooks of the term *naqba* (catastrophe, referring to the establishment of Israel in 1948). That study is required after all the tumult caused by the unfathomable act of Yael Tamir, Israel's current minister of education (up to the elections in Israel in February 2009) as a means for promoting "peace ... Now!"

On second thought, perhaps Minister Tamir's comment is not quite as preposterous as one might think due to the fact that she had a formidable precedent by which her remarks could be judged. All she needed to do was see the outrageously anti-Zionist hate-filled conduct of one of the previous ministers of education, Shulamit Aloni who recently reiterated in even more severe and outlandish terms her disgust with the Israel (Aloni, 2008). Aloni never was, and never will be, an academic in Israel. Consequently, the damage wrought to this nation and its citizens by her hostility to Jewish tradition, Zionism, and Israel was, and is, all the greater. At the time of this writing, Tamir is spending her final days in office, along with Prime Minister Ehud Olmert (who was interrogated by the police many times, even after Israel's war in Gaza in which Olmert played the role of a patriot). Tamir probably added many acts of Jewish self-hatred at the end of her stay in office in order to enhance her infamous record as minister of education of Israel (despite being the granddaughter of one of Zionism's heroes in Palestine/Israel, Dov Hoz).

We know a great deal about how Arab adults represent Jews and Israelis in their drawings and caricatures (Stav, 1999). Should we expect the drawings of Arab children to be so different from those of the adult society? Children everywhere who hear adults discuss dreadful events perpetrated on their country by another nation or group most likely will depict people from that group in a negative light. Children's drawings in the United States of the Germans and Japanese during World War II typically represented the images of "the enemy" in a very negative manner, to put it mildly. Aren't such drawings and the perceptions they reflect stereotypical? Of course they are. Consider the fact that human thought in general about other people, groups and nations, even thoughts about your own nation, by necessity employs stereotypes as a basic cognitive means of categorizing the myriad events transpiring in the environment and within the human psyche. Despite the French deconstructionists, the world cannot be comprehended as a vast collection of finite events disconnected from one another. Thought about groups of people becomes possible by categorization and stereotypes. Otherwise we would be reduced to thinking only about individuals, and our mental ability to deal with groups or nations would be seriously impaired.

Recent history has seen a worldwide increase in the use of negative stereotypes referring to Arabs because for the last decade or more many nations, primarily but not exclusively in the West, have been subjected to Arab or Muslim terrorism in different forms. The media have brought into the homes of people across the world scenes of the disasters perpetrated by Muslim terrorists from different countries, including the Palestinian Arabs. Time and again the world is treated to another story of kidnapping by Muslim terrorist groups, in Israel, the Gaza strip, Lebanon, Iran, Afghanistan, and elsewhere where the victims are used for financial or political extortion, torture and death by decapitation. By now, not only is it common usage to employ stereotypes in reference to the terrorists, but people have come to expect that the terrorists will be Muslims, whether the terrorism occurs in Spain, the United Kingdom, the United States, Israel, Lebanon, Indonesia, India, Afghanistan, Pakistan or elsewhere. It reflects how many Western societies have come to perceive and think about the Islamic world in reference to actual events, not on fantasies or "ingrained" hatred. Significant numbers of Muslims carried out these terrorist acts.

Some heads of state have said repeatedly that most Muslims are law-abiding citizens. The sheer fact that government officials feel compelled to make statements of that kind indicates that the public at large has come to believe that Muslims are potentially dangerous and a threat to Western society, and sometimes to Muslim societies as well. We cannot blame prejudice for these stereotypes, but rather palpable fears and suspicions based on prior experience. The fact that Islamic groups have proclaimed their devotion to jihad emphasizes the power of Huntington's concept of the "clash of civilizations." Psychology researchers, who voice accusations that Israel's textbooks include negative stereotypes about Arabs, and who draw an analogy between Hebrew textbooks and those found in Nazi Germany, exclude the worldwide context in which we live from their mental horizon. That, of course, is in addition to Bar-tal's personal bias expressed so unabashedly by stating that Israel's schoolbooks are similar to Nazi textbooks. Bar-Tal certainly intended to convey the message—by implication—that Israel itself is like Nazi Germany. What would have been this Polish Communist's fate in Germany had he told them what he is telling us now?

Similarly, one may ask what would have been Avrum Burg's fate had he, as the anti-Zionist he is today, would have been in his father's shoes? Burg, it may be recalled, once (during the 1990s) served as the director of the Jewish Agency for Israel but since then has metamorphosed into his present condition. As Glick (2007) pointed out, Burg's "leadership" was grossly ineffective, to employ kind language, and private Jewish organizations finally undertook to do something serious to stimulate and assist immigration to Israel from North America.

People tend to forget that the anti-Semitic stereotypes in German society and in its textbooks emerged long before Nazism. It was not the stereotypes that led to anti-Semitic outbreaks and the persecution of Jews. It was the persecution of Jews and the anti-Semitism rampant in German society during the entire nineteenth and early twentieth centuries that produced the stereotypes in European schoolbooks, before and during the Nazi's control of Germany and much of Europe (Vital, 1999). Indeed, Germany began its history of anti-Semitism in the early Middle Ages, as will be discussed later. Stereotypes of Arabs in Palestine/Israel were influenced by Arab persecution of Jews in the form of close to a century of armed attacks, murder, riots, and so forth (Israeli, 2002, 2003, 2006).

Bar-Tal and associates have a penchant for turning things upside down, proclaiming the bottom to be the top. To determine where the top or the bottom is located, or to distinguish causes from consequences, has always been a problem for social "scientists" who think in correlations instead of in cause-and-effect chains of events. That very same metaphor can be applied to the volume edited by Ben-Amos and Bar-Tal of Tel Aviv University's School of Education, called *Patriotism: We Love You, Homeland* (2004: republished in Hebrew by Hakkibutz Hameuchad) and praised, inter alia, by the late Baruch Kimmerling, surely one of the outstanding anti-Zionist Israelis of the twentieth century. For Bar-Tal, patriotism is essentially the motivating force behind a war. Patriots are prepared to (joyfully?) forgo their personal comforts and go to war, even to sacrifice their lives, on behalf of their country. No war or other armed conflict, assert the editors, can be conducted without the soldiers' sense of patriotism (including that of their generals, it appears). Of course, that is in addition to matters of domestic security, calculated de-legitimization of the enemy, cultivation of the population's sense of being a victim, and so forth. The conflict between Arabs and Jews (Israelis) relies on patriotism which—it is alleged—is the prism through which Israel conceptualizes the environment.

Ben Amos and Bar-Tal only edited the book entitled *Patriotism* (in Hebrew, 2004). The book contains fifteen chapters whose authors, not all of whom have the reputation of identifying with extreme leftists positions on Israel and the Arabs, write about that subject. As a comment apart from what appears in the following paragraphs it should be noted that the chapter by Micha Popper (pp. 195-211) differs markedly from the other chapters by virtue of the author's broad, multifaceted definition of patriotism that does not seek to establish a connection between patriotism and war, or with some instinct contradictory to human nature. Popper's chapter is, thus, something of an anomaly in this book, to the credit of the editors.

To Control the Homeland is a Patriotic project: To Rescue the Jewish People is the Goal of Zionism. Yigal Eilam, a well known historian in Israel, argues we must accept a distinction between Zionism's disregard for the concept of the Land of Israel versus its concentration on the Jewish People. Zionism asserted that that the Jewish People had to be changed significantly by means of leaving the Exile, moving to Israel and settling on the land. Thus, the Land of Israel was not Zionism's primary focus. The Jewish State, claimed David Ben-Gurion, was only a means to an end of settling the land of Eretz Yisrael. The State was a far more effective means for doing that than the British Mandate. Hence the Land of Israel could not be of equal importance, in the ideology of the Zionist movement, with the Jewish People, and so Ben-Gurion and his like-minded colleagues were willing to accept the plan to partition the Land of Israel and have the Arabs control their portion. (Ben-Amos and Bar-Tal, 2004, pp. 48-49)

Ben-Gurion later rejected a newer British suggestion giving the Arabs the right to maintain a majority in the population of Palestine (The British White Paper of 1939), and he initiated a struggle against the British plan, a struggle that he asserted was not directed at freeing the land from British control or for achieving independence for the Jews residing at that time in the Land of Israel. Ben-Gurion's struggle (in May, 1939) was explicitly for the purpose of undoing Britain's act of treachery against the Jewish people, against the masses of Jews who did not (yet) reside in Palestine.

Jabotinsky (as early as 1936 in a speech delivered in Warsaw) attacked the Labor wing of the Zionist movement for its Palestine-centered policy instead of focusing its attention on the millions of Jews "stuck" in the Golah. However, Yisrael Eldad, leader of the Lehi (Freedom Fighters of Israel) ridiculed that stance in 1950: "The presence of foreign soldiers on the soil of the homeland is not tolerated by anyone belonging to a non-Jewish nation. That idea was difficult to absorb by Jewish residents of the Land ... establishing a State is the solution to our problem ... saving the (Jewish) People is not an Idea (cited by Eilam on p. 51 in the book edited by Ben-Amos and Bar-Tal, 2004).

Eilam is not always transparently clear in his discourse, but seems to wish to present the notion that patriotism differs from Zionism because, in general, the Zionists sought to save the Jewish people while Patriotism means identification with a country or nation. As a psychologist, this author (S. Sharan) wonders what happened to history and to our awareness of the fact that we often do not know the exact motives or unexpressed thoughts of history's main cast of actors? We do not know exactly why Ben-Gurion assumed particular positions during the years of negotiations with the British. His lengthy diaries do not tell us everything. It seems quite reasonable to surmise that he did not wish to arouse greater antagonism on the part of the Arabs and/or of the British by asserting Jewry's demand for extended sovereignty over the Land of Israel. That is especially possible in light of the large number of Jews in Eastern, and even in Western, Europe who could potentially become immigrants to Palestine.

Nor can wars be "explained"—even to some small measure—as a function of patriotism. Patriotism is more often than not quite dormant, acquired in most countries by young elementary school students. It is a mental-emotional phenomenon aroused by the events that lead to war, not the other way around. If so, how can the political scientists and sociologists whose praise is cited on the back cover of the Ben-Amos/Bar-Tal book, justify their praise when the book itself is a travesty of logic, history, political reality, and the nature of human social behavior? Is it because they all came to praise Caesar *a priori* due to the ideology they knew would be expressed in it, while no one intended to bury, that is, criticize the book. Of course only favorable passages were selected for the cover to promote sales of the book, an approach found for just about every book published.

We may wonder if any astute reader's thoughts were attracted to this anomaly of the cart pulling the horse. But—to psychologize for a moment—couldn't that have been the authors' very intention, to impress on readers the view that patriotism (clearly demonstrated by many people in Israel) leads to violence? If that is the case it follows that, in the opinion of the editors, some thought or feeling, that is, some psychological state, explains why the misguided Jews keep fighting wars with their Arab neighbors when there "should have been" peace between them. Remarkably, neither editor suggested that the political-ideological goals of the Arabs promoted the wars with the Jews, as mainstream historians of the Arab-Israel wars have written repeatedly (O'Brien, 1986; Sachar, 1979). The entire history of the Yishuv during the British Mandate period finds the Jews buying territory from the Arabs and engaging in agriculture. The relentless attacks by Arab marauders pressured the Halutzim to form groups for self-defense. I challenge the editors of *Patriotism* to find examples of Jewish patriotism in Palestine from 1880 to 1948 that demonstrate their thesis that Jewish patriotism led to war or conflict rather than the far more fundamental psychological need for self-defense that responded to violent provocation.

There is no convincing evidence on behalf of the distinction between Zionism that allegedly sought to free the land form foreign control on the one hand, and Palestinian Jewry's struggle to rescue and preserve the Jewish people on the other hand. Yes, the two notions can be distinguished and not be considered identical. Yet, we should ask, just what do we gain in historical understanding from that distinction? Clearly the answer is nothing of note. The entire discussion in Eilam's article ignores the broader historical-social context in which these differences emerged. From today's perspective (2008), the fate of the Jewish people after the Holocaust, a fate now being powerfully affected by both cultural and national assimilation, and the need to maintain Israel as a Jewish nation, are inextricably interwoven. Both goals of safeguarding the integrity of the state as a Jewish nation, and serving as the only Jewish nation for Jews everywhere to consider their home, now or in the future, are complementary regardless of mental distinctions made for the purpose of writing historical essays. In reality the distinction is largely "academic."

The editors of the volume *Patriotism* succeeded in selecting many chapters by authors who underwrite the editors' views with the kind of semi-religious devotion that the authors attribute to patriots. Yael Zerubavel (Ben-Amos and Bar-Tal, 2004, pp. 61-99) initiates her discussion of patriotism with the definition: "Patriotic sacrifice is an altruistic act that contradicts the human instinct for survival." Can it be said in truth that patriotism necessarily involves sacrifice? We are willing to wager that patriots may or may not view their identification with their country or nation as a sacrifice but rather as a privilege, or as an opportunity to fulfill him/herself, and so forth. And can observers honestly classify "devotion to a cause that one considers worthy" to be contrary to basic instincts of the human race? If that is true, we should hardly expect countless millions of people in many countries around the world to exhibit patriotic behavior or express patriotic thoughts or emotions.

If a given act stands in opposition to fundamental human instincts such as the instinct for survival, we venture to say that it is patently unrealistic and absurd to claim that such behavior characterizes countless millions of people. How can readers relate to these genuinely learned essays when their authors become embroiled in such grossly deviant definitions of the concept they wish to clarify? Perhaps we should consider all citizens of Israel as patriots because they pay (or are supposed to pay) taxes. We surmise that there are not a few patriots who avoid paying taxes if they can. This strange world does indeed manifest numerous contradictions, not the least of which are the definitions of patriotism offered by an elite group of scholars whose work appears in this book. Nor need soldiers defend their country from its enemies out of a sense of patriotism: they can be imbued with a desire to protect their homes, their children, their friends as well as protecting their country from terrorists, or perhaps even out of a desire for revenge.

It seems quite natural to anticipate that many American soldiers felt they wanted to avenge the deaths of close to three thousand of their countrymen who died in the attacks of 9/11. The aforementioned types of motivation need not be viewed as having any necessary relationship to patriotism, although patriotism certainly need not be excluded as an element in the soldiers' thoughts or feelings. The present authors wish to ask: What motivates the editors and authors of various chapters in the book under discussion to make such transparently flawed statements and present such unacceptable definitions?

In a series of quotations from works of both poetry and prose composed in the late 1920s by the towering figures of the Hebrew literary world at the time, such as Yitschak Lamdan and Avigdor Ha-Meiri, Professor Zerubavel highlights their recurring mention of death resulting from the patriotic devotion of Jews at the time to the "conquest" of, or return to, Jewry's ancient homeland. More pointedly, death resulting from this "conquest" of the homeland was held up to be a heroic one, a model for Jewish heroism in an age where the national-collective destiny was primary compared to the less important fate of the individual

(Ben-Amos and Bar-Tal, 2004, pp. 64-65). The quotations are accurate, as is the fact that they were invoked as examples of heroism to serve as a model. What arouses puzzlement is, once again, the restriction of the historical-geographic horizons to the "Zionist" writers and "activists" of Palestine-Israel. Zerubavel ignores many important events, resulting in the presentation of a decidedly partial and insufficient background for comprehending the opinions, attitudes, assertions, and strivings of the early Zionist writers and leaders.

Yehezkel Kaufman (1936) defined the classic criteria for identifying anti-Semitic assertions (cited above). In light of his widely accepted definition one must point out that those very same conditions of potential death of many individuals in the course of their patriotic efforts obtain in the matter under discussion here, namely the Arab-Palestinians' press for a new Arab nation in Judea and Samaria. If the Arab-Palestinians continue their acts of terrorism against Israel, how many more of them, and of Israel's soldiers, will die as a result of that dangerous activity? Or should the Jews of Israel just lie down quietly and let the Arab terrorists wreak their murderous deeds on us?

Alternatively, let us assume for the moment that Israel participates in the establishment of a new Arab nation in the territory of Judea and Samaria. No nation can exist for long without some semblance of an economy needed to feed its citizens. Yet, no economy exists at this time—or, it seems, will exist in the foreseeable future—on which to base a new nation. Moreover, whatever may be the strivings of some Arab leaders to "restore a People to its homeland," and however much the world extols the "noble" ambition of self-determination, the many Muslim nations that exist at this time in almost each and every case demonstrate that democracy is simply not part of their culture or strivings. Hence, no one should delude themselves into presuming that the new Arab nation, if established, would be a democratic rather than an authoritarian theocratic nation, as are most of the Arab and Muslim countries today. However, as is widely acknowledged by people who view the matter with a modicum of objectivity, a new Muslim-Arab nation in Western Eretz-Israel will, almost inevitably, serve as another terrorist state that will, very quickly, serve the goals of jihadist Islam and of Iran. Hamas has been doing precisely this for quite some time. It is more than obvious that an Arab-Palestinian state will arise on the ruins of Israel and definitely endanger Jordan. From a Palestinian vantage point, there is no possibility of Jewish existence as a whole (Oren, 2008). That disaster is sadly being advocated not only by egregiously misled nations friendly to

Israel, but also by a not negligible part of political leaders and supporters of the extreme left in Israel's electorate. That phenomenon cannot be identified except as another indication of Jewry's suicidal impulse or perhaps death wish (Megged, 1994; Sharan, 2003; Stav, 1998).

In the social sciences it is often difficult to evaluate single events that lack essential similarity and meaning to other events. If we broaden the scope of the present discussion and appeal to events of World War II and later, it can be shown unequivocally that precisely the same patterns bemoaned by Professor Zerubavel emerged in many other countries. The leaders, poets, novelists, songwriters, and journalists of the day expressed their apprehension about the human toll to be paid for the successful resolution of a national, or even international conflict. In the case of Britain during the Blitz, the man in the street saved others, escaped the bombs, or died, and he knew quite clearly that those were his options, given the huge number of precedents. British, Russian, New Zealand, Australian, American, Polish heroes of World War II did not embrace patriotism and then perform their heroic acts. They were proclaimed heroes ex post facto because they fought their enemy with bravery and were consequently known as patriots.

Several authors of chapters in the Ben-Amos and Bar-Tal book claim that patriotism can lead to a willingness to sacrifice one's comforts or even one's life for the protection of the community. The implication of this mode of presentation is that the attribution of heroism and accepting the likelihood of death consequent to participation in the events, was stimulated by thoughts of patriotism, and much less by the threat of the enemy over-running your country and devastating your life, the lives of your family members, and the lives of countless numbers of your countrymen.

### How did European Nations Try to Resist the Nazi Onslaught?
### How did Germany Try to Counter the Russian Onslaught?

The critique of the authors' ideas referred to here is not restricted to any particular historical period, as Professor Zerubavel attempts to do in her chapter (p. 63). In fact, it is precisely during the past two or three decades, when patriotism in Israel allegedly declined, that soldiers in Israel have displayed what can be characterized as patriotic behavior in defense of their country. That observation is valid without the author knowing what the soldiers themselves thought about their own behavior. The citizens of Israel witnessed their soldiers' patriotism without conducting an investigation into their state of mind.

It seems a bit redundant and trivial to point out, as do the authors of a chapter in this book, that patriotism involves cognitive, emotional, and behavioral elements (Oren and Bar-Tal, p. 363). The only other dimension of human psychological existence is the unconscious, if you accept that Freudian notion. Oddly enough that dimension is omitted by the authors. Certainly the unconscious plays a role in patriotism as it does in many other broad and almost all-inclusive concepts we have about ourselves as people. It also plays a significant role in the lives of those who write about patriotism, such as the editors of the book referred to here. Authors who possess a relatively high level of self-awareness often include in their work a discussion of their own motives, goals, and methods that affect them in the preparation of their works, without, of course, presuming to know what their unconscious motives may be. An example of such an approach is found in the book by the well-known academic expert on education and psychology, Professor Seymour Sarason of Yale University (Sarason, 1995).

It is most significant that the editors of this book, and the authors of the specific chapter discussed here, failed to include any material that would permit readers to comprehend the intellectual, ideological or emotional background of their work. However, discerning readers will most likely reach reliable conclusions about that in the course of perusing this book, particularly after they encounter a chapter title such as "Manipulations of Patriotism in Israel Society" (pp. 363-398).

To what does the title of the aforementioned chapter refer? True, the authors issue the caveat that their assertion of "manipulation" does not refer to a phenomenon that is necessarily typical of a given group of patriots. They seek to clarify their meaning by indicating that it refers to a situation where the claim of patriotism results in the exclusion of some other group from the realm of the patriotic. Once again we wish to state that all such terms—such as wealthy, poor, evil, moral, patriotic, treasonous, dark, democratic and so forth—imply the existence, at some time or in some place, of a person or persons who differ and hence are not included in that group. That is the fundamental yin and yang of human thought and existence recognized, identified, and explained thousands of years ago. Just why do the authors make the effort, or occupy space in this book, to explain that phenomenon once again? It must bear some relation to their personal point of view, unless one attributes it to sheer pedantry.

Similarly, the term patriotism implies, perhaps covertly for some, that there are many people or nations who are not included in the positive aspect of the duality. Those people or nations are not Democratic, not wealthy, not white, not patriotic, not talented, not black, not Christian, Muslim, or Jewish. They are also less legitimate, or are beyond the pale, compared to those who are included. That bears no repetition. It is certainly the case if one assumes, as one must, that whoever reads this book must have lived on this earth for a while and most probably was graduated from elementary school.

Gad Barzilai (Ben-Avner and Bar-Tal, 2004, p. 345) makes the "astounding" statement that the citizens of nations at war typically display patriotic sentiments toward their country, and that at such time patriotism "becomes restricted" or "limited" to the nation favored by the dominant political party. Did the author forget that the dominant political party (in a democracy) is the one that must declare or direct a war against an enemy nation? Just toward whom would a citizenry express its sense of devotion to the country that is, at least in their perception, fighting to defend them against harm? Would they express "patriotic" sentiments toward a minority party that lost the election? Such a display would constitute an act of national divisiveness in a time of crisis. And who says the citizens must necessarily refer to any particular political party at all, whether it won or lost the latest elections? Don't most citizens in time of war address their patriotism toward the nation per se and not toward political parties?

In the United States, at this time, the Democratic Party is largely opposed to the war in Iraq, but in public it affirms its loyalty to the military and to the political establishment of the country of which the Democratic Party is essentially a part. All political groups, be they part of the "Establishment" or not, even if they are small or numerically insignificant, declare their patriotic devotion to their country. It is simply a gross distortion of reality to claim that "the legal definitions of devotion to the state have declined [i.e., become limited to] and reflect the inclinations of the political establishments, in order to emphasize the national need for the purpose of drafting collective citizenry for war." Isn't it patently clear that no democratic nation—not even a small city-state such as Singapore—can maintain a government "of the people" without political parties? Any party must "establish" itself, i.e., join the official political process and have its representatives listed on a ballot.

Of course there are non-governmental organizations (NGOs) in almost all democratic countries, but those organizations, by definition, do not participate in the official electoral process. No one can elect them to office as an organization, only as individuals. Assuming for a moment that such a deviant case existed somewhere, it is close to certain that a case of that kind would not emerge in time of war. Even extremists on both sides of the political spectrum would hesitate before being prepared to suffer the rage of the populous. Barzilai's assertions appear to derive from some never-never land that he wished would exist so he could conveniently employ that example as a whipping post. Barzilai also mentions that in Israel an Arab is considered less patriotic than a Jew. Despite Barzilai's use of the singular (Arab, Jew), he clearly wants to refer to all Arabs in Israel and all Jews in its plural form as a collective or social-ethnic group. But that is precisely the point: the Arabs as a collective are considered by the Jews to be less patriotic toward Israel than the Jews because Israel is a Jewish nation and is now, and has been, at war for many decades with Arab nations.

Moreover, the Arabs have (again as a collectivity, not as individuals) demonstrated persistently, for a century at least, their animosity toward, rejection of, and unwillingness to recognize the Jewish nature of the State of Israel. What additional evidence is needed by the members of an ethnic-nation like Israel (or like Finland, Norway, Sweden, Holland, Switzerland, the Czech Republic, and so forth) to reach the rational, clearly demonstrated, conclusion that a particular ethnic group other than their own (the Arabs, in this case) is in fact not patriotic toward the given nation (Israel). Any other conclusion would border on a suicidal view. The people of Finland knew very well that the Germans living in Finland were not Finnish patriots, even though, formally, Finland fought on the side of Germany in World War II. All the Germans in Finland were sent to the northern part of the country, and lo and behold, when the opportunity arose, Germany attacked Finland from the north although Germany is south of Finland. That was no coincidence. Are the Arab terrorists who originate in Um El Fahum but belong to Fatah, Hamas, or some other terrorist organization—are they terrorists by chance, or because they are Arab patriots?

The last point made here does not provide Neta Oren and Daniel Bar-Tal, authors of the chapter entitled "The Manipulation of Patriotism in Israel Society" (Ben-Amos and Bar-Tal, 2004, pp. 363-398) with a great deal of support for their theory that the Jews of Israel defined patriotism in a monopolistic fashion, i.e., did not include the Arabs of Israel in their comprehension of that term (compare Israeli, 2008 in English, or 2002 in Hebrew). Strangely enough, say the authors of the chapter under discussion, the notion of patriotism can exclude people who do not share the patriots' insistence on sustaining the elected leadership. Undoubtedly that can be true in some European countries with a particular kind of parliamentary system where the government can be toppled by a vote in the parliament that does not support the dominant political party. In the U.S. bicameral system, the minority party's victory in the Congress does not constitute a threat to the continuity of the government, so that in no case can the people who voted for, or identify with, the minority party be excluded from being considered patriots. Hence, it is definitely not the case that only members of the dominant party are considered to be patriots.

There is much evidence for the claim that the Jews of Israel disregarded completely the question of whether Israel's Arab population was to be considered patriotic to Israel or not. There are many Israel Arab members of all political parties, although a large portion is concentrated in the extreme Left, such as the Communist Party that has Arab representatives in the Knesset. Obviously, those Arabs' patriotism might be questioned by many Jewish citizens of Israel. However, the political-social lives of the Israel Arabs are not affected by that opinion in any public way, although they certainly may be affected psychologically in various ways.

Just what, then, does it mean when Oren and Bar-Tal state that the people who do not support the prevailing ideology are not considered to be patriots? Just what does it mean to the Arab members of the Knesset that perhaps a majority of Jews believe that they, the Arab members of Knesset, are not patriots? Does it mean they would not be elected, that they will be persecuted or mistreated, that they will be ridiculed or feared? Yes, patriotism does have both cognitive and emotional sequelae for many or most people, but the behavioral consequences, particularly in the case of Israel Arabs' political life, are few if any. The authors' assertion that "any expression of criticism of the ideology, policy or leadership of the country is perceived as non-patriotic or treasonable" (p. 364), and that the Jews of Israel believe that they have a monopoly on patriotism in the country, is patent distortion and grossly misleading.

Utterly preposterous is Oren and Bar-Tal's claim that a person perceived by others as not being patriotic is not considered to belong to his/her own people/nation, and is considered to be a traitor. That might be true in dictatorships, not in democratic countries. In democratic countries, people who are viewed as not patriotic may be shunned by some, but they are not accused of treason. Many countries have had their traitors, and they are not shunned because they are left to be anonymous, or because their traitorous behavior does not consist of a betrayal of national security. If the authors of the chapter referred to here have evidence to the contrary, the onus is on them to present that evidence along with their assertions. That claim is so blatantly contrary to normal experience that the need for evidence is too pressing to be postponed.

For example, the term "un-American" when referring to someone's behavior, does not imply, under any circumstance, that a given person is, or should be, excluded from the American nation. Nor do people consider him/her to be a traitor. Nor is an unpatriotic person ever thought of as excluded from the people of Israel. A famous rabbinic dictum, formulated about 1,500 years ago, unequivocally states that "A Jew who sins is nevertheless a Jew." That statement certainly includes all of those Jews who criticized, disagreed with, or otherwise failed to behave according to the norms of Jewish society and its leadership. That rabbinic norm was never abrogated and most definitely prevails today in Israel. Wisely, Israel does not ask Arabs to serve in its military, although some do of their own free will.

The statement that persons believed by others to be unpatriotic are, overtly or covertly, excluded from the nation is so transparently false that its propaganda purposes cannot be missed, that is, dissemination of falsehood for "political" or "ideological" reasons and goals. Assume for a moment that someone is arrested in some country for incitement and given a sentence of "exile" for five years or longer. The very fact that a person convicted of incitement is sent away, out of the country, as punishment proves that he/she is considered part of the nation/people. A person not considered part of the nation cannot be "exiled." They can be expelled but not "exiled." Napoleon was "exiled" but not expelled. Otherwise he could have gone wherever he wished and not forced to live on the island of Elba. Whether such punishment is justified or not is an issue that cannot be discussed here.

In their chapter, the authors, Oren and Bar-Tal, wrote about a subject that appears to reveal more about the authors themselves than it does about the object of their discussion, namely the events surrounding the attitudes expressed by Israel's political parties toward the Communist Party in Israel. The latter was the brunt of considerable de-legitimization by the other parties, particularly since it proclaimed itself to be a non-Zionist party. The Zionist parties asserted that the Communist Party's declaration, and particularly its objection to Israel's Sinai Campaign in 1956, constituted a threat to the nation's security and hence was an act of treason, as was stated in the semi-official newspaper of the day, *Davar*, on November 8, 1956. The newspaper claimed that the Communist Party was subject to the directives of a foreign power and identified with the aims of Israel's enemies (p. 371). This attitude toward the Communist Party serves as an example—so say Oren and Bar-Tal—of "the manipulation of patriotism" because the anti-Communist position identified with Zionism. Moreover, the manipulations are the instrument of the political right exclusively. It is the left that is unequivocally devoted to peace, say these authors (p. 388). The hawks are trying to eat the doves, and in Israel that phenomenon is particularly blatant, more so than in other countries, because in Israel it is accompanied by a singularly powerful drive to delegitimize other political groups (p. 392).

The authors do not engage in any assessment of the political-military conditions prevailing during the period they discuss, nor do they evaluate the extent to which the behavior of either the Zionist political parties or the Communist Party did in fact have a bearing on historical events and on the political-military fate of Israel. The authors concentrate on ideology, while political reality is ignored. Does ideology exist in a social-national-military vacuum? From a strictly intellectual-analytic perspective, it is surprising to see such a radical disregard for the social-political-military ecology manifested in this chapter, and, indeed, in a good part of the entire book. A rebuttal of the authors' interpretations requires no more than a quick reference to any standard history book of the period (O'Brien, 1986; Sachar, 1979).

In our estimation, the reply to the question posed at the beginning of this work, namely—why write about the anti-Zionists?—appears to be of greater importance the more we delve into their publications. As the distortions increase in depth and scope, so the reply must grow in significance. 'Tis true, 'tis pity! It seems that we are engaging in apologies, but in truth this is more a probe into historical reality as a counterbalance to egregious misrepresentation of that reality. But writing history per se does not suffice. Rather, the problem confronting the Jewish people is survival which occasionally requires polemics against one's enemies, external or internal, after the genuinely professional historians have done their work.

Readers of this book may not be aware of the fact that very few Jews currently reside in Muslim/Arab countries because most of them departed long ago. Ergo, the question of their service in the military organizations of Muslim countries did not arise, although Jews did serve in the armies of some Arab countries before Israel was established and before the Muslim countries became infected with fierce anti-Semitism. In medieval Muslim Spain, for example, large numbers of Jews served in the Muslim army, and at one time a Jew (Shmuel Ha-levi ben Yosef ibn-Nagrelah,

Ha-Nagid, 993-1056) was the commander-in-chief of a Muslim army that fought against the Christians. More recent manifestations of Jews' relationship to military matters in Muslim countries are discussed by Bernard Lewis (1984, p. 135).

No doubt, the public school system presents a largely—but not exclusively—patriotic version of a nation's history. Is there such a thing as a neutral history, one that takes no position whatsoever regarding the nation's past, its values and strivings for the future? Perhaps that question deserves in-depth research in a variety of countries. The results of that research can be anticipated to a large extent but not absolutely. We expect the results of such a study—if it could be carried out—to be negative: Countries do not present their national history or culture in negative terms. Public education everywhere does not wish to alienate the youth from its own country. Neither does it wish to cultivate a narrow-minded, self-centered, inflated version of its history and accomplishments alongside a grotesque depiction of its enemies. That might have been true in antiquity, or even in the Middle Ages, but it is decidedly not true since the advent of relatively modern approaches to historiography. It would not hurt the authors of the chapter in question to acquire more information about nations' curricula in regard to the topic of patriotism before asserting what a given curriculum says or does not say about it. It is more than reasonable to suggest that nations' curricula are not uniform in this respect, but that they are, in general, not at the extreme ends of any distribution, as Oren and Bar-Tal imply (p. 367).

Reading the chapters of this book written by Israeli academics leaves little doubt that the book reflects a clearly conceived plan to belittle, denounce, and condemn Israel for its alleged inhuman and nefarious mistreatment of the Arabs in Israel. The editors' goal was to be achieved by the systematic disregard of Arab behavior except "in their role" as victims. Bar-Tal and Teichman's volume on Jewish children's representation of Arabs in their drawings suffers from the very same flaw: they did not study Arab children's representation of Jews so they had no basis for comparison. In any case, to their minds no comparison was needed. The Jews treat the Arabs, and represent them verbally or graphically, very badly, and no reference is required to the Arabs and their propaganda or behavior to prove that.

Of course that position is scientifically and morally indefensible and reflects a deep-seated prejudice that the editors and authors of the chapter here never even mention. Events performed by Israel regarding the Arabs are all described in unilateral terms. This is a perfect volume for the new

Arab-Palestinian movie industry whose exclusive message is the mistreatment of the Arabs by the Jews, and the Ben-Amos/Bar-Tal volume is a book about blame, not about social science research or theory. That aspect of the book is a transparent façade, a backdrop for its main focus. Had the book been written by Arabs, it would fall naturally under the rubric of propaganda that is broadcast daily by Abbas and colleagues.

The question relates to stereotypes and prejudice. Just when prejudice against blacks in the United States declined markedly, the sinister presence of the Arab terrorist rose up to catch the attention of the free world. No doubt that law-abiding Muslims in many countries are badly affected by the frightening image of the jihadist Muslims wreaking terror on the West. But not since Charles Martel halted the Muslim conquest of Europe at Tours in 732 c.e. has the West been so palpably threatened by Islam.

Moreover, stereotypes are not tantamount to prejudice and antagonism although they can accompany such feelings as they can accompany other feelings as well about given people, groups or nations. Statements to the effect that the Chinese people are industrious, or the Germans pay attention to details, the Swedes or Irish are drunk a good deal of the time or the Japanese are obedient, are also stereotypes (albeit not necessarily negative ones) that make it possible to think about social and national existence on this globe. "Investigators" at Tel Aviv University like Bar-Tal and Teichman (2005) want to impress upon the world and on the Jews that Jews are suffused with hatred.

The anti-Zionists' transformation of Arab hatred for Jews into Jewish hatred for Arabs provides them with a self-image of being defenders of the downtrodden and accusers of the aggressors, namely their own Jewish brothers and countrymen from whom they wish to distance themselves. The transformation of their hatred for Jewry and Israel into Jewish hatred for Arabs displays another of Anna Freud's mechanisms of defense called "Identification with the Aggressor." That mode of relating to one's own impulses has been called "the most pernicious of the dynamic process" (Dor Shav, 1998) that allows anti-Zionists to argue that Arab terrorist attacks on Jews are justified. For anti-Zionists, the Arabs allegedly practice terrorism primarily to "achieve their national goals or express their profound despair" which endows their terrorist activity with moral stature (Uri Avnery, Jeff Halper, Neve Gordon, Lev Grinberg, and others).

## Ideology, Not Poverty, Breeds Terrorism

After so many years of Arab terrorism in different parts of the globe, one can only wonder how some people persist in clinging to the idea that terrorism stems from "despair," referring primarily to poverty, lack of social mobility, or some form of emotional or economic deprivation. The September 11, 2001 devastation wrought on the United States, and the many successive explosions set off by homicidal bombers in Africa, Spain, England, Lebanon, and elsewhere, in addition to the years of homicidal bombings in Israel, demonstrate beyond a shadow of a doubt that terrorism is motivated by ideology and not by poverty. Poverty breeds crime, not terror. Muslim terrorists are both educated and middle-class, some with degrees in higher education, such as the medical doctors who perpetrated the terrorist acts in Glasgow in July 2007, or those who hijacked the airliners that attacked targets in the United States on 9/11, and most of the suicide bombings in Israel.

The despair of the Palestinian Arabs stems from their inability to eradicate Israel, not from their alleged abject poverty. But no evidence that testifies to these conditions is permitted to creep into the world view of the Jewish anti-Zionists in Israel, which bespeaks not only prejudice in favor of the Arabs, but the fact that their historical narrative is subjugated to their fanatical religion of anti-Semitism and anti-Zionism. Precisely that characterization applies to the review by Ariel Hirschfeld (Hebrew University) of an Israeli film in which he displays an extraordinary talent for distorting the feelings and intentions of Jews ("religious" Jews in particular) in an utterly grotesque manner, while expressing the most profound empathy for the Arab victim (in the movie under review) of Jews' insensitivity and indifference to his plight.

Of course Hirschfeld is not alone in his empathy for the Arab victims of Israel. That same "empathy" permeates the Muslim world that vows vengeance on the infidel Jews for killing their peace-seeking, passive, impoverished and helpless co-religionists! Palpable expression of this passivity and peace-loving stance was demonstrated recently in the "successful" bombing of the Marriot hotel in Islamabad where scores of foreigners were eradicated by the will of the All Merciful. Following the horrendous acts of torture (of Jews connected to the Lubavitch movement) murder and bombing (276 people dead) in the city of Mumbai (Bombay), it has emerged (December 2008) that the terrorists, ironically enough, were (some fourteen were killed and one captured) Pakistanis.

Hebrew University professor Yaron Ezrachi (2008) and his like-minded colleagues will always be happy to join the chorus of naysayers who seek to oppose and denounce the Zionist enterprise of Kibbutz Galuyot and of defending the Jewish population here from the mistreated Arabs who are suffering, penniless, and literally drowning-in-donations in the territory they call Palestine. The Arab Palestinians invest their energies, time and money, particularly the billions of dollars contributed to their "cause" by the United States, the EU, Saudi Arabia and Iran, and less directly by Russia too, in building their armies, purchasing weapons and paying terrorists.

Mahmoud Abbas, head of the Fatah terrorist organization and chairman of the Palestinian Authority paid the salaries of Hamas members in Gaza (July-August 2007) after receiving 650 million U.S. dollars from Israel as "tax returns." (Does the U.S. transfer huge sums of money to Canada and Mexico whose citizens cross the borders to work in the United States? Large numbers of Frenchmen from Alsace-Lorraine work in Germany. Does Germany return the funds withheld from their salaries to France?) The Palestinian Authority does not engage in economic planning and development lest it become economically independent and no longer in need of charity from abroad. The PA could have been economically independent several times over with the vast sums it collected ever since the Oslo agreements in 1993. However, financial issues apart, no one is surprised at the terrorist activities of Mahmoud Abbas and the PLO. His 1982 Ph.D. dissertation at the People's Friendship University in Moscow, during the Communist regime, is entitled: "The Other Side: The Secret Relations between Nazism and the Leadership of the Zionist Movement" (cited by Wisse, 2007, pp. 158 and 201).

Most relevant to this discussion is the fact that the anti-Zionist academics bemoan the Arab Palestinians' plight without ever mentioning what they did with the "aid" they received that fell into their lap more abundantly than the manna fell from heaven as the Biblical Israelites wandered in the desert. Perhaps what is wrong with the PA is the same thing that is wrong with not a few countries in the Arab-Muslim world: A preoccupation with antagonism toward others, maintaining large numbers of men under arms to protect them from attack by fantasized enemies (Huntington, 1996, pp. 256-258), and a distinct paucity of attention and effort to self development in social-economic spheres of life. Of course the previous statement is a generalization or a stereotype. All diagnoses of mental or other disorders are stereotypes because they are shorthand terms for a multitude of phenomena considered under a category.

The characterization of disregard for socioeconomic development in Muslim countries does not apply, for example, to Dubai or Qatar. Yet, that fact does not detract one iota from its validity as a reasonable description of current conditions in the large Arab countries of the Middle East. Included in the latter description is oil-rich Saudi Arabia that still imports most of its food because it does not bother to develop its own agriculture. Why should it? It is easier to extract wealth from under the ground or from property, industries and securities bought in other countries—than to cultivate the soil. Anti-Zionist academics are completely embedded in their empathy with the Arabs that blinds them to the many factors that maintain the Arab Palestinian political-economic situation at a primitive level. Disregard for that aspect of the environment, like their disregard for the factors that dictate Israel's need for self-defense, and like their disregard for the bottomless hatred of the vast majority of Israel's Arab neighbors, Christians and Muslims, allows the Jewish self-haters to continue to denounce Israel and the Jews as contributors to Arab Palestinian "poverty." With friends like these (Alexander, 1993) the Jews of Israel don't need any enemies.

## People are Known by the Company They Keep

Udi (Ehud) Adiv of Matzpen, an erstwhile spy from Syria, grew up in kibbutz Gan Shmuel of Hashomer Hatzair, which, at the time, was a communist greenhouse where the pro-Arab communist Simcha Flappan, founder and editor of *New Outlook* magazine, lived since 1930 (Rael Jean and Erich Isaac, 1993). Surely there were many members of the kibbutz who were not card-carrying members of the Communist Party. The spy Uri Davies or Davis, formerly of Matzpen, formerly a Jewish resident of Sahknin, recently converted to Islam and married a Muslim woman in Ramallah (October, 2008). The Arab "legislator" (i.e., agitator) Jamal Karsli appears in a photograph, arm in arm, with Israel's anti-Zionist demonizer Ilan Pappe. He is formerly of Haifa University and now of Exeter University in the United Kingdom where he is surrounded by like-minded academic colleagues. Spies for the Arabs, communists who seek to undermine Israel in favor of the Arabs, and the academic anti-Zionists of the likes of Ilan Pappe, act in concert.

They have all been striving for the same destructive goals for decades, ever since the matrix of communism, Trotskyism, pro-Arabism, and spying for an enemy nation was introduced by Moshe Sneh in the early 1950s (Lord, p. 44). Consider, too, a conference held in 2006 entitled "Contemporary Capitalism: USA, Europe and the Middle East in the Beginning of the 21st Century" that took place at Ben Gurion University. The conference was a Marxist attack on the United States and capitalism, and on capitalism in Israel. In attendance were, inter alia, Neve Gordon, Oren Yiftachel, David Newman, Uri Ram, and Shlomo Swirski, the old-time preacher of the Marxist Orthodox Church, and others from the list of our anti-Zionists. Ilan Pappe also decided to join the Communist Party in Israel. He was tutored at Oxford University by the Arab historian Albert Hourani, during which time he came to the conclusion that whatever he had learned as a young man in Haifa about Israel's war of Independence with the Arabs was not true. He had ample opportunity in England to interact with Arab intellectuals who helped him congeal his positive view of the Arab plight imposed by the aggressive and domineering Israel army. In 1996 Pappe joined the predominantly Arab anti-Zionist Communist Party. He wound up his chapter of life in Israel with a book on *The Ethnic Cleansing of Palestine*, and then moved to England where he now teaches at the University of Exeter (Wilson, 2007).

Kenneth Levin (2005, 2007) has brilliantly documented the ideological debt of Jewish anti-Semites to socialism and communism. The intellectual debt of Israel's anti-Zionists to a long tradition in the social sciences of neo-Marxist, post modernistic "critical" thought has been carefully examined and documented by Ofira Seliktar (2005). Anti-Zionists also hobnob with representatives of the far right in the United States not only of the extreme left, namely neo-Nazi groups with whom Noam Chomsky was and is in league (Alexander, 1993; Neuwirth, 2005). Harvard professor of law Alan Dershowitz wrote about Ben Gurion University's Neve Gordon: "[He has] gotten into bed with neo-Nazis, Holocaust justice deniers, and anti-Semites. He is a despicable example of a self-hating Jew and a self-hating Israeli."

The association of anti-Zionists with neo-Nazis follows the pattern of Arab anti-Semitism in World War II set by Amin al-Husseini, as discussed above. Our contemporary Jewish anti-Semites have broadened their horizon to include communism as an ideological foundation for their ideas, so they have evolved a homegrown mixture of Red and Black, pseudo-communism and neo-Nazism. If they would have their way, Israel would soon become known as the only place on earth that manages to maintain both gulags and concentration camps, without either of them existing in reality.

Actually a short history lesson can demonstrate that the Gulag served as the precedent from which Hitler developed the concentration camp. The communists were the Nazis' instructors in the technology of mass persecution (Viereck, 1941/1965). Alfred Rosenberg, the central founder of Nazi ideology, was one of the primary figures in the Russification of German culture. Not that Germany needed Russian precedent to persecute Jews. After all, Catholicism conquered Germany 600 years before the advent of Luther in the late fifteenth and early sixteenth centuries, and Luther is one of the major anti-Semites of Western history prior to the modern era. Germany remains heavily Catholic to this day. Pope Benedict XIV slipped up by naming a British bishop (Williamson) who is a Holocaust denier to the rank of archbishop, and then, after fierce objection by the Anti-Defamation League and other Jewish organizations, the pope accepted an apology by the bishop for making a not politically correct statement in public. However, the bishop said he would have to study the problem of how many Jews were killed in the Holocaust after his assertion that the number was about 300,000 was rejected by the pope. Never did the Vatican require that the bishop retract his assertion.

The merger of communism and Nazism has its roots in the early years of the twentieth century (Viereck, pp. 266-272). Noteworthy is the fact that Hitler characterized his new movement as socialist: National Socialism! He and his immediate associates, Alfred Rosenberg most of all, were more Russified than commonly acknowledged. Who would have ventured to guess that our contemporary Jewish-Israeli anti-Semites would, knowingly or unknowingly, re-embody that singularly lethal combination for Jews, namely the ideological merger of the anti-Semitic far left with the far right?

## From Where Did They Come?

How did the anomaly of Jewish-Israeli anti-Zionists/anti-Semites grow? Who or what cultivated them? A dozen years before Israel was established, the great Zionist leader and ideologue, Berl Katznelson, referred to the anti-Zionists of his day in a public address that appeared in the Labor Party newspaper *Davar* (1936):

> Is there some nation among all the nations whose sons engage is such distortion, mental and emotional, such that everything their nation does, every creation and all of its suffering, is despised and hated, and everything that their nation's enemy does, every robbery, every murder, every rape, fills their heart with a feeling of admiration and devotion?... while here [in Palestine, later Israel] all the germs of self-hatred cling to him....

In truth, from whence did this anomaly spring? The problem of origins plagues many academic disciplines, and rarely are we fortunate enough to learn the truth. How did I, or you, or he, or they get the way we are? To find a convincing reply to that question, as difficult or impossible as it may be in respect to the development of individuals, is next to impossible when the question is asked about a group or a nation. Many people think that if we only knew the answer we would be able to correct some given situation and prevent its recurrence. That is highly doubtful.

Nevertheless, we can exercise our curiosity and seek a solution, whether we find one or not.

Before focusing specifically on the anti-Zionists, some comments are in order regarding the social-historical condition of the Jewish people in general and in Israel in particular. Jewry's experience with statesmanship and with conducting a sovereign nation is limited in time and began, in the modern world, only sixty years ago in 1948. For centuries Jews have excelled in many walks of life: in finance and commerce, in a broad spectrum of professions, in the sciences, music, the arts, and so forth. However, that striking and remarkable success—which by any measure constitutes an unparalleled chapter in human events—did not provide the Jewish people with a history of, or experience with, the conduct of national sovereignty for its own people, even though they counseled those who led other nations. Jews counseled the heads of states in both Christian and Muslim countries (Baron, 1952-1983), but, alas, had no opportunity until the advent of Israel to do so in their own sovereign nation (Bukay, 2004).

Jewry did one thing in its 2,000 year exile that no other nation did, and that was to survive. No Western or Middle Eastern nation survived for two millennia except Pharonic Egypt. Nor did any nation ever survive exile. That survival was made possible by Jewry's brand of monotheism and way of life (Halachah), by its self-consciousness as descendents of the Biblical Hebrews and by many other factors that can be called, in short, instruments of exile (Klei Golah: Arfa, 1947/2005) that Jewry cultivated alongside the instruments of redemption (Klei-G'eulah) (Kaufmann, 1929-31). Those terms—exile and redemption—embody the two faces of Jewry's survival: it's adjustment to conditions of exile, and its anticipation of leaving it and returning to its historic homeland, the Land of Israel. Contemporary Jewry has both worlds, for better or worse. Two millennia after the destruction of its national sovereignty by the Romans in 72 A.D., most Jews still remain in the exile. They no longer agree to call it by that name since, in their view, they have been successfully integrated into many different nations. The State of Israel, for most of its citizens, constitutes redemption from the exile. What remains is a source of distress to a few Jews with a cultivated sense of their own history and national character is that those "instruments of exile" that developed over so many centuries are not easily discarded. Several decades after settling in Israel, patterns of thought and behavior adopted by Jews to survive in an alien and antagonistic environment continue to manifest themselves. Those patterns are particularly noticeable in the behavior of

Israel's socio-ideological subgroups, and in its government and political leaders, albeit not in all of them.

We can identify four major subdivisions within Israel Jewry (that apply as well to no small degree to Jewry worldwide):

1.  *The Ultra-orthodox (Haredi) wing.* These Jews express total indifference to political reality, as if it didn't exist. Their life is concentrated on what they believe to be the behavior regulated by the Law (Talmud) which is divinely inspired and mandatory. National-political existence is a rebellion against God's wishes. He will redeem the Jewish People in His own good time. All temporal self-government (except for that of the Gentiles which one must obey) is to be shunned. Only God is King.

2.  *Jewish nationalists or Zionists who are patriots of Israel.* These Jews are proud of their country that finally, after the two millennia of exile, has made it possible for them to govern themselves and live in their own country where they are a majority. Patriotic Jews display an entire spectrum of religious beliefs, although few can be seen to be ultra-orthodox. The Jews have returned to their Land, and the Land has returned to them. We do not (or—should not) suffer from the Jews' complexes developed in the Exile. It must be defended in the face of its enemies, just as the citizens of other countries defend their homeland despite the fact that it is not threatened with total annihilation by its enemies as Israel is and has been. This subgroup need not be discussed in detail because our focus here is on the self-hating Jews, on those who oppose the ideas that brought their people back to their land.

3.  *Secular leftists.* This wing of the Jewish people can be seen as consisting of two somewhat distinguishable groups who nevertheless end up with the same ideological result, namely—Escape while the going is good. That translates into these Jews' transition from relying on our own strength for our security and not relying on other nations to come to our aid, to a position of perpetual crisis and panic that leads to capitulation because we have no alternative.

a.  Liberalism and Moralism. They want to prove that, unlike the way Jews were treated in the Exile, Israel can relate to minority groups in the country differently, with considerable tolerance, and not as we were treated. Those Jews want to be accepted by the Gentiles abroad, to appear as members of the enlightened and cultured world. The left is allegedly in vogue and attractive, moderate and moral. The rightists are all "extremists." In reality, however, the liberals do not belong to the left: They did not embrace a Marxist ideology, or a socialist one.

Obviously, they have dressed in the current style, hoping that they can continue to enjoy their life surrounded with material pleasures as well as peace and security without "taxation." The enemy is distant and, to maintain their distance from us, we can relinquish parts of our "vast" territory, of dubious significance, to the less fortunate Arabs.

Those Jews who are poor want to stick to their ground because they do not have anything else. Those blessed with material benefits do not need the ground—as long as other people leave us be. In short, we know who sides with us politically—our neighbors with money, not the poor slobs who side with the "extremists."

The pleasure-loving peace seekers travel to all of the world's exotic locations to bath in luxury at the expense of various governments who, not long ago, sought Israel's destruction and participated in one way or another in their/our "not sufficiently rapid" elimination. These days, those nations finance the trips of our peace seekers. They learned that the "struggle" for peace is lucrative and accompanied by fame and popularity (exemplified countless times by Shimon Peres).

b.    The politics of cultural ignorance. Just what do the anti-Zionist Jews know about the Arabs and the culture of Islam? It can be demonstrated that they, young and old, know precious little, and do not really know how the Islamic world is perceived by the West. How many citizens of Israel appreciate the profound bias evident in the printed and electronic media, and that the bias disseminated by the media contradicts Israel's national interests? Israel's education of its youth has achieved unparalleled failure in cultivating Jewish and Zionist consciousness, knowledge and values, as well as identification with, and pride in, national symbols. Nor has it succeeded in cultivating the internalization of the fundamental principle that internationalism is anarchism and that, exactly as in the natural world, only the strong ("the fittest") and the determined survive. Whatever success Israel has enjoyed in those realms cannot be attributed to its educational system.

c.    The anti-Semitic Anarchist Revolutionary Wing. This group expresses a radical messianic ideology that seeks to bring about a better world that doesn't exist anywhere in our galaxy except in their dreams. A similar vision once characterized the now defunct communist movement whose downfall was predicted by many people with two eyes in their head.

The same is true for anarchistic utopian ideology in general. In Israel the anarchists are engaged in a struggle against anything that smacks of particularism and nationalism, including activities that conflict with the vital interests of Israel as the Jewish State (Lord, 2000; Yariv, 1953). That position is not far from one that is prepared to forgo the existence of Israel as a political entity. For these Jews, Israel's so-called "integration into the region" where it is completely surrounded by Muslim countries is the decisive factor. Arab national governments—all of which are dictatorships that support and promote the murder of Jews in and outside of Israel—are preferred to the Jewish-Zionist government.

The revolutionary and anti-Jewish anarchists were viewed by one scholar as having evolved as an alternative to a wave of a Jewish nationalist spirit that arose in the wake of the Six-Day War. Those anarchists intended to proceed aggressively against the Jewish-religious nationalists. The former group claimed to be the embodiment of Democracy rather than of Nationalism, and it determined that it alone could say what the social-cultural norms of Israel should be. Those norms should be those of a secular, atheist religion, an alternative to Jewish identity (Schweid, 1996). By means of its near total control of the media in Israel, the post-Zionist group succeeded in being adopted by the leading political party to the effect that they had an encompassing world-view to offer the nation. Henceforth, the Jewish-religious and the Jewish-nationalist "camps" were to be considered as fringe elements along with Zionism itself. They were to be seen as archaic and lifeless, nationalism having been "transformed" into a racist and murderous chauvinism. It seemed as if a mutual admiration society had been set up between the media and the Left, in which the Left provided the media with "scoops" that the media could portray as "larger than life."

The pinnacle achievement was the outrageous Oslo agreement that resulted in more than 1,200 Jews killed in Israel by Arab terrorists. They were directed by Yasser Arafat who signed the Oslo agreement along with Yitzhak Rabin. He had been convinced by Shimon Peres (and Yossi Beilin) that the agreement was to Israel's benefit and would lead to peace with the Arabs. One of these days a board of inquiry will examine the question of how Israel was so egregiously misled that it stood on the brink of collapse. That was the beginning of the phenomenon called "democratic totalitarianism" by Jacob Talmon (1956). It might be noted that Arafat made a superhuman effort to observe the conditions of the agreement for forty-five minutes!

The "leftist" truth constitutes a form of cultural terrorism in Israel. The left asserts that it has a monopoly on truth and the rest of the social-political groups are fascists. Moreover, the left represents the majority will and they alone comprehend what the majority truly needs. Mack and Snyder (1957) taught that cultural conflict is the worse kind of conflict there is. But in our day, cultural terror is worse than its predecessor cultural conflict.

The cultural terror of the left succeeded beyond its dreams in gaining widespread influence over Israel's information media where it has imprinted its doctrines to the near exclusion of all other views. The leftist labor leader, one-time head of the all-powerful Histadrut, the late Yitzchak Ben-Aharon, burst out on television after Menachem Begin's party won the elections in 1977, that he, Ben-Aharon, would never accept those results. He repeated much the same declaration when Netanyahu defeated Shimon Peres in 1996. Yossi Beilin undertook a putsch against the elected government, by once again acting secretly and funded by anti-Israel EU countries. He prepared (in Europe) the so-called Geneva Agreement or document (October 2003) which blatantly expressed his (and his cohorts') unwillingness to accept the will of the Israel electorate and to thereby function contrary to the rules and requirements of a democracy. Of course, Beilin was not the only Leftist who followed anti-democratic views. Yuli Tamir—a leftist activist after her return to Israel with her doctorate from Oxford University at the time (1999)—was a member of the Knesset, (in November 2008, she was the incumbent minister of education). She was quoted in the newspapers to the effect that "we welcomed the Oslo agreement despite it not having been born democratically … there were severe democratic flaws in this process … we adopted it enthusiastically, and rightfully, in my opinion" (Tamir, 1999). Nor is Shimon Peres to be left out: "Oslo is a political truth, a necessity" (Peres, 2002).

Ironically, the political Left in Israel has watched its power dwindle after a series of personal, social and national catastrophes for which Olmert and his government were responsible. The more their power declined, the more they imposed their views on the national ethos by means of the printed and electronic media. Alas, many signs and manifestations in Israel's national and international behavior appear to embody mental and behavioral habits acquired during its 2,000 years of national Exile. Ben-Gurion perceptively noted that Jewry had to take the giant step from occupying various levels of social status within nations to become a nation on its own (Ben-Gurion, 1974).

It seems that taking that step is accomplished—perhaps—over the course of many years, perhaps even centuries, as some nations have taught us. Neither the leaders nor the citizenry of Israel have had the time to internalize the possibility and responsibility of national sovereignty. Instead, Israel looks for quick solutions to its distressing political-international situation. Amazingly enough, Israel tried to reach agreements with our most bloodthirsty enemies (such as Arafat), who almost simultaneously with writing their signatures on an agreement, abrogated them, such as Arafat's (unannounced) rejection of the Oslo agreement forty-five minutes after signing it. Israel went marching on as if nothing had happened. The so-called Oslo accord was secretly prepared by that "peace-loving" self-appointed arbiter of Israel's destiny, Yossi Beilin, and his mentor, Shimon Peres, the foremost figure of self-delusion and historical distortion that Jewry has seen, at least in the modern era. Beilin finally announced (November, 2008) that he is retiring from politics as head of the very left-wing political party Meretz, but he hoped to continue to influence political opinions through his many connections in and outside of Israel.

In his capacity as president of Israel, Peres continues to preach peace to this nation. He might preach to the Arabs as well if they would let him, but that will not happen. Peres persists in representing his very own one-sided image of Israel in his globetrotting career. He appears to have a supersonic jet that whisks him from Jerusalem to the UN headquarters in New York for a photo opportunity with Bush and Livni, a little hobnobbing with the elites, and then back to Jerusalem. Upon returning from one of his jaunts abroad he expressed another bon mot in his unique fashion, unbelievable as it may sound, that we should "close our eyes" (i.e., to what the Arabs are doing to Israel) "and make peace" (i.e., despite terrorism). Obviously it has not occurred to him and to the Left that if you close your eyes you can fall off a cliff. Moreover, Israel did "close its eyes" for a long time. Tragically our youth had to be sent to fight our peace-loving friends the Arabs, and many closed their eyes forever.

The anarchist perceptions, few as they may be, constitute a formidable group. To recap—among them are Ilan Pappe, Zehava Galon, and Shulamit Aloni (former minister of education), the well-known writers Amos Oz, A.B. Yehoshua, and David Grossman; Yossi Sarid, who inherited the Meretz Party from Shulamit Aloni (also a self-proclaimed anti-Semite), Avraham Burg, once head of the Jewish Agency, a member of the Knesset and son of the Religious-Zionist leader Dr. Yosef Burg; and Amram Mitzna, a retired general who became mayor of Haifa and is now retired. All of the above and more are strongly supported by the *Haaretz* newspaper begun in Germany by the Schocken family, benefactor of many great Hebrew writers (first and foremost, Shmuel Yosef Agnon). Later the newspaper evolved under the editorship of Amos Schocken into an extreme leftist organ of the anti-Zionist journalists, such as Akiva Eldar and others (Hornik, 2004).

## We Belong to the Enlightened Germany

The phenomenon of Jews praising the "enlightened Germany" actually belongs to a different historical era, the period of the Nazis. In the middle of 1939, Jews in Germany said, in effect: "What can the Nazis still do to us? (i.e. that they have not done already—authors). We number

a million in Germany. Can anyone seriously believe that they will succeed in eradicating us?"

In 1944 Jews in Amsterdam put on their finest clothing and gave tips to
their German guards who huddled them onto railroad cars to Auschwitz.
The same happened in Hungary. Quite a few Jews returned to Germany
after the war, insisting that "this is our home." Some of the descendents
of Jews from Germany who came to Israel after World War II are willing
to embrace any gimmick and bow down to the Golden Calf of "peace"
even if Israel will pay in blood for their behavior. Unlike the Jewish capos
(guards) in the concentration camps, who acquiesced to perform that job
in order to survive, at least for a few more days, Israel's anti-Zionists
assumed their task out of self hatred and a cultivated ignorance about
Israel Jewry's condition.

Let us return to the Oslo agreement. Along with Beilin's Geneva initiative, the Oslo agreement demonstrates beyond a shadow of a doubt
some characteristics of Jewish behavior. The crimes committed in the
name of the Oslo agreement are too numerous to count. In that vein we
can cite the remarkable statement by Amnon Dankner (2001):

> The Ashkenazi elite [in Israel] displayed contempt, disdain and ridicule for anyone
> disagreeing with them. They defined those people as primitive and as war mongers.
> Members of that elite wanted to trample under foot any opposition to, or disagree-
> ment with, every suggestion of ideological heresy or criticism connected with the
> Oslo agreement. Peace became an article of faith, a religious principle, around which
> the prophets assembled, those who envisioned The New Middle East. The victims
> of Oslo were sacrifices for peace. A cruel enemy who broke any agreement was the
> "partner of peace for the brave.

Nightmarish propaganda suffused with hatred is "a natural response
after years of occupation." When reality slapped the pursuers of peace
in the face, it was claimed that we were to blame.

For the past few decades, the left has been a huge and profitable
enterprise of hatred, ridicule, and contempt to the Middle Eastern Jews
in Israel, to those with rightist views, and to society's underprivileged.
By contrast, a strange phenomenon flowered of identification with,
and participation in, the suffering of the Palestinians. As their sense of
solidarity with, and love for, their Israeli brethren died in their hearts,
their pity for the conquered nation flowered. The left devoted itself to
one thing, peace, in a compulsive and repellant way, while employing
ways of disregarding and repressing reality. Despite the collapse of the
Oslo agreements, literally and figuratively, their architects still try to
convince us that the agreements are active and unvanquished, and that
we can achieve Peace Now.

The entire membership of the elitist Left should look deep into their souls and ask themselves how they got into that situation. How do they manage to feel the tickle on a foot that has been amputated? How did peace become the sole principle of their world, while losing their self consciousness?

The enigma of Jewish self-hatred defies comprehension. One suggestion in the way of explanation was offered by Theodore Lessing (2004). He commented about factors leading to, and the circumstances of, the tragedy of the assimilated Jew in the modern world who was prepared to disregard his own essence in order to be accepted by the gentile environment. Relating primarily to the Jews in Israel, the revolutionary anarchists here remain deeply alienated from, even hostile to, Judaism and their Jewish identity. In Israel it is best to ignore them. On the international scene we must neutralize the damage they do and explain that all nations have their fanatics, and the Jews do too. One recent example is the behavior of Avraham Burg while a member of the Knesset, whose sanctimonious and demonstrably vicious statements were made when he appeared on the Israeli television program *Politika* (February 3, 2004) and denounced the pro-Zionist Christians. His depth of antagonism towards that group is matched only by his love for the anti-Semitic Arab Palestinians, the enemies of his own nation.

## The Jewish Death Wish: Love Thy Enemy

1.  *The Stockholm Syndrome.* Captives taken by terrorists gradually identify with their captors and deny their despicable and inhuman behavior. In Jewish tradition, kidnapping is liable to the death penalty. Jewry's sages interpreted the commandment Thou Shalt Not Kill as referring to kidnapping, not just to outright murder. In regard to the Jews, it is quite possible that guilt plays an important role in Israel Stockholm-like behavior as a nation. Israel's extremely trying security situation, propelled by a cruel and uncompromising terrorist enemy, and the internal tension generated by the security situation, provides the background for the nation's self flagellation. Some voices in the country accuse us ourselves—that we are guilty of creating the crisis. The victims are surrendering to the terrorists who have enslaved their victims' minds.

    As the threat to our lives increases in viciousness, our anti-Israel Israeli brethren shout our guilt louder and blame their political opponents (i.e., Jews on the "right') for fomenting Arab hatred of the Jews. The make-believe agreements with the Arabs, such as the Oslo or Geneva agreements, unilateral withdrawal from "Arab-owned" land, conducting negotiations with Arab groups as if there were no terror (Vaihinger, 1911), and absconding in fright from the battlefield. We all know that terrorism will suddenly disappear because the terrorists have rational demands that we can meet with just a little effort. Our panicky response to terror is an illusion, as is the fact that our panic, and our media, intensify terror and endow it with enormous power beyond its real threat. So we'll make the effort and all will be well, and no further analyses are necessary. It is unacceptable to our peace loving fellow Jews—and non-Jews—to view terrorists as despicable murderers who deserve to be liquidated. Even the weapons of the Hamas terrorists in Gaza were not eliminated in the recent war there.

2.   *Threat, Displacement and the Dissonance of Repression.* As an instrument of survival the Jews developed an exaggerated degree of self-criticism. A fundamental motif of Jewish prayer (particularly on the Day of Atonement) is: "We were exiled from our land because of our sins," or "We are guilt-laden, we have been faithless, we have robbed, and we have spoken basely. We have committed iniquity," and so forth, and we beseech God to redeem and save us. In contemporary Israel that motif has been translated by the pursuers of Peace into the notion that Arab antagonism toward the Jews cannot be utterly pathological. That is impossible and irrational. Hence, there must be something and/or some people among us responsible for generating that hatred. Of course, the "conquest" (of Judea and Samaria) is responsible; the "settlers" are responsible. If Israel returns to the 1967 borders there will be peace between the two states that will be located in the Western part of the Land of Israel. The repressed Palestinians act out of sheer desperation,

The above type of "mental blindness" can be understood only as a loss of nerve, a sense of having lost control over events (as if there ever was such a thing), the inability of the mind to comprehend what our eyes behold and admit our mistakes. Too many Jews display an unwillingness to cope with a complex reality accompanied by the need to behave in a socially acceptable manner. Too many Jews have fallen in love with theories that explain everything instead of employing their reasoning and responsibility, as well as living by a policy of gambling with our nation's life and the lives of its citizens. If our basic goal had been to reach the status of a normal nation in a sovereign state, we would have behaved normally like other sovereign nations that exerted all the energy at their disposal to safeguard their national independence. But the Jews behave in a manner diametrically opposed to normality, not like a responsible nation devoted to securing its national interests. But our anti-Zionists are not prepared to fight for our nation's political values. Normality in their eyes means to understand the stress experienced by our enemies and their needs, at the cost of self annihilation.

## The Cultural Elite

Arab cultural elites reject Israel unequivocally. With the exception of a handful of remarkably brave and articulate intellectuals living primarily in the United States for the past few decades, (such as Fouad Ajami, Joseph Phares, and a few others) the Muslim elites in Muslim and in Western countries support Arab terrorism or war against Israel. Edward Said wrote:

> There is no symmetry in the (Arab) conflict (with Israel-authors). One side is guilty and the other side is the victim. The victim's war, which is legitimate must be uncompromising. Israel has conquered the entire land of Palestine. The "territories" are not relevant. Israel must relinquish the Jewish State and Zionist identity (Said, 2000).

By contrast, the cultural elites in Israel fill a decisive role in pushing public opinion and the political leadership to support the extreme Arab-Palestinian aspirations and to reach an agreement that is tantamount to capitulation. The most cursory examination of the subject will reveal that writers like Yizhar Smilansky, Amos Oz, A. B. Yehoshua, David Grossman, and other "cultured" members of Israel society consistently asserted that we—the Jews—are guilty, namely those Jews who are the conquerors. The exploited Palestinians are guiltless, even righteous. Amos Oz published an article in the *New York Times Magazine* (July 11, 1982) to the effect that Israeli society deteriorated from an exemplary classless society to a chauvinistic, nationalistic, militaristic society dominated by medieval clerics. Regarding Gush Emunim. Oz descended to the depths of *Der Sturmer*:

> [Gush Emunim is] a messianic junta, insular and cruel, a bunch of armed gangsters, ciminals against humanity, sadists, pogromists and murderers, that burst forth from some dark corner of Judaism…from out of the cellars of bestiality and defilement…in order to bring about the rule of a thirsty, mad worship of blood (Oz, 1989)

Following the severe terrorist explosion in Israel of September 11, 2000, Oz repeated his position that neither radical Islam nor Arab culture is the enemy, but rather "fanaticism" [Jewish fanaticism] because the most important step to be taken on a humanitarian basis is to grant the Palestinians the right to self determination. Contrary to all information available to the media and to the world, Oz indicated that all of the Arabs and Muslims were deeply upset and sorry over the terrible terrorist act, as was all of humanity (2001).

The poet Yitzchak Laor said about the Israel Defense Forces that "On our holiday of freedom [i.e., Passover] we will celebrate … with the blood of Palestinian youth in our matzot.".

Natan Zach, another poet, remarked: [They are] "stupid rejectionist front, evil, chauvinistic and full of lies" (Zach, 1990).

Udi Aloni, the son of Shulamit Aloni, directed a film that was screened in Berlin, of all places, where Israel was compared to Nazis on the grounds that Judaism has roots in genocide (2003).

These pathological phenomena on the part of "cultured people" were diagnosed by the writer and poet Dr. Yochai Oppenheimer who wrote (2003) that:

> I can't remember any protest meeting in which writers or poets participated. But you will see them at public protests on behalf of the Arabs. The destroyed house of Palestinians ignites their imagination more than the empty refrigerator [that belongs to Jews who live] in Katamon [neighborhood of Jerusalem]. To write about the suffering of the Palestinians is considered to be the pinnacle of a sensitive morality consideration. By contrast, a hungry Jewish boy from one of the development towns in Israel, economic distress in Meah Shearim [district of Jerusalem] or the exploitation of workers from foreign countries, does not cause them to come out of their shell. I know poets who engage in giving equipment to the children of [Arab] refugees, nut they would never think of doing that for hungry (Jewish) children in the Negev. There is something noticeably distorted about the kind of altruism that leads poets to prefer to be photographed with olive pickers in the "West Bank," and not in a soup kitchen in Jerusalem.

In a presentation he made in Sweden, Dror Feiler from the communist kibbutz Yad-Hannah that still adores Stalin denounced the Judeo-Nazis in Israel. However, when anyone accused Feiler or Sweden—never neutral in respect to anti-Semitism and is remembered for its activities during the Nazi era—we are reminded that many "artistic" creations, far worse than that of Feiler, are set up in Israel quite frequently. These "creations" are funded by Israel's taxpayers to the tune of hundreds of millions of dollars. Those funds shower Israel with calumny and hostility, disseminate poisonous slander in the world and present our nation as a Nazi racist storm trooper.

The Tel Aviv Art Museum held an exhibition where Israel's flag was seen as interwoven with a swastika and money-hungry Jews wreaking destruction on the peace of the bleeding world. Next to this exhibition appeared the anti-Semitic paintings of artist David Veckstein who displayed to the world the essence of the racist and greedy Jews. For the sake of art, the Arabs are always the victim and Israel is the criminal and murderer.

A significant portion of the "new European anti-Semitism" is actually propelled by anti-Zionist Israeli leftists who assist the protest activity and the anti-Semitic demonstrations of Arabs and Muslims in Europe. The facts bear repetition: The anti-Semitic protests in Europe are conducted by Arab-Islamic factions backed up by fanatical anti-Semitic leftists. Most Europeans are not to be found in those protest gatherings, which is not to say that they do not harbor anti-Semitic attitudes and opinions. However, they much prefer to live in peace and calm after the trauma of World War II.

In the past, the anti-Jewish marches were the work of the fascist Right, but today they are almost exclusively the work of the Left fed by fanatical Jewish anarchists. To condemn European anti-Semitism is to ignore reality. We are still afraid of identifying the true nature of the phenomenon which is an Arab-Islamic one, a product of a violent and murderous culture that sanctifies blood and death (erroneously called martyrdom). Any research into the protests in Europe will demonstrate the (Arab-Muslim) identity of the protesters. Here are two quotations elaborating the issue. The former Kuwaiti communications minister, Sa`d Bin-Tafla:

> The violence of slaughter and bloodshed is a cultural phenomenon. The religious faction sets the rules: to achieve victory or martyrdom in order to restore the Islamic Empire, from China to Andalusia; the Arab media assists them by painting the world in black and white; and Arab culture stokes the fire. Zionism and Western imperialism have nothing to do with all these and many other issues among the Arabs.

In the words of the Bahraini liberal, Said al-Hamad, this is:

> The "culture of backwardness," which dominates the Arab world, and led them into wars and violence against the West. The "culture of backwardness" includes "culture of terrorism," which adopts beheading and lynching people; and the "culture of hatred," which propagates in the minds and consciousness of the youth hatred for the world.

The following statements quoted from Muslim thinkers exemplify the Islamic world threat. Ibn Taymiyah, the Islamic religious scholar of the Hanbali School, wrote:

> The command to participate in jihad war occur innumerable times in the Qur'an and the Sunnah. It is the best religious act that man can perform. Since its aim is that the religion is Allah's entirely and Allah's word is uppermost, therefore according to all Muslim jurists, those who stand in the way of this aim must be fought and killed.

Ibn Khaldun, the renowned fourteenth-century historian and philosopher, observed:

> In the Muslim community, Jihad as the holy war is a religious duty, because of the universalism of the Muslim mission and the obligation to convert everybody to Islam either by persuasion or by force.

In the introduction to Sahih al-Bukhari, it is stated:

> So, it is incumbent upon the Muslims to follow the path which Allah's messenger adopted to avoid polytheism and heresy in all its shapes and to take the Qur'an and the Prophet's traditions as torches in front of us to guide us. We have to teach our brethren and convey the message to non-Muslims all over the world as much as possible in order to save them from the Hell-fire.

Hasan al-Banna, the founder of the influential Muslim Brotherhood organization, noted as follows: "The Muslim must make all efforts by jihad war and ideological preaching of da`wah to subdue the whole world"

## Abu al-A`la al-Mawdudi, the Indian-Pakistani religious scholar:

Islam wishes to destroy all states and governments anywhere on the face of the earth which are opposed to the ideology and program of Islam... The goal of Islam is to rule the entire world and submit all of mankind to the faith of Islam. Any nation or power that gets in the way of that goal, Islam will fight and destroy.... This is Jihad.

## Ayatollah Rohallah Khomeini of Iran:

I am decisively announcing to the whole world that if the infidel powers wish to stand against our religion, we will stand against their whole world and will not cease until the annihilation of all them. Either we shake one another's hands in joy at the victory of Islam in the world, or all of us will turn to eternal life and martyrdom. In both cases, victory and success are ours.

Israel's academics are no less involved in this revolting phenomenon than the left-wing artists. The former's vociferous participation results in enormous damage and endangers the very existence of Israel by expressing extreme anti-Israel attitudes. Those attitudes serve as the main focus of the international public's denunciation of Israel. Some people from the same leftist groups distance themselves from Israel and refuse to stand up for their country's best interests, while simultaneously maintaining relationships that will guarantee their acceptance in liberal-academic circles. That tactic demands that those leftists not become ensnared personally in public events that reveal their identity. Only a small number of academics in Israel are prepared to work tirelessly to protect their country and to be involved in political processes contrary to hostile trends circulating on the international scene.

The academic who was probably the most visible 'hero" of the extreme leftists was the late Yeshayahu Leibowitz who spoke about the Nazification of the Jewish State. He insisted, unflinchingly, that: "I call upon you to take up arms before they herd you like leprous dogs into concentration camps … yes, take up arms" (1985). He was the one who coined the term Judeo-Nazi. But in Israel there is reward for hatred of Zionism: Leibowitz was awarded the Israel Prize in 1993. The call to employ weapons was made by a number of Jew-hating "citizens" of Israel, in addition to the infamous statements of Leibowitz and Sternhell who said that tanks should be sent to the settlement of Ophrah to eliminate it (1988). Michael Harsgur, a self proclaimed communist, said on the radio (Channel 2, December 22, 2003) that the Israel army should move against the settlements and not stop. Meron Benvinisti wanted Israel dismantled and a bi-national state set up in its stead (2002).

Israel, said the late Tanya Reinhart (2003), was carrying out a genocidal war against the Arab Palestinians who can't even enjoy the weather. A special place in this rogues roll call should be reserved for Tel-Aviv University Professor of Philosophy Asa Kasher who succeeded in having his anti-Zionist views penetrate into almost every corner of Israel's society, particularly the Army. There seems to be little doubt that his absurd guidelines for soldiers adopted by the army, as to when they are ethically permitted to open fire on terrorists, cost the lives of several soldiers who were shot before they dared attack. Yehudit Harel, the daughter of Holocaust survivors, wrote to Kofi Anan when he was the secretary general of the U.N. who cooperated more with the Arabs than any of his predecessors, asking him to save the Palestinians who were being subjected, according to her opinion, to an unprecedented scope of crimes against humanity being carried out by Israel.

However, it is clear, as Alan Dershowitz, professor of law at Harvard University, stated on Israel TV (channel 1) that Israeli academics outside Israel who express anti-Israel claims, are causing inestimable damage to their homeland. Their hostile position serves as the basis for justifying Arab assertions that Israel is committing crimes against them. Dershowitz recommended that Israel not employ academics for purposes of providing information about Israel during their visits abroad. That point was referred to by Eliezer Schweid (1995). Amos Perlmutter viewed the attack of Israel academics on the state as an attack on its right to exist (1995).

# 4

# Anti-Zionists and Social Research

*"Jews don't learn from logic, they learn only from catastrophe."*
*—Ze'ev Jabotinsky*

*"Israeli society is afflicted with the Munchausen syndrome."*
*—Rabbi Shlomo Fuehrer*

Contemporary Palestinian politics displays two main strategies toward Israel: the secular one known as the Phased Strategy of the PLO-Fatah and the religious ideology of Hamas. Both approaches affirm the total obliteration of the State of Israel as a sovereign independent nation. However, both strategies include reducing the Jews to a status of *dhimmis* (people "protected" by Islamic rule). Both wish to establish an Arab-Palestinian state in Palestine in its entirety from the Mediterranean Sea to the Jordan River; both discount resist any possibility of Jewish existence as a nation entitled to a state. The two approaches differ only in the future status of the Palestinian state as a religious or a secular one.

Israel is the only state in the world that is under existential threats of annihilation on a daily basis. The Arabs and Palestinians have lost many wars. If Israel loses even one, she will exist no longer. From an ideological perspective, the Palestinian objective is to transfer the historic rights of the Jewish people to the Land of Israel, accrued over four thousand years of existence to the Palestinians who have no history, only a present. This policy aims to appropriate the identity and legitimacy of the Jews and transfer it—though in reality there is no such thing—to the Palestinians. They demand to be the sole legitimate occupants of Palestine.

The opinions of the anti-Zionist academics seem to exist in a near vacuum. Events in the international domain as well as the behavior of the Arabs, whether they call themselves Palestinians or by the names of the different Arab nations of the Middle East, (Iraq, Syria, Jordan, Saudi

Arabia, and so forth) are almost completely ignored, creeping inadvertently now and then. Israel's academic anti-Zionists assert that what the Jews, in or outside of Israel, say and do erupts out of the depths of their own prejudice and hatred, not in reaction to acts or statements made by the Arabs. The reader of the publications written by members of this group is amazed at their disregard of any possible explanation of Israel Jewry's behavior toward the Arabs as a reaction to events transpiring in the environment. In that kind of world Jews are not defending themselves or their country, but are perpetrating pogroms on an innocent and helpless Arab population. All "laws" of action and reaction are suspended by the anti-Zionists in favor of the "psychological" sources of prejudice deep in the historically or even genetically determined psyche of the Jews. Indeed it was suggested (Hammerman) that Jewish aggression against the Arab Palestinians stems from ingrained persecution beginning with Biblical times.

Given that the acts of aggression against Israel and Jews perpetrated by Arab groups and nations remain beyond the ken of the anti-Zionists except as resistance to Jewish/Israel aggression against the Arabs, there is no palpable explanation for Israel's behavior other than as some bizarre acting out of biological impulses. If one excludes the panorama of historical events (and not just the behavior of one group in a given location) as the primary arena and motivator of human behavior, one inevitably must have recourse to biology, genetics and inherited psychological characteristics. It is more than obvious that the anti-Zionists have cultivated an unmistakably racist view of Jews, Israel, and Zionism even as they denounce Israel as racist.

The reason why the persecution is ingrained rather than originating in the environment, as described very clearly in the Book of Esther, is not discussed. Indeed, from this author's perspective, one of the amazing and distressing characteristics of the Jews is that, in the face of endless persecution throughout the ages, they have trusted and continue to trust their non-Jewish hosts in many countries of their long sojourn in the Exile, including German Jews from the first half of the twentieth century (Volkov, 2002). Equally astounding is that Israel's Jewish leaders trusted agreements with the Arabs time and time again. One betrayal after the other has not imprinted on their minds the folly of their ways. The very same condition prevails to this day: forty years of terrorism and Holocaust denials by Mahmoud Abbas, as Arafat's close associate; the murder of hundreds of Jews, betrayals, cunning deception and publicly paraded corruption, has left almost no mark on the Jewish-Zionist leaders of this country. To what "ingrained" hatred of the Arab Palestinians do the anti-Zionists refer?

The use of the term "hate" by members of the Israel anti-Zionist academics highlights once again their imperviousness to events in the Muslim world. Do the anti-Zionists read books? What about Brigitte Gabriels' recent volume *Because They Hate: A Survivor of Islamic Terror Warns America* (2006), or Dore Gold's *Hatred's Kingdom* (2003) about Saudi Arabia's culture of Wahhabi fanaticism and support of worldwide terrorism against the West? Many U.S. congressmen and senators objected to the American initiative (July 30, 2007) to give Saudi Arabia 20 or so billion dollars for the purchase of new weaponry precisely because that country is the financier of worldwide anti-Semitism and terrorism. At this writing it appears that Arabian wealth decidedly outstrips that of the United States. Relatively low oil prices at this time (end of 2008, beginning of 2009) may have lowered Saudi Arabia's daily income of billions of dollars, but Arabia is far from being engulfed in an economic crisis of the kind now being experienced in the United States, England and other Western countries.

The anti-Zionists do indeed present matters in reverse of reality (Plaut, 2007). Psychoanalysts such as Anna Freud (1936) would call this phenomenon "reaction formation" in which a person defends him/herself against his own thoughts or impulses by transforming their meaning into their opposite. The need to direct this aggression elsewhere since the original intent is laden with intolerable feelings, such as aggressive impulses against someone or something,. The anti-Zionists cannot publically acknowledge Arab hatred toward Jews and Israel. Hence, they invest enormous time and energy, and money, in the effort to convince the world that global terrorism and Islamic fanaticism financed by Saudi Arabia are not real, only a figment of our imagination. Therefore, Arab hatred is altered from "them to us" in objective reality into "our hatred for them" in the reality attributed to Israel Jewry by the Jewish anti-Zionist academics here.

This phenomenon is undoubtedly unique or at least extraordinarily unusual: A significant portion of a democratic nation's intellectuals asserts that the relentless hatred publicly expressed and disseminated by the Arab nations—including Egypt whose publication of anti-Israel and anti-Semitic material (such as the Protocols of the Elders of Zion) is unmatched anywhere in the world—actually is a reaction to Israel's or Jewry's hatred for them. How reality can be so egregiously distorted and transformed into one huge lie remains an enigma, regardless of how we might seek psychological/psychiatric explanations. Indeed, no nation would tolerate such behavior on the part of any of its citizens in times of war. Who in the United States claims that Americans hate Iraqis? Not even the most extreme detractors of George Bush have made such a claim, and certainly not as an explanation why Iraqis attack American or British soldiers in Iraq. The anti-Zionists, for their own reasons, have adopted the Arab propaganda hook, line, and sinker. That brings them in line with the Arab nations on the one hand, and with the European nations on the other, against their own country. Perhaps that gives them a sense of protection from the threats directed against Israel from those countries.

Academic personnel concerned with social-science research, as well as with research in the Humanities, have published work highly critical of Israel. However, researchers without an ax to grind have pointed out the fundamental prejudices and distortions inherent in the anti-Zionist "scientific" publications. Efraim Karsh wrote at length about the anti-Zionists' manufacture of Zionist history in the post-Zionists' publications, including partial quotations that alter the context of the remarks referred to (Karsh, 1997). Similar observations were made by the first author of this work regarding the anti-Zionists' claims regarding the "myths" upon which Israel was allegedly founded and developed (Sharan, 2003). Readers interested in knowing the precise contents of these "myths" can find them scrupulously documented by Oz Almog (1997).

The Israel media consciously and intentionally falsifies Israel's image and presents her as a Nazi nation. B. Michael, a journalist, is one of the outstanding and extremist despisers of Israel. The skull cap he wears on the top of his head apparently endows him with the feeling that he has the license to publish weekly Satanic indictments of Israel in the country's most popular newspaper. One example is as follows:

> We hold thousands of people in prison who have not been tried by a court. We kill on the average of five people a day. We regularly and routinely destroy the homes of innocent people. We keep millions of people in a condition of poverty and misery, as well as in a state of starvation and sickness. We grant human rights and citizenship only to the dominant group. We subdue millions of people and the theo-fascist and armed storm troopers at transfer stations unabashedly treat them with extreme cruelty. The conquered people are without the protection of law. We reached new heights with which the hangmen can operate. Execution without trial has become routine. (Michael, 2003)

A group of organizations, such as "B'tselem," "Physicians for Human Rights" and others almost daily publish "investigations" of Israel's alleged atrocities without ever relating to the Israeli side of the events or, for that matter, to evidence needed to support their claims. Their sole point of reference is the "observations" expressed by the Arab Palestinians opposed to Israel. The "investigative" journalist whose articles appear in *Ha'aretz*, Gidon Levi, interviewed a number of the "miserable victims" of Israeli fascism, although it should be noted that he has no command of Arabic. The so-called investigations provide support for the leftists' demented illusions. Contrary to the small army of Jews who served in Hitler's military machine who hoped to gain some life for themselves or for their families from their betrayal of their own people, or they may not have had any choice in the matter, Israel's leftists freely, even lovingly, contribute to the cause of their country's enemies, definite proof of their fanatical anarchistic beliefs.

When radical leftist writer, Ronit Matalon, returned from her visit to Gaza (April 2001), she asked members of the B'tselem organization if they were aware of the fact that the Palestinians deliberately sent children to face Israeli soldiers. Kidnapping children to use as human shields for Hamas fighters against Israel in the December 2008 war in Gaza was commonplace and shown repeatedly on television. The B'tselem people answered Matalon by saying that they admitted knowing about the dreadful behavior of Hamas but asked her not to write about it because it harms their cause (Matalon, 2001). That is why the Leninist-Marxist post-Zionist, Nir Bar-am, could attack the "mendacity of the Left" (2004). According to the latter's view, the Arabs pose a demographic threat to Israel, so he —Bar-am—proposed that the criteria for Jewish identity be made more flexible, and to call it "Israeli" rather than Jewish (i.e., to employ a term that clearly points to a bi-national State). That term will reduce the fundamentalist and isolationist trends that characterize Israel's Arab population (*Ma'ariv*, February 9, 2004). It takes a singularly unique form of sophistry to produce a rationalization of that kind.

A listener to the Israel radio became incensed with hatred at what Israel was alleged doing to the Arabs. She turned to a bereaved father and said:

> "I am glad your son was killed" (*Ma'ariv*, 2003). The source of that dreadful event can be traced to the grossly distorted messages broadcast by Israel's media. They simply call all of the political groups "the peace camp." However, it is far more accurate to call them "the camp for the elimination of Israel," or "the camp for war on Israel."
>
> "We still await the results of research on the role of Jews in Stalin's criminal regime, the great murderer (perhaps even "greater" than Hitler) of human history. But it is certain that many Jews did cooperate with it. That is the consequence of a bizarre ideology that suffers from moral ignorance" (Shavit, 2001).

Expressions like "the struggle for national freedom," "the right to self-definition," "conquest of the West Bank and Gaza by Israel," still fascinate the mass media without the slightest attempt to explain the circumstances that affected events at the time. In particular, no comprehension is revealed by the media of the Palestinian-Islamic fanaticism. General Ya'alon stated that if we continue to tell ourselves the truth about our own history and remain faithful to it—that the heart of the Israel-Arab conflict was never the conquest of 1967, but rather that of 1948, and that thus far the Arabs' refuse to recognize Israel's right to exist in any territory—we will be victorious. There is no problem of colonialism, of which Israel is falsely accused, nor is there such a thing as a repressive conquest. Rather, the subject of the conflict is an Arab ideology of extermination of the (Jewish) People and of the State (of Israel).

Cultural pluralism, like multiple nationalism or like the phrase "a nation of all it citizens," is the basic slogan of the post-Zionists who wish to destroy Israel as the nation of the Jewish People. That is unadulterated militaristic anti-Zionism. The writer Aharon Megged observed that Israel Jewry is engaged in an unprecedented historical process: the emotional and moral identification of Israel intelligentsia with a people that has vowed to destroy us. Their central message is that Zionism is a colonialist and evil plot (*Jerusalem Post*, 1994).

Professor David Horowitz was correct when he said: "The Left is our doom…. There is no Left more destructive than the Israel left. How can a country make peace with someone who wants to kill you? The Left has no concept of reality" (Horowitz, 2001).

Western countries genuflected towards the Nazis before the outbreak of World War II in an effort to avoid the trauma of World War I. Today the West is repeating that behavior in respect to the Arabs and Islam in view of their numerical superiority, economic power and their influence in the UN and other international bodies (OPEC, for example). The West was recently (November, 2008) treated to the pitiful scene of British Prime Minister Gordon Brown making his rounds with his hat in hand to the sheiks of the Gulf States begging for a hand out. The West has forgotten—not everyone of course—that appeasement and sycophantic behavior were prominent in the days leading to World War II. The same scenario can repeat itself in the near future. The West will pay a heavy price for ignoring the Islamic threat to its very cultural-religious and political existence. The West is in the midst of a deep slumber from which it must rouse itself before it is too late (Bat Ye'or, 2002, 2005; Lewis, 1990).

Perhaps the most penetrating observation about the violence associated with Arab-Islamic extremism was provided as early as 1955 by Nathan Azriel Carlebach, first editor of the *Ma'ariv* newspaper in Tel Aviv in an article entitled "You Can't Converse with Allah" (October, 1955):

> Did anyone ever arrive at anything with the Muslims? Nevertheless, they all keep trying. That's the sign of provincialism—they can't rise above the walls around their town. It is also expression of the diplomats' ignorance. They imagine that other nations are a direct reproduction of themselves. In fact there is absolutely no understanding, now or ever, between the world of Islam and the world of Western civilization.
>
> For generations Muslims have been taught to rape the nature of Man: Not to use the power of thought, and not to seek individual rights. Muslims do not strive for a better world, not is there any concept of development. There is no initiative or attempt to improve anything. The motivation of Western man to "bring forth (more) bread from the earth" were chocked off in Islam. Europeans got caught in the fatal error of viewing Muslims as their own mirror image. The Golem of millions of Muslims has arisen in the four corners of the earth. The danger lies in Muslim psychology that is cased in illusions, disturbed by a sense of inferiority and delusions of grandeur. Islam denies the sanctity of everything found in Western culture until the day comes when Islam conquers the West (demographically, and, hence, politically), and can claim—as it actually does already—that all Western achievements in all fields of human endeavor were created by Muslims.
>
> The danger to the West lurking in Islam is far greater than that of communism. You can talk to the communists on a rational basis of give and take, but not with Allah. You can forgive the boors in the U.S. State Department who cannot comprehend Islam. But we cannot forgive our own people. We must know. We are assisting the world to perceive Arabs who are the figment of our imagination and wish fulfillment. We add sin to our crimes when we distort the picture and shrink the breadth of the disagreement by turning it into a conflict over borders. The Arabs present arguments against us that … (appear to be) … acceptable to the Western mentality. Alas, who knows better than we that borders are not the substance of Israel's conflict with the Arabs. Even had there been no "conquest" (of Arab territory-authors), and even had there would not have been "refugees," the Arabs would have continued to object to our existence with the exact same degree of force.
>
> Above all, we sin against the world and ourselves with our provincialism. With our own hands we restrict the true enormity of the catastrophe and its global dimensions. We are only its peripheral, almost coincidental victims. As long as we will not provide the Free World with this information, we will remain the first victims of our ignorance.

The world has yet to learn that appeasement of the Arabs won't work. Apparently that lesson is still to be learned, despite what the world learned about the failure of appeasement with the Nazis by Neville Chamberlain.

## The Anti-Zionists and Communism

As noted earlier, some of the Israeli-Jewish anti-Zionists today are of communist persuasion. Communism attracted significant numbers of

Jewish intellectuals in Russia, in the United States and among Palestinian Jews, all of whom turned a blind eye to the extreme anti-Semitism embedded in communism by Marx.

It was ... the Jewish sections of the Communist party in revolutionary Russia that led the fight against Zionism. If it were not for these sections, the liquidation of the Zionist movement would have been a slower process (Julius, 2008).

During the period of the British Mandate for Palestine and the early years of Israel's existence, one source of the phenomenon at hand is the influence on young people in Palestine/Israel of communist ideology, or, at the very least, of left-wing socialist ideology. That was the ideology proclaimed at that time by political groups and parties such as Hashomer Hatzair and Mapam, as well as by the Communist Party itself.

There are still Communist parties in Israel, such as the Hadash Party whose constituents are largely Arab but not exclusively so, including Dov Hanin of the communist Hadash Party. Dr. Ahmed Tibi, a close associate and advisor to Yasser Arafat, is a representative in the Knesset of that party. He was re-elected to his post in the Knesset in the national elections held in February 2009. Information about the childhood of the Jewish-Israeli anti-Zionists is not easily accessible so that the nature of their early experiences, in terms of being exposed to communist ideas that incorporate anti-nationalist and anti-Zionist views, cannot be reconstructed at this time. Tanya Reinhart was one of the foremost anti-Zionist academics, a student of Noam Chomsky and professor of linguistics at Tel Aviv University. She was born and raised in Haifa where she was a member of a communist youth group, and remained a communist all her life. Her life story also combines a communist background with exposure to neo-Nazis through Noam Chomsky, and with Arab terrorism (recall, Chomsky visited Hassan Nasrallah in Lebanon in May, 2006, see Seliktar, 2006, and Alexander, 1993). Ilan Pappe's personal history might read something similar to that of Tanya Reinhart. Yossi Schwartz of the Tel Aviv University Law School advertises his Marxist ideology in public. In all likelihood, Kimmerling too was exposed in his early life to communist ideology. The late Baruch Kimmerling preached that Israel should discontinue the Law of Return, and change its national anthem, its flag, and its ethnic character to become a multi-ethnic nation instead of a Jewish one. Eliezer Schweid is no doubt correct when he noted that post-Zionism is a mask to conceal—albeit not so effectively—assimilation into some kind of cosmopolitan Jewishness that is trying to escape from its own history

(1995). Secularism has, in part, evolved into an anti-Jewish ideology. Post-modernism and post-Zionism are now interrelated.

In 1996 a group of Orientalists in Israel's universities announced that Yasser Arafat had canceled the Palestinian Covenant. Perhaps that was no surprise since Arafat had already "fooled" President Bill Clinton with a transparently mendacious charade. That group in fact can be called "The Committee of Orientalists to elect Shimon Peres as Prime Minister." The latter activity is, of course, entirely legitimate, whereas the former announcement was an egregious falsehood made in public about a subject that is within the committee members' professional purview. That is scandalous.

The post-Zionists succeeded beyond their wildest dreams because they "conquered" the printed and electronic media almost in their entirety. More than 95 percent of the video footage sent by APTN and Reuters to their satellite communication systems is supplied by Arab-Palestinian film crews. They do not suffer from any compunction about objectivity, and identify absolutely with the Palestinian Authority's criminal activities.

The powerful news media such as CNN, Sky News, France 24, etc. (with the sole exception of Fox News) are frequently very hostile towards Israel, as it is clearly reflected in their broadcasts. Viewers are rarely provided with background information in order to better comprehend the meaning of the events described in its news programs regarding Israel. The definitions and concepts are biased and distorted, presented in a highly selective manner, facts and events are distorted and conclusions are reached that are not merely grossly unfounded but actually not more than fabrications.

Once again, Linguistics emerges—perhaps by coincidence—as a preferred discipline for anti-Zionists. Professor Ron Kuzar teaches linguistics and English at Haifa University. He asserted that since the Jews stole Palestine from the Arabs, they forced many Arabs to leave Israel and find "refuge" in surrounding Moslem countries. Israel is presently celebrating its sixtieth anniversary, and a propos that celebration, Arabs who so wish should be welcomed back into Israel. At least that would ameliorate somewhat the catastrophe of the Arab refugees.

Need we point out that the so-called "return" of Arab "refugees" to Israel would quickly result in the elimination of Israel as a Jewish nation and install another Islamic nation in its stead? Nor would the elimination of Israel constitute a by-product of the influx of Arabs, but would be the fulfillment of a well-planned move whose explicit purpose is to destroy Israel. That "plan" was expressed publically in 1949 by none other than the Egyptian minister of foreign affairs Muhammad Saleh Ed-Din, who wrote:

> Let it therefore be known and appreciated that, in demanding the restoration of the refugees to Palestine, the Arabs intend that they should return as the masters of the homeland, and not as slaves. More explicitly, they intend to annihilate the State of Israel.

There are dozens of anti-Zionists at Haifa University, even after the departure of Ilan Pappe. Haifa University boasts of the presence of Micah Leshem, an experimental psychologist who deals primarily with the question of the intake of salt by rats. It seems that his academic background prepared him to accuse Israel of being a racist nation (Leshem, 2007), about which he actually knows nothing. His document on the Internet can be assessed as a hate-filled diatribe with no foundation in research, just an arbitrary collection of slogans. It betrays a great deal about the pathology of the extreme Left in Israel's academia, but nothing about reality. In this country he is free to dump endless quantities of venom into the worldwide web without the need for proof of any kind, although he claims to be taking a great risk and demonstrating enormous courage. Among his more lucid pronouncements one finds statements such as: "Zionism is the mother of all dogmas." Leshem appears to believe whole-heartedly in the veracity of his accusation.

One of Israel's dogmas—as found in other nations as well—is that the government is obligated to defend the nation's citizens from its enemies. Another dogma states that, if necessary, citizens can have recourse to courts with judges who can be objective in terms of upholding the law. If these are not the dogmas to which Leshem referred, perhaps someday he will be kind enough to clarify what he meant. Leshem's assertion quoted above might be the function of displaced anger against all of the gentile nations who showered the Jews for centuries with persecution. But Leshem, for reasons most probably unknown to him or others, is unable to direct that rage against its true object. Instead, it is more convenient for him to unburden himself by accusing his own People. A famous psychoanalyst once called that "abreaction." Another psychologist of considerable repute, Leon Festinger, wrote about the phenomenon whereby true believers (members of a cult) "focused on the obsessive rejection of tangible reality" and became oblivious to facts that contradicted their version of history. Those facts are unable to soar into the upper reaches of the academic ivory tower to cause the disillusionment of self-hating Jews like Leshem and his colleagues (Kuhn, 1962. See also Festinger, 1956).

Jewish anti-Zionists, however, do not listen to Arab pronouncements, and certainly disregard "ancient history" such as the remarks of an Egyptian foreign minister made sixty years ago (when the so-called "refugee" problem began). Instead, the anti-Zionists focus exclusively on the alleged plight of Arabs, and the almost three generations of their descendents, who once lived—they or their forebears—in the territory that has been Israel since 1948. They do not pay attention to Jewish history, such as Jewry's millennia-old documented desire and intention to return to their ancient Homeland, or the conditions under which Jews who survived centuries of persecution in Europe and the Middle East. "Conquerors" are not entitled to moral considerations, and it is common knowledge that the Arabs are "natives" not conquerors! The Arabs trumpet aloud the notion that they resided in the Land of Israel since time immemorial, especially since the Philistines or Canaanites were Arabs (while simultaneously asserting that the Arabs are the descendents of Ishmael who was mistreated by Abraham. Few people observe that it is blatantly bizarre to claim that the Arabs are, at one and the same time, descendents of Abraham's son Ishmael and of the pagan Canaanites or Philistines. Furthermore, that claim also affirms that the Israelites were the ancient inhabitants of the Land of Israel called Canaan at the time of Abraham, Isaac and Jacob, approximately 1800 BCE and following (Kitchen, 2003).

The anti-Zionists would also dub the white man of North America as conquerors, from the point of view of the American Indians. However, the enormously large number of white people in the United States, who obviously are not black, red (Indians) or Hispanics, must be ignored by anti-Zionists because the whites have long ceased to be conquerors even if we agree that they were at one time in the distant past. It seems that, had additional millions of Jews returned to the Land of Israel from the Exile, the anti-Zionists would have not emerged at all, and their revision of history would never have become known to anyone. The whites can no longer be thrown out of North America, as they were once by the native Indians (Algonquin) when the overly self-confident and fierce Vikings reached North America in the tenth or eleventh century. But the Jews, riddled with anxiety rather than with over-confidence, can be thrown out of "Palestine" (i.e. Israel). According to the anti-Zionist and clearly anti-Semitic academically employed Jews in Israel, that is what would, and should, occur when the Arab Palestinian "refugees" re-enter Israel (Sharan and Bukay, 2008).

### History, Zionism and Muslim Claims to Israel's Territory

Anti-Zionism brings to the forefront the fundamental question of whose history are we to recognize as legitimate and reasonably objective (i.e., can be "scientifically" documented within recognized limits), and whose history is myth, propaganda, or, at best, concocted to achieve ulterior motives? For anti-Zionists, the Arab version of history is the authentic one, whereas Jewish-Zionist history was doctored to make the Jews/Israelites appear to be the genuine heirs to the Land of Israel. Indeed, the anti-Zionists assert that the Arabs are the true descendents of the ancient Philistines. They were expelled by the criminal brutality of the early kings of Israel and occupied territory on the periphery of Eretz Yisrael. In modern times, when it became possible to cultivate what until recently appeared to be irrevocably arid soil, the Arabs began to trickle back. Hence, they are the autochthonous inhabitants of this country and their expulsion again in the wake of the Jewish invasion of Palestine is, exactly as the Arabs claim, a catastrophe that, morally, deserves to be corrected. Their "return" must be viewed as imperative, if "justice" is to be done. That version of the past undoubtedly deserves recognition for its sheer novelty.

The above revisionist version of the Arab's history and their relationship to the Land of Israel is reminiscent of the various attempts to revise history initiated by several regimes in modern Europe to support their claims to ownership of territories they wished to annex and/or religious-ethnic groups they wished to dominate That kind of revisionism was typical of Nazi Germany and Communist Russia (Sharansky, 2008; Shiloah, 1991; Vital, 1999). In our day far-reaching historical revisionism has been incorporated into the public statements and ideology of terrorist leaders in the Middle East including the late Saddam Hussein, the late Yasser Arafat, Mahmoud Abbas and, of course, Mahmoud Ahmadinejad. Readers are reminded of the statement made earlier (page 65) regarding the PhD dissertation of Abbas about Zionism and Nazism, a dissertation submitted to the People's University in Moscow (Abbas, 1983). Soviet-style revisionism dictated the entire higher education of Abbas and the content of his dissertation, so that Israel's anti-Zionist academics share that mentality with the Arab Palestinians. Abbas is not the only Arab politician to assume that position (Jamal, 2004, pp. 399-452).

While we are on the subject, the question of the territory called Palestine by the British and later called Israel by the Jews, we turn to a chapter, in the book edited by Ben Amos and Bar-Tal, by geographers Oren Yiftachel and Batya Roded called "We are Judaizing You, Homeland" (Ben Amos/Bar-Tal, 2004, pp. 239-274). The chapter is based on the principle that the territory of Israel, (without defining borders) belongs in equal measure to Arab Palestinians and to the Jews. Furthermore, the Jews achieved domination over territory that belongs to the Arab-Palestinian minority. From that point of view, the case of the Jewish-Zionist conquest of Palestine does not differ from the Chinese takeover of Tibet, the Muslim takeover of Malaysia, or the Tamil battles for control of Sri-Lanka (Ben-Amos/Bar-Tal, 2004, p. 243). The authors of the chapter decided to ignore undesirable historical facts. Those facts not merely challenge the authors' view but render it historically and legally indefensible, such as the decisions of the League of Nations and later of the United Nations, to grant Palestine to the Jews as their National Home. Unfortunately for Yiftachel and Roded, the aforementioned events regarding the Jews and Palestine bear no resemblance to what occurred in Sri Lanka, Tibet, or Malaysia. The sources from which their assertions derive were not disclosed. Clearly, someone knowledgeable about Tibet is not likely to agree with them, such as the Dalai Lama. He can certainly be approached for an opinion on the subject.

Another "methodological" observation is in order before returning to the content of the chapter. The chapter's authors employ a series of Hebrew/Israeli songs written by various songwriters and poets/librettists as their source for portraying Israel's perception of its territory. Of course the authors also cite a list of bibliographical references. It cannot be fortuitous that the songwriters and librettists cited are/were largely devoted Zionists, such as Naomi Shemer whose songs are mentioned more than any other songwriter, while the authors of the items in the bibliography are overwhelmingly noted Leftists who are/were critical of, or who actually denounce or ridicule, Israel as a Jewish-Zionist entity. The publications of Yuli Tamir (Peace Now), Daniel Bar-Tal, the Tel Aviv University former communist and present pro-Arab anti-Zionist, are included in those mentioned, inter alia, as scholars who defined the concept of Patriotism.

Aren't the authors' a priori intentions transparent in this fundamental fact alone, without reference to the substance of their comments? It should be obvious to any analyst of this "study" that the songs are intended to serve as examples of Israel's Jewish-Zionist nationalist ideas, while the intellectual-scholarly works provide the scaffolding for an a-nationalist or even anti-nationalist, non-Zionist perspective. Examining this chapter by Yiftachel and his co-author is not unlike comprehending someone's fierce anger by the look on their face before they utter one word. No research can be accepted as valid that prejudices its outcome in advance by employing a decidedly biased methodology. Using a group of subjects who share a single ideology, or a collection of scholarly publications all derived from a single school of thought, would never pass muster for publication in a respectable social science journal as a study of a nation's views about its own political-cultural attitudes. That is precisely what the two authors of this chapter asked readers to do, and, obviously, that is what the editors accepted or invited to be included in their anthology. With one or two notable exceptions, this volume should be renamed as *Patriotism: A One-Sided View for Anti-Zionists*.

Professor Yiftachel and co-author launch a pointed attack on the "ethnocratic" nation that marginalizes minorities and assumes ownership of the national territory (p. 244). Israel, these authors believe, is a prime example of the despised ethnocracy because it emphasizes the distinction between the secular "state" and the nation (of the Jewish People). In a multi-cultural nation no overlap would exist between the nation (or the People) and the State. Members of all ethnic groups are citizens (A nation of all its citizens) so that no particular group dominates the State. Of relevance here is the authors' claim that ethnic-national perceptions of the national territory and of identity are cultivated by Israel's authorities. These perceptions are not the consequences of patriotic notions derived from citizenship. Ethnic concepts of identity and history are divisive because they exclude minority groups and atomize universal humanity (p. 245).

Yiftachel and co-author are obviously much aware of the fact that Israel is an ethnic nation identical to an entire group of ethnic nations in the world, in the West as well as in the Middle East and Far East. Indeed, the Jewish-Zionist position of Jewry's ethnic-national identity and ownership of the Land of Israel over the past few thousand years never said otherwise, so that the two authors are actually regurgitating what the Jews have always said about themselves. Moreover, Yiftachel and Roded return once again to the super-Leftist motif that, from a geographical-political perspective there is a universal humanity that is not subdivided into separate units which are part of an alleged (mystical) unity. I wonder if they are also aware of the fact that constitutional democracy requires the existence of sovereign nation-states.

No democracy can survive if all of humanity would be included in one nation at least not as long as people remain human. Can people imagine that a nation can survive without a history, without people knowing their historical-cultural-religious roots, without the dimension of time filled with collective memories? Where does their particular language and written-spoken traditions come from, where do their ancestors come from, what values, strivings, identity do they wish to transmit to their children? Perhaps our anti-Zionist Jews consider those questions superfluous, irrelevant or outdated? If so, once again they are probably unique on this planet since no other group, tribe, country, nation or group of nations (e.g., Europe, Scandinavia, the United Kingdom) survives for long without providing some reasonable response to those questions for its inhabitants.

Even if the nation-state encompasses several subgroups who have elected to maintain one government, each subgroup still seeks to know about, study and transmit its unique historical tradition to their offspring. The statement that lack of historical knowledge results in a lack of interest in the future ("Those who do not remember the past are condemned to repeat it"—George Santayana—quoted by William Shirer, 1960, page vii) remains valid for all, or at least most, of humankind.

We submit that a large majority of humans presently alive on the planet Earth understand that the entire planet is divided among nations, each with its national, cultural and historical identity and interests, and Israel, from that point of view, is indeed one of those nations. An organization called the United Nations does exist, but the last time I looked it was anything but United. Its predecessor had a less presumptuous title, namely The League of Nations. Universal Humanity certainly exists on the anthropological level, insofar as all people are homo sapiens. If Professor Yiftachel and colleagues think that the same concept prevails at the level of nations, or in regard to cultural or ethnic groups, the burden of proof is squarely on his shoulders. Human history patently belies such an approach and any attempt to undertake a demonstration of the falsity of that premise or assertion is foolhardy, just as it is absurd to try and prove that everyone alive had a mother.

In his chapter on "Law as a Means for Shaping Patriotism," (pp. 341-362), Gad Barzilai sets forth a string of arguments that require several readings before the reader can conclude that he/she gained a reasonable idea of what the author tried to say. He quotes Erich Fromm at length (p. 342) who asserted that patriotism was the worship of irrationality (Fromm, 1975, pp. 63-64). Apparently Barzilai doesn't know that Fromm was unable to determine his own national identity. Born in Germany, as a young Jew he became close for a short time to Franz Rosenzweig (d. 1929) who knew little about being Jewish but gradually learned a great deal and became a kind of Zionist (Glatzer, 1953, pp. 353-358). Fromm went to the United States where he became a psychoanalyst but gradually understood that he could not accept Freud's theories. Eventually he wrote several widely read and quoted books (*The Escape from Freedom*, *The Sane Society*, et al.), where he developed a psychoanalytic approach of his own. After many years in the United States he decided to move to Mexico (as had Trotsky before him) where he died.

It seems that Fromm and others with profound doubts about their identity appeal to anti-Zionist writers in Israel such as Barzilai, Bar-Tal, Ben-Amos and their mental associates. Barzilai points out that patriotism cannot be part of, and is even opposed to, Marxism since Marx was a "universalist" opposed to national identities. Yet, on the same page (343) Barzilai notes that patriotism often means the right of the nation state to punish people who are not patriots. How can a free nation punish some of its citizens for not being patriotic and yet remain legitimate in the eyes of its (other) citizens? Only a dictatorship can do that and get away with it. The author of the chapter under discussion then quotes other well-known anti-national sociologists (who wrote twenty-five to forty years ago) such as Foucault and Habermas, to underpin his own anti-nationalist position. Strangely, Barzilai at no point mentions anything about criminal behavior and the fact that a nation's citizens want to be protected from crime and criminals. Nor does he discuss the constitutional basis for punishing criminals through the agency of the law and its provisions for safeguarding society. Yet, nowhere does the author appear to be an anarchist, so that this reader is inclined to ask if Barzilai understands that his chapter reflects some critical contradictions.

## The Reds in Israel

The revealing work of Amnon Lord (1988) leaves little room for doubt that in pre-State Palestine and in Israel's early years, the far-left wing of the Zionist movement (Mapam-Hashomer Hatzair) was singularly concentrated on its loyalty to the Soviet Union and to communism, and viewed the Jewish State as a potential tool for the cultivation and spread of communist doctrine. The communist persuasion of Hashomer Hatzair before and after the establishment of Israel in 1948, and its fierce loyalty to Stalin and to the Soviet Union, aroused the wrath of Ben-Gurion who denounced them in a series of articles in the daily press (later collected and published as a booklet: Yariv, 1953).

In the 1940s, the youth groups affiliated with Hashomer Hatzair in and outside of Palestine, including those in the United States, went marching in the streets singing quite loudly: "The worker marches forward to freedom and to the revolution!" Jews were to go to Palestine from the Golah to live as communist Jews. They had no ties with non-communist Jewish organizations or with synagogues in the broader Jewish community. When the reality of the Jewish communist experiment soured for them in Israel, many returned to their home countries straight from the kibbutz without stopping in the bourgeois cities of Tel Aviv or Haifa, and certainly not in the religious ghetto of Jerusalem. In their minds, they had not settled in the Jewish nation of Israel but in the communist settlement of the kibbutz.

It is important to mention that not all left-wing Jewish socialists were attracted to communism. Ben-Gurion and the Israel Labor Party were all socialists and opposed to communism. In the United States as well many well known Jewish socialists rejected communism vehemently and were devoted Zionists, such as Chaim Greenberg (1889-1953) who was a friend of Ben-Gurion. Greenberg was a Labor-Zionist theoretician and widely recognized as one of the moral leaders of world Zionism. His collected essays include a strong condemnation of communism written in 1936 (Greenberg, 1953, pp. 251-261). In Palestine too, socialist theoreticians, not only politicians like Ben-Gurion, wrote against communist ideology and its Marxist, anti-humane and anti-Zionist implications and orientation (Kaufmann, 1930; 1936). Kaufmann and Greenberg wrote their denunciation of Marxism and Communism almost simultaneously.

Just what influence did the initiation into the communist religious doctrine have on the Jews of Palestine, later Israel? That initiation could have taken place in Russia or Germany where Jewish radicals became the priests and prophets of communism. Five out of a total of twenty-one members of the Communist Party's Central Committee were Jews, namely Sokolnikov, Sverdlov, Trotsky, Uritskii and Zinoviev. Kamenev had one Jewish parent (Vital, p. 703). In addition to the leadership of the communist movements in some European countries, communist ideology enveloped large sections of East European Jewry (Vital, 1999). Many Jewish communists arrived later in Palestine, where they indoctrinated their youth and exerted considerable influence on some of Jewry's institutions in Palestine, including the Haganah (Yitschak Sadeh, for example) with their social-political convictions (Lord, 1988). That initiation had broad and multiple implications for these people's entire world view, affiliations, loyalties, values and life goals, all of which affected the lives of some of the anti-Zionists discussed here as well as the lives of many Jews in Israel. Large numbers of Jews who adopted Communist ideology were opposed to Zionism. But, quite tragically they also adopted a deep anti-Semitism according to which religious and Zionist Jews were perceived as enemies (Epstein, 2003; Sharan, 2003; Wisse, 2007; Vital, 1999).

This essay cannot provide a thorough treatment of communist ideology as it affected Jews, Zionism and Israel, but it is relevant to highlight a few fundamental ideas that bear directly on our discussion here. Readers who wish to pursue that topic further are referred to several extensive treatments of the subject (Dothan, 1996; Epstein, 2003; Isaac, Rael and Erich, 1993; Lord, 1988; Shiloah, 1991; Vital, 1999, see in particular pp. 703-754; Yariv, 1953).

On the theoretical level, Marxist-communist ideology negates the significance of separate nationalisms and focuses instead on the trans-national "unity" of the working class or proletariat. It is a neo-messianic ideology that foresees the redemption of the workers from their "chains" through revolution that will redress the evils of the industrial revolution and its enslavement of the masses who do not benefit from the fruits of their labor. The prophetic brotherhood of Man will be realized by the dissolution of national boundaries when the representatives of international workers will replace the capitalist nation-state, as preached by socialism. Although Kaufmann, (1936) who certainly belonged to the Labor party and was consulted frequently by Ben-Gurion, had long ago analyzed and debunked the Marxist-socialist doctrines and mentality and his essays were readily available in Hebrew.

For example, Shimon Peres, and his sidekick Yossi Beilin cunningly dragged Yitzhak Rabin into the Oslo agreements, all of which took place carefully hidden from public view. That infamous agreement with the Yasser Arafat, yielded a forty-five-minute break from terrorism and the violent deaths of at least 1,500 Jewish citizens of Israel. Quotations from statements made by Ziyad Abu 'Ein in 2006 on an Arab TV station (cited by Wisse, page 168) disclose unequivocally, that the Oslo agreements provided the means whereby the PLO obtained legitimacy and weapons that made it possible for it to carry out the Intifada (Arab uprising) in Israel and in the territory of Judea and Samaria. So many years later the situation with the Arabs has deteriorated even more, and our government still insists on pursuing its march of folly. The present Israel government (of Ehud Olmert which at this writing has only a few weeks left in office) insists on continuing its "negotiations" with arch terrorist, Holocaust denier, politically unstable PA Chairman Mahmoud Abbas. He still wants Jerusalem for his new state in Judea and Samaria which, in fact, are a Hamas province in all but name. The Gaza War (2008-2009) did not change that situation in any essential way.

Many Jews in Israel knew at the time of the Oslo agreement what a dreadful mistake was being made. In retrospect it is a pity they could not have prevented the agreement from being adopted and given such thunderous accolades by the Western world including the Nobel Peace Prize for Peres and for Arafat, the arch terrorist himself. After that decision, the Nobel Prize for Peace can be viewed only with enormous cynicism and with a healthy dose of disdain. The Jews call it Land for Peace. That is a serious misuse of the words peace and piece. One side believes it will get peace for pieces, while the other side wants pieces but will give only temporary peace until the waiting period is over when it can renew its demand for another piece exchanged for another short period of peace. Aren't the Jews of Israel, extraordinarily lucky that the Arabs remain absolutely recalcitrant and won't agree to anything Israel gives them, either money or territory (Vital, 2008)? If the Arabs would contemplate making peace with Israel, they might even receive most of the country from its current political leaders and conclude an agreement with the State of Tel Aviv.

The Israel electorate told Peres to his face that he was a loser, but the Kadima dominated Knesset elected him as president of Israel. The political party called Kadima actually did everything in its power to pull Israel back in time to the point where its existence was threatened by the Arabs (long before it was threatened by the Iranian president). Peres told a packed hall of students at Oxford University's Balliol College (November 20, 2008) that a new era of peace is dawning on the world, and he was cheered. Both Peres and the students preferred to disregard the recent return (November, 2008) to London of Prime Minister Gordon Brown to London after pleading on his knees, hat in hand, for contributions from the Emirs of the Emirate States. Peres then went on to tell the British Parliament how grateful Israel was for the help England offered the Jews in brining Jewish refugees from Europe after World War II to Palestine! Peres and the Oxford students totally ignored the battles raging in Afghanistan and Iraq, the nuclear threats of Iran and North Korea, the relentless waves of rockets fired at Israel from Gaza (even after the alleged "conclusion" of Operation Cast Lead), the Syrian conquest of Lebanon, and so forth. But, the illusionary world of Shimon Peres seen through rose-colored glasses urged us to close our eyes so we would not see the rockets landing in Ashkelon, Sderot and nearby while making peace with the Arabs. That strange Peresian world has been known since the days of his clandestine land purchases for his brother's contracting business in Ramat Aviv, and the millions he raked in from investments in electricity and water companies in the Palestinian Authority and elsewhere in the Arab world (back to the Emirates).

"The Independent Jewish Voices" (IJV) opening statement in 2007, for example, endeavored to "reclaim" the "tradition of Jewish support for universal freedoms, human rights and social justice ... justice, justice shall you pursue (Deut. 16:20) ... as a Jew I feel a particular duty to oppose the injustice that is done to Palestinians..." (Hodgson, 2007). The historian Eric Hobsbawm explained when IJV was launched:

It is important for non-Jews to know that there are Jews...who do not agree with the apparent consensus within the Jewish community that the only good Jew is one who supports Israel (Hodgson, 2007).

Anthony Julius, a prominent London lawyer, goes on to treat the Jewish anti-Zionists' reference to universalism. They assert that: "the true Jew is the universalist ... one who has disavowed all the trappings of linguistic, religious, and national identity" (Rose, 1991), That ambition is captured in Karl Kraus's slogan, "Through dissolution to redemption!" He formulated that quip as the conclusion to the following statement:

Only a courageous purge of the ranks and the laying aside of the characteristics of a race, which through many centuries of dispersion has long ceased to be a nation, can bring the torment to a stop. Through dissolution to redemption! (cited by Julius from Wistrich, 1990).

Oren Ben-Dor teaches legal history at Southampton University. In his view, Israel should be reconfigured. Israel is a "terrorist state like no other" because it hides its primordial immorality by fostering an image of victimhood. In 1948 most of the indigenous people were ethnically cleansed from the part of Palestine that became Israel. This action was carefully planned...." Ben-Dor wishes to convince readers that the Palestinians have 'no option but to resort to violent resistance...the main problem in Palestine is Zionism..." (Ben Dor, 2006).

Julius points out that Ilan Pappe, like other former Israeli self-imposed ex-patriots now in England, has chosen to devote himself to the role of advocate for the interests of Israel's adversaries (Pappe, 2006). The latter heap praises on the Jewish anti-Zionists who are perceived as "an embattled remnant ... who know the truth about Israel, the truth about Jews... (Julius, op. cit.) Another such embattled ex-Israeli is Akiva Orr about whom Tariq Ali said: "[he] had long abandoned Israeli patriotism...."(Ali, 2003, cited by Julius). Orr argued that to be Jewish is to be religious. There is no such thing as a secular Jew and Israel has not supplied a secular identity to Jews. In fact, Zionism "is no more than a heresy of Judaism and the ethnocentrism of Jewish Israelis" (Julius, 2008). For Uri Davis, who recently converted to Islam and married a Moslem woman, everything connected with Zionism and Israel is racist. Davis is another anti-Zionist enamored of the term apartheid for characterizing Israel. Zionism in his eyes is an abomination. In light of Israel's apartheid legal system it is not entitled to exist. It should be replaced by "a democratic Palestine."

Jacqueline Rose, a British Jew, published three anti-Zionist books: *States of Fantasy* (1996), *The Question of Zion* (2005) dedicated to the memory of Edward Said, and *The Last Resistance* (2007). Clearly, she is a woman of considerable ability, and her formulations often display an enviable command of language. The gross distortions of reality and history in her books convey the depth of her animosity for Zionism and Israel. Like other anti-Zionists, she compiled a list of grievances against Israel. Israel "desires its potential citizens … to come home, with as much fervor as it banishes the former occupants of its land from their own dream of statehood" (1996, pp. 2, 13).

Israel suppresses dissent, she claimed. But she also noted that Israel "mostly silenced the voices of dissent ... and that the voices of dissent and opposition are very strong in Israel" (2005, pp. 53, 69). Rose subscribes to the Arab/Muslim use of the term Naqbah, catastrophe, for describing the 1948 establishment of Israel. Hence, Zionism "is a notion of redemption … bound up with ruin, dread and catastrophe" (Julius, 2008).

Rose is enamored of, and apparently cannot resist, the analogy between Jew and Nazi. Every exercise of power is latently Nazi. Indeed, everything that one opposes can be described as Nazi, which Jacqueline Rose in fact does, as do her Israeli "colleagues" Idith Zertal and Akiva Eldar (2007). These egregiously distasteful allegations that stem from an unbridled anger (for events, traumas or experiences that we, the readers cannot know) will not be pursued here.

It is worthwhile noting that the strengthening of democratic national life is indeed modern Messianism because in today's world there is no alternative unless populations agree to accept an arbitrary monarchy or totalitarian government. The nation state is the contemporary world's sole form of macro-political-social organization. Nationalism not only predates Zionism, but the latter adopted its modern form and structure from existing nations. Of course all nationalisms on this planet are "material and carnal" in Rose's words, and not "spiritual." Had she been writing a poem, those words could be appropriate, but in a political document they are bizarre. Is there a spiritual nation anywhere? What kind of "creature" is a "spiritual" nation? If we wish to focus on material reality and disregard our mental or "spiritual" constructs, one could claim that there is no such thing as a nation because it is only an idea, albeit one that leads to a multitude of concrete behavior in all organic life, particularly in the human species. Granted, humanity does live by myths, and the nation-State is one of the abstract, mythical ideas by which we live.

*The Myth of the State*, a book on political philosophy Ernst Cassirer (1946), is only one of numerous myths dominating our collective existence, at far as our limited understanding permits. If Ms. Rose proposes to jettison the myth of the State—and condemns Israel and Zionism for adhering to it—then she unambiguously places herself in the category of anarchist in the strictest sense of that word. In our accepted vocabulary and in our human society, both in the West and in the East (Russia, China, India, etc), anarchy is tantamount to social-political chaos accompanied by an outbreak of anti-social behavior that would result in wholesale slaughter.

Social critics may draw attention to ideological controversies over the nation's form of government. As Ernst Cassirer emphasized, the manipulation by the state of various myths in order to support its political power is a potential danger today as it has been through centuries of human history. Democratically elected presidents as well as the infamous dictators of Western and Eastern nations manipulated myths for the purpose of public relations. Often there was more than a kernel of truth in the myths. Indeed, all great ideas are subject to manipulation by anyone and everyone, given the opportunity. It does not require a particularly long or accurate memory to recall the manipulations in modern times made by sundry groups and nations of the word Socialism, including, of course, the Soviet Union, Nazi Germany, regimes in South America, Africa, the Far East (Mao Tse Tung) and so forth. Democracy can also be a myth and exist as a slogan rather than as a social reality.

Some countries hold elections to demonstrate that they are democratic. Elections are part of the myth of Democracy which is based on equal representation of the population together with the rule of Law and the subordination of government to the Law. Dictators can be "elected" to office. Election processes and results can be manipulated like all other human institutions. In the university where I taught for thirty-four years department heads were elected. My objection to elections when there was only one candidate was summarily ignored. The claim was made by colleagues that one could always vote "no." To me that reply was no more than a repetition of elections in the Soviet Union when the population voted for Stalin. They too had only one candidate for whom they could vote with the option of voting "no." Who would dare to vote that way? Besides, whoever the candidate was, he/she would always be elected since there was no opposition. Some universities are typical Bolshevik organizations.

After two millennia of Exile, where the Jews themselves developed ideologies that sanctified Jewry's political limbo, Zionism had to combat many other subgroups within Jewry in its struggle to be adopted and implemented (Baron, 1960). Many Jews never became reconciled to the Jewish State and a few relatively small groups in Israel today have still not "recognized" Israel as an independent political entity. J. Rose's reference to such ideological controversies within the Zionist movement or in reaction to it, is to point to the—by now—historically obvious. Indeed there seems to have been some social-political influence of the Sabbatean messianic movement of the seventeenth century on the Jewish nationalist movements in Europe that emerged in the nineteenth century (Scholem, 1941, 1957). Gershom Scholem, Israel's famous historian of Jewish mysticism whose pioneering research and analysis brought the figure and history of Sabbetai Zevi to light with a depth and breadth that had not been know previously, published his major works seven decades ago and onward. Those works are well known to anyone who takes an interest in Jewish history. One should note in passing that Scholem's "connection" between Sabbateanism and the later Zionist movement remains a reasonable hypothesis but a more palpable linkage between the two remains to be established if that connection is to be considered as historical fact.

Furthermore, Messianism is not part and parcel of a particular political ideology on one versus the other side of the political spectrum. Zionism as the ideology and social-political movement devoted to rebuilding Jewry's repossession of its ancient—and modern—homeland (Herzl's Altneuland, 1902) was dominated at one time or another by socialists, by national idealists, by people who had an almost exclusively cultural-historical view, by capitalists, by Jews seeking a way to safeguard Jewry's physical survival and others. The greatness of Zionism for the Jewish People is precisely its ability to serve as an umbrella ideology for diverse groups in the Jewish People who seek diverse ends, all of which converged in the return to what the British called Palestine, namely the place historically known as the Land of Israel.

Messianism colors Zionism at every turn, a fact which Ms. Rose calls "chilling." She wrote that the struggle for the land (Land of Israel) "has nothing to do with the Palestinians themselves at all" (Rose, 2005, p.

133). With whom, may I ask, does it deal? With the ground? Perhaps her thought was that Jewry's/Israel's struggle is still with the Turkish government (up to World War I) or with the British government (that left Palestine sixty years ago)?

## The Anti-Zionist Grasp of Anti-Semitism

The Biblical prophets were supporters of Jewish self-government and denounced reliance on foreign powers. They proclaimed to us and to the world that nations and their leaders, as well as the populace, should pursue justice, and, if they do, their land will prosper. Justice is not the purview of individuals only, but of nations. A nation exists by virtue of the devotion to it of its constituents, of its people. Individuals' ethics have very limited impact on society if the larger social-political unit of the nation fails to observe ethical standards. In fact, ethical individuals can become demoralized when the body politic neglects its responsibility to be ethical. In today's democracies, ethics must reign supreme in the courts, or there can be no justice or righteousness. The courts are not regulated by the citizens but by the institutions of government. Hence, contrary to the so-called "universalist" anti-Zionists, the nation and not the "international community" (which is the world's most acrimonious platform—the U.N.) implements justice. The Jewish people, whose historical literary sources concentrate largely on the pursuit of justice, were unable to observe those rules due to its lack of power at the national level. Its courts could deal with individual cases exclusively. To disavow nationalism is to destroy Jewry's devotion to justice, not to strengthen it, as the anti-Zionists would have us believe. The latter have chosen to support Arab-Palestinian justice, not justice for or by a Jewish nation.

Stalin was undoubtedly an extreme anti-Semite on par with Hitler and the Nazis. Leon Trotsky was aware that he too, a completely peripheral Jew, was an object of Stalin's anti-Semitism. Yet, for him there were no solutions to "the Jewish problem" other than revolutionary struggle that he advocated as late as 1937-38 when it was an empty slogan that led nowhere except to the gulag. The anti-Zionists of today, not unlike Trotsky, refuse to acknowledge the utter pointlessness of communism. But Trotsky himself was not an anti-Semite. Rather, he could "smell" anti-Semitism in others, something contemporary anti-Zionists are unable to do. Instead, they contribute to it significantly (see Julius, 2008).

The typical anti-Zionist view of anti-Semitism emphasizes the following points: (a) anti-Semitism is caused by Israel; (b) Jews should not be concerned with anti-Semitism; (c) contemporary anti-Semitism is trivial; (d) many acts of ostensibly anti-Semitic character are not in reality Jew-hating; (e) the anti-Semites are right about Israel. Hence, the Jewish State is causing Jews everywhere to be the object of antagonism, as stressed by an English-Jewish academic, Tony Judt, who teachers at New York University: "it is a Jewish State not a Christian one which is holding [the Jews] hostage for its own actions.... Israel is bad for the Jews" (Judt, 2003).

Attacks on Jews in Europe and elsewhere by Muslim youth are "misdirected efforts" to wreak revenge on Israel. In a speech at the University of Chicago, Judt remarked that;

> "there is an Israel lobby ... there is ... a set of Jewish organizations behind the scenes to prevent certain kinds of conversations, certain kinds of criticism ... there is a de facto conspiracy ... and that sounds awful like ... The Protocols of the Elders of Zion ... well if it sounds like it it's unfortunate, but that's just how it is..." (Judt, 2007: cited by Julius, 2008).

Judt also argued that Israel imported late nineteenth-century nationalism, when people dreamed of forming nation states, into a world that has moved on to open frontiers and international law. Israel is an anachronism. It must dissolve itself. Zionism is a dead end. It seems he never heard the words spoken by John F. Kennedy: "Ask not what your country can do for you; ask what you can do for your country." Nor do Atzmon and the other anti-Zionists ask the Jewish population of Israel whether his position would be welcomed by the majority of Israel's citizens. Then again, they can be coerced into accepting this enlightened view so they can enter the twenty-first century whether they like it or not. Yet, despite the loudly trumpeted and widely published claims of the Jewish anti-Zionists, in Israel, England or wherever there is a Jewish community, they remain a minority now, and in the foreseeable future.

What is not trivial is the racist antagonism directed at Muslims and blacks (Greenstein, 2007). Attacks on Jews outside Israel are motivated by public outrage and cannot be criticized. Suicide bombing is the reaction to Israeli action that causes Arabs to be humiliated and frustrated ... in the occupied territories. (Breugel, 2004)

As Anthony Julius notes in his very astute and restrained manner, the Jewish anti-Zionists not only contribute to anti-Semitism, they also "provide cover to the anti-Semites" because they, the anti-Zionists are Jews, and they endorse the anti-Semitic positions as true as if they, the anti-Zionists, had the knowledge or authority of an expert (Julius, 2008). How can non-Jews be called anti-Semitic when Jews voice the very same opinions?

Two Israeli anti-Zionists, Akiva Orr and the late Israel Shahak commented on the inhuman and immoral features of Judaism and Jewish law. Orr said that Jews think that God requires of them to sacrificing their own children to him, to test the strength of their convictions. (Orr, 1983), and Shahak (1997) asserted that Judaism required Jews to mistreat non-Jews. The anti-Zionist Talmud scholar in England, Daniel Boyarin, called Shahak's book "a scandal, it's a slander, it's the sort of thing the worst anti-Semites could write." The latter's writings, Scheonfeld wrote, have become

"a basic staple of the anti-Semitic library... are widely available in English, French, German and Arabic, and have been posted on the Internet by anti-Semitic groups...." (Scheonfeld, 2004, pp. 134-135).

Shahak's book was published by Pluto Press, founded in 1969, a publishing arm of International Socialism later called the Socialist Workers party in the United Kingdom. Later still that publisher became independent (Pluto). The British Socialist Workers party has repeatedly invited an ex-Israeli Gilad Atzmon whose anti-Israel sentiments and writings are legion. Two of his critical statements will suffice here: "I am not going to say whether it is right or not to burn down a synagogue. I can see that it is a rational act" (Doward and Hines, 2005).

And later, he observed:

To regard Hitler as the ultimate evil is nothing but to surrender to the Zio-centric discourse. To regard Hitler as the wickedest man and the Third Reich as the embodiment of evilness is to let Israel off the hook...Israel and Zionism are the ultimate Evil with no comparison.... The current Israeli brutality is nothing but evilness for the sake of evilness.... if we want to save this world, if we want to live in a humane planet, we must focus on the gravest enemy of peace, those who are wicked for the sake of evilness: the Israeli State and world Zionism.... We have to admit that Israel is the ultimate evil rather than Nazi Germany. (Atzmon, 2006)

## Marxist or Nazi Historians U.S. Style

Israel is not the only country that bears the brunt of attacks by Marxist ideologues from the academic world. Recent publications in the United States carefully describe and document the effects of neo-communist and Marxist academics on education and on the policies pursued by many universities. They assert, inter alia, that the United States "is an oppressor nation, the Third Reich incarnate" (Horowitz, 2007, p. 93) paralleling what several of the anti-Zionist professors in Israel write and say about Israel (See also Horowitz, 2006).

This basic tenet of radical socialism was expressed as early as the second half of the nineteenth century by Aharon Shmuel Liberman

(1845-1880), editor of "The Truth" (*Pravda*!) the first socialist periodical in Hebrew that appeared in Russia: "for us socialists there is no division into nations or races ... the "zhid" ... is a cosmopolitan: No country on earth can tie us to it by some special patriotism ... (we) can be only cosmo-socialists..." (Shiloah, p. 23; Vital, pp. 410-411).

Lenin's ideas about the withering of the state are a direct continuation of this notion that preceded him by five decades:

> the one true common denominator of the Jewish members of each of the three major Revolutionary parties, the Bolsheviks, Mensheviks, and the Socialist Revolutionaries, was their fixed, quite passionate determination to disengage themselves from specifically Jewish interests and from the Jewish collectivity itself in any of its forms. (Vital, p. 727)

This doctrine molded leftist Zionists' ideology in Palestine-Israel, as expressed succinctly by Ben-Gurion:

> The document that Mapam signed (that) demands that all the workers in Israel must also sign it ... is not a minor matter. That document impresses itself on, molds and crystallizes all of our moral and political perceptions, determines all of our human and Jewish relationships in the world, in the Jewish world and in the international sphere ... and suspends our free judgment regarding everything done by a mighty power [i.e., the Soviet Union]...that is completely beyond our control ... if Mapam had its way ... it would have, in fact as well as in theory, dissolved the sovereignty of the State of Israel and erased the image of the Jew and of the human being in us. (Yariv, p. 28)

In short, for Jews in Israel, communism was a negation of Jewish nationalism, namely, of Zionism, and the Israeli communists rejected Ben-Gurion's condemnation of the principles of their manifesto. Hashomer Hatzair, in Ben-Gurion's eyes, was identified with the Soviet Union and with Stalin as its unopposed leader.

Inside the Soviet Union, the Bolshevik Jews displayed frightful savagery toward religion and toward religious Jews, including the deliberate desecration of Jewish and Christian buildings and hooliganism directed at humiliating religious people (Epstein, 2003; Hazaz, 1956/1968). The Russian theologian and priest, Sergei Bulgakov offered a penetrating interpretation of Jews' enthusiastic participation in revolutionary activities in Russia (see Epstein, 2003, pp. 129-133). He observed that the Jewish revolutionary intellectuals had completely disconnected themselves from Jewish history and from their Jewish roots under the influence of radical socialism and humanism. But, argued Bulgakov, even their bestial behavior toward Jews and Christians manifested their religiosity, albeit in a reversed negative sense. They believed that they would "occupy the temple in place of God," meaning that the revolution would redeem the world instead of the God of Israel or of the Christians, while the religious believers should be eliminated. They saw themselves as redeemers of the world while seeking the historical suicide of the Jewish People. They conducted a war of "Jews against their Jewishness." Bulgakov's assessment written early in the twentieth century (perhaps in 1919) has been confirmed often by recent thinkers, particularly in regard to the total ignorance of anything Jewish and of Judaism by Jewish communists (Aharonson, p. 293).

The internationalist character of communist ideology, and its idealization of the world's workers as forming a trans-national brotherhood, leads almost logically to the view that the "impoverished" Arab Palestinians (hence proletarians) would be viewed with great empathy by the anti-Zionist Jews in Israel with a strong communist background or ideology. Jews are not entitled to a separate nation while the Arab Palestinian "proletariat" is "homeless." Nor would a new Arab nation in Judea and Samaria suffice because that leaves the Jews in possession of their ethnocratic nation that rules over many Muslims, Christians, Druze, and others. Hence, even with an Arab Palestinian state that would essentially terminate the so-called "occupation," the Jews would continue to "occupy" Israel, and Israel should not exist, in the eyes of a Marxist-communist anti-Zionist. This form of trans-nationalism is not a local version of the United Nations, but one that entails demolition of existing nations to be replaced by a global government (Fonte, 2003). Since other nations fiercely defend their right to exist on their historic national soil, it suffices if the Jewish country will be dismantled as a first step in the direction of socialist-communist trans-nationalism until the advent of the millennium. In that way, the original communist ideal of world redemption through the abolition of national governments can be realized in part, and the Israeli Jewish anti-Zionists can boast of participating in this glorious endeavor through their struggle for the removal of Israel from the community of nations and the handover of the territory of Israel to the "proletarian" Arabs.

Perhaps the core notion of Jewish self-hatred is that the Jews have no moral right to place their own survival and self-interests above that of their enemies. Defending oneself or one's country against those who unabashedly announce in public that they intend to kill you is universally considered to be an act of cowardice. Isn't that so?

The other side of the coin comes from the Nazi onslaught on the Jews. The Yiddish expression that "it is hard to be a Jew" must be rephrased in post-Holocaust times to read: It is frightening to be a Jew. Some people, observed Freud, cope with Fright by Flight, namely, attempt to escape from the source of the fear. For not a few Jews, that means escape from being Jewish. Surely, the Nazi slaughter of the Jews must have generated an incalculable burden of fear that Jews tried to deal with by aligning themselves with their enemies. Our contemporary anti-Zionist Israeli Jews must have said to themselves something like the following:

If we will be accepted by the Arabs, even admired for our courage to reject the dominant culture of our own People, to oppose the Zionist hegemony as the reigning narrative, we will be exonerated and will not have to fear our enemies. By transforming my enemies into friends, at least in my own mind, I rid myself of the fear of being a victim. The fact that my former enemy remains an enemy of my country and of my People requires that I go one step further and perceive my fellow Jews and my country as my enemy.

Without specific evidence, that psychological scenario cannot be attributed automatically to given individuals, but it is most definitely within the realm of psychological possibility as one explanation of how the anti-Zionist and anti-Semitic Israel Jews reached the depths to which they have sunk. It seems they perceived quite clearly that they are part of the delegitimized group that denounces the existence of a Jewish state in Israel. Naturally, they behave in accordance with their own perception of themselves and with their own convictions.

In short, the ant-Zionist Israeli-Jewish academics, largely of Marxist-communist persuasion or inclination, revel in identifying Israel with Nazism (see the explanation offered in the illuminating chapter by Epstein, 2003). Israel's schoolbooks are Nazi-inspired, our youth groups are Hitler Youth, the life-long socialist-Zionists from Poland were (allegedly) Nazis, and Judeo-Nazi soldiers, who unashamedly obey the orders issued to them by their officers, are persecuting the helpless Arabs.

On their part, the Arabs, along with their Israeli-Jewish supporters, including a handful of American-Jewish professors thrown in for good measure, proudly parade their hatred for Jews and Israel before the world, on television and in the press of almost every country. The world gleefully looks down on this drama—of anti-Semitic Jews who joined the chorus of Holocaust denial and support for the Arab aggression against Jews and Israel—from the top floors of the European Parliament or the United States State Department. Jeremiah (17: 9) probably had in mind our Jewish-Israeli anti-Semites when he wrote: "Most devious is the heart; It is perverse—who can fathom it?"

In the modern era, George Orwell's penetrating comment can be applied to our anti-Zionist academics and their insistence on preaching the necessary destruction of Israel as Jewish state, and on drawing analogies between Zionist Jews and the Nazis: "*One has to belong to the intelligentsia to believe things like that: No ordinary man could be such a fool.*"

For all that, the questions asked here regarding the origins and development of Jewish-Israeli anti-Zionists, remain unanswered. The histories of the people identified with anti-Zionism must be studied and understood before a picture can be drawn of how this dreadful phenomenon emerged.

# 5

# Indoctrination in Education: Anti-Zionist Textbooks in Israel's Secondary Schools

*"The Jewish dovish Bolshevism is much worse than classical Bolshevism because it is the Bolshevism of people who presume to be enlightened."*
—Ezra Dalumi

*"We are witness to a phenomenon that apparently is unique in history: Emotional and moral identification of Israel's intelligentsia with an enemy obviously bent on destroying Israel."*
—Eyal Meged

Critics of world education and in Israel, in particular, assert that it is criminal to employ public education as an instrument for indoctrination. However, and regrettably, the Palestinian Authority and Muslim nations in general, as well as Israel's educational system, are daily users of indoctrination against Zionism, Judaism, and Israel. From that point of view, the Muslims, the anti-Zionist, and the anti-Semitic Jewish educators share common ground. First we discuss the Arab-Muslim views on the subject of Jews, Judaism and Israel as it is expressed in school textbooks. Following that will be a discussion of Israel's textbooks that have been heavily influenced by Israel's anti-Zionist academics.

## Jewish Anti-Semitic Perceptions

Classic Christian European anti-Semitism made its way into the Arab world at the end of the nineteenth century and was amplified by the Arab-Zionist conflict. It increased its spread during the 1930s after the Nazi rise to power in Germany, and particularly after the establishment of the State of Israel in 1948. It includes elements of classic European anti-Semitism combined with Islamic motifs, and has become more prominent in the past three decades, following the escalation of radical Islam. It is directed against Israel as a Jewish-Zionist state and as an enemy of the Arab-Muslim world. Verses from the Qur'an and the Islamic traditions are spread to delegitimize Zionism and the State of Israel and to dehumanize the Jewish people.

Arab-Muslim anti-Semitism has a broad field. It is not only popular among the lower classes nor is it the exclusive province of intellectuals, opposition groups, or radical Islamic movements. Anti-Semitism is marketed in a variety of ways (books, the Internet, television) and helps fan the flames of hatred for Jews and Israel among Muslim communities far beyond the Middle East. There is a link between anti-Semitism, anti-Americanism and anti-Western sentiment in general. Al-Qaeda, the global jihad and various radical Islamic groups claim that the struggle between Islam on the one hand and Judaism and Christian Crusaderism on the other is an integral part of the ancient, multidimensional struggle between Islam and the "infidel" West.

The following statements represent Islam's position:

Sheikh Dr. Yusuf al-Qaradawi (Bukay, 2007, pp. 294-302) is a highly recognized religious authority in Sunni Islam today, with millions of followers. He is known for his fatawat edicts regarding the use of violence and terror against civilians.[1] This is the reason why his declarations and rulings are so important, with his tapes and videos available for the Muslim communities all over the world. According to al-Qaradawi, all martyrdom operations (`Amaliyat Istishhadiyah`) are allowed even when casualties are civilians:

> Israeli society is militaristic in nature. Both men and women serve in the army and can be drafted at any moment. If a child or an elderly person is killed in such an operation, he is not killed on purpose, but by mistake, and as a result of military necessity (darurah). Necessity justifies the forbidden.[2]

On the one hand, Qaradawi has declared that "Islam, the religion of tolerance, holds the human soul in high esteem, and considers the attack against innocent human beings a grave sin," (*Surat al-Ma'idah*, 5 verse 32) at the same time, he systematically denies that Palestinian homicide bombings constitute terrorism, and insisted that all the deeds of the Palestinians against Israel are legitimate.[3] "Anyone killed while fighting the American forces and annihilating Israel would die as a *mujahid*."[4]

He strongly supports Palestinian homicide bombings, including against civilians, and claims they are a legitimate form of resistance: "I consider this type of martyrdom operation as an evidence of Allah's justice. Through his infinite wisdom he has given the weak a weapon the strong do not have and that is their ability to turn their bodies into bombs as Palestinians do."[5]

Qaradawi also heralds the imminent conquest of Rome by Islam, in accordance with the prophecy of Muhammad: "Islam will return to Europe as a conqueror and victor, after being expelled from it twice – once from the South, from Andalusia, and a second time from the East, when it knocked several times on the doors of Vienna. Islam will return to Europe. Islam will return to Europe, this time by *Da'wah* and not Jihad, and the Europeans will convert to Islam. Then they will disseminate Islam in the world."[6]

On al-Jazeerah TV, April 25, 2004, al-Qaradawi explained his support of homicide operations on his weekly religious sermon:

> The martyrdom operations in Palestine are sacred. By these operations Allah has compensated the Palestinians for their lack of strength. This is a divine justice.[7]

We are a nation of jihad and martyrdom. We stand alongside our brothers in Hamas and al-Jihad al-Islami al-Filistini to destroy Israel.[8]

> The Jews of today bear responsibility for their forefathers' crime of crucifying Jesus. Even though the Muslims believe that Jesus was not crucified, a crime was committed, and the people who paved the way for this crime are the Jews.[9]

Our war with the Jews is over land. We are fighting them in the name of Islam, because Islam commands us to fight whoever plunders our land. All the schools of Islamic jurisprudence agree that any invader who occupies even an inch of land of the Muslims must face resistance and be destroyed. That is what we are fighting the Jews for. We are fighting in the name of religion, which makes this Jihad an individual duty, in which the entire Islamic nation takes part, and whoever is killed in Jihad is a martyr. This is why I ruled that martyrdom operations are permitted.[10]

Muhsin Abu 'Ita, the Palestinian cleric declared:

> It is strange to find an entire chapter in the Qur'an bearing the name *Bani Isra'il.* It is even more peculiar that this chapter does not talk about the Jews of the Qaynuqa, Nazir, or Qurayza tribes. It talks about the Jews of our times, of this century, using the language of annihilation. In this chapter, the Jews were sentenced to annihilation, before even a single Jew existed on the face of the earth. This Qur'anic chapter talked about the collapse of the so-called state of Israel, before this state was even established. From here stems the importance and oddity of this chapter. The blessing of Palestine is dependent upon the annihilation of the pit of global corruption in it. When the head of the serpent of corruption is cut off here in Palestine, and its octopus tentacles are severed throughout the world, the real blessing will come. The annihilation of the Jews here in Palestine is one of the most splendid blessings for Palestine. This will be followed by a greater blessing with the establishment of a Caliphate that will rule the world.[11]

**Wail al-Zarrad**, a *Palestinian cleric*:

As Muslims, our blood vengeance against the Jews will only subside with their annihilation, because they tried to kill our Prophet several times. What is the best solution
for these people who have perpetrated every possible thing against us? The Jews are
nothing but human scum, who came as scattered gangs to occupy our land. By Allah,
if each and every Arab spat on them, they would drown in Arab spit.[12]

## Sheikh Muhammad Ibrahim al-Madhi, PA TV, June 6, 2001:

We welcome, as we did in the past, any Jew who wants to live in this land as a
*Dhimmi*, just as the Jews have lived in our countries, but the rule in this land and in
all the Muslim countries must be the rule of Allah alone.

## 'Abd al-Fattah al-Khalidi, "Qur'anic Truths regarding the Palestinian Issue"

In each Jew there is a complex of ethical depravities and behavioral corruptions so
astonishing that it is doubtful that this can be found in other people. These traits have
taken permanent root in their character. These depravities, corruptions, deficiencies,
sicknesses, have their special taint in the Jews' astoundingly complex personality....
This is the result of determined inherited "genes" carried by every Jew everywhere
and throughout all of history...

## Sayyid Qutb, "Our Struggle with the Jews"

Behind the doctrine of atheistic materialism was a Jew; behind the doctrine of animal-
istic sexuality was a Jew; and behind the destruction of the family and the shattering
of sacred relationships in society ... was a Jew. The war which the Jews launched
against Islam was longer, more extensive, and of greater ferocity than the war which
the polytheists and idol worshipers perpetrated, then and now. As for the modern
period, the intensity of the struggle between the Hindu idol worshipers and Islam is
vividly apparent, but it does not equal the viciousness of world Zionism.

## Sheik Ali Al-Faqir, a Palestinian, former Jordanian minister of religious endowment:[13]

We declare that Palestine, from the River to the Sea, is an Islamic land, and that
Spain—Andalusia—is also the land of Islam. All Islamic lands of Dar al-Islam from
China to Andalusia that were occupied by the enemies will once again become Islamic.
We proclaim that we will conquer Rome, like Constantinople was conquered once.
We will rule the world, as has been said by the Prophet Muhammad. Its beginnings
were in Palestine, in Iraq, in Afghanistan, and in Chechnya. What has begun will be
completed. It will not stop. The Zionist entity is beginning to decline, and it will wane
and come to its end. America has begun to realize that their end is near. The EU will
come to an end, and only the rising force of Islam will prevail.

## Yunis Al-Astal, Hamas member of Parliament MP and a cleric:[14]

Allah has chosen the Palestinians for Himself and for His religion, so that they will
serve as the engine pulling this nation forward. Soon, Rome will be conquered, just
like Constantinople, as was prophesized by our Prophet Muhammad. Today, Rome is
the capital of the Crusader, which has declared its hostility to Islam, and has planted
the brothers of apes and pigs in Palestine in order to prevent the reawakening of Islam.

Rome will be an advanced post for the Islamic conquests, which will spread through Europe in its entirety, and then will turn to the Americas. I believe that our children will inherit our Jihad and our sacrifices, and, Allah willing, the commanders of the [Islamic] conquest will come from the Palestinians.

Sheikh Muhammad Bin `Abd al-Rahman al-`Arifi, imam of the mosque of the King Fahd Defense Academy, declared:

We will control the land of the Vatican; we will control Rome and introduce Islam in it. Yes, the Christians will yet pay us the *jizyah* in humiliation, or they will convert to Islam.[15]

Islam establishes religious tolerance and honors man as such. Allah's justice is for all his creations. We did not invent the hostility towards the Jews. We are fighting the Jews because they seized the land, expelled its people, and plundered it. There can be no dialogue between us and the evil-doers People of the Book, who commit crimes and barbaric slaughter that are taking place every day.[16]

The liberation of Jerusalem will be achieved by realizing the divine path in the souls of the Muslims, to lead the battle against the brothers of apes and pigs. By Allah, Jerusalem will be restored only through Jihad. The foundations of the monstrous entity will be shaken only by the love of martyrdom for the sake of Allah.[17]

Sheikh Muhammad Tannoun, Chief Mufti:

In 1948, Palestine was lost, its inhabitants were dispersed and killed by the most despicable creatures on the face of the earth—the offspring of apes and pigs.[18]

Palestinian Legislative Council Speaker, Ahmad Bahr:

Jerusalem, which was first conquered by `Umar and then liberated by Saladin, was lost by the brothers of apes and pigs, who had the audacity to defile and occupy it. By Allah, Jerusalem will be restored only through Jihad. The foundations of the monstrous entity will be shaken only by the love of martyrdom for the sake of Allah.[19]

## Holocaust Denial

Holocaust denial, accusing Israel of carrying out a holocaust against the Palestinians, and drawing a parallel between Israel and Zionism on the one hand and Nazi German on the other are central themes in contemporary Arab-Muslim anti-Semitism. The motifs used in anti-Semitic propaganda are taken from neo-Nazi literature, media and rhetoric. Accusing Israel of carrying out a holocaust against the Palestinian people is fostered by the Palestinian and Arab media.

Amin Dabur, head of the Palestinian "Center for Strategic Research" explained that

The Holocaust—the whole thing was a joke. The Jewish leaders planned the Holocaust to kill disabled and handicapped Jews by sending them to death camps so they would not be a burden on the future state of Israel. This is Hamas TV's sinister twist on Holocaust denial. The Holocaust served to make "the Jews seem persecuted" so they could "benefit from international sympathy.[20]

The Palestinian-Jordanian author, Ibrahim 'Alloush:

> The Holocaust is a lie. The Holocaust is exploited to justify the Zionist policies and to justify the enemy state's right to exist. There is evidence and scientific research that proves the Holocaust is a lie. I support the legitimate resistance, and primarily martyrdom operations.[21]

The Holocaust denial in the Arab-Palestinian Ideology and Strategy is not a manifestation of irrational hatred, but planned, intentional, and premeditated and cold-blooded instrument. It has major goals that lead to the same conclusion.

First, the denial of Israel's legitimacy, its creation and continued existence: This is expressed clearly in the notion that no Holocaust occurred and all is a myth created by the Zionists. Hence, there is no justification for the establishment of Israel in the Arab land of Palestine. The second goal is the elimination of the Zionist entity, to "wipe Israel off the map." To achieve the goal of wiping out the Jewish People and destroy Israel it is necessary to eradicate the memory of the Holocaust and to label it as a myth. That makes it possible to demonize Israel and the Jews. The Arabs and Palestinians are taking the same path taken earlier by Hitler, who first engaged in a campaign to demonize the Jews before actually murdering them. The Arabs are conducting a virulent, anti-Semitic campaign of demonization before they attempt to annihilate the Jews.[22]

As one means to achieve this end, the Arabs employ state-controlled television and other mass communication media to disseminate the blood libel that depicts Jews as using the blood of non-Jewish children to bake Passover matzos, and kidnapping non-Jewish children to steal their body parts. Jews are described as being pigs and apes. They are accused of persecuting the Prophets, murdering Muhammad, and tormenting Jesus on the Cross. The message of achieving the goal of demonization of Jews and Israel is vital for their elimination. Holocaust denial is vital, in order to wipe out the image of the Jews as victims and as worthy of a State. Even if the Holocaust is not a myth, it cannot justify Israel's existence. If Europe has committed injustices against the Jews, why must the Muslims and the Palestinians pay the price for it? If Europe committed a crime, it is only appropriate to place a piece of Europe's land at their disposal.

The other side is denying Palestine as the Jewish homeland. The State of Israel is an absolute evil, a tool in the hands of the West to dominate the Muslims. Israel perpetrates ethnic cleansing of the poor Palestinian People. Such a regime must be eliminated from the pages of history. Zionism is a Western-colonialist ideology with secular ideas and fascist methods. It was founded by the English, with the help and direct guidance of America and Europe. When the Zionist regime will be wiped out, humanity will be liberated.

All of these allegations are part of a central anti-Semitic motif in the Qur'an. The centrality of the Jews' permanent "abasement and humiliation," and of being laden with Allah's anger, is a basic motif in Muslim exegetic literature. That motif is intended to justify and legitimize the annihilation of the Jews: "Thou wilt surely find the most hostile of men to the believers are the Jews" (5:82).

## Israeli War Crimes: Nazism

In a July 6, 2006 article in *al-Hayah*, columnist and former editor Jihad al-Khazin compares Israel to Nazi Germany.

> The Israeli offensive against the Palestinians is similar to the Nazi offensive against the Warsaw Ghetto. The whole Gaza Strip is a Nazi-like concentration camp. The Israelis' crimes are similar to the Nazis', no matter how the numbers may differ. The government of Fuhrer Olmert will not send the people of Gaza to gas camps only because oil is expensive. Olmert's government might decide to force the Palestinians to wear something like a yellow Star of David, with the word 'Jew' written in the middle. Hence, I suggest a crescent with a green background, and the word 'Arab' or 'Muslim' written in the middle.[23]

In another article, Jihad al-Khazin, asserts that Israeli political and military leaders are actually grandsons of Nazi killers who assumed Jewish identities and fled to Israel.

> Ehud Olmert's government perpetrates Nazi practices against the Palestinians and the Lebanese. He is a young Fuehrer. The Nazi political and military leaders realized in 1944 that defeat was imminent. They assumed the identity of Jews and fled to Palestine as Jews who had survived the Holocaust. I cannot find any other logical reason for Israel's Nazi-like practices. The U.S. Congress and government support Israel to the point of becoming an accomplice in its war crimes."[24]

In an article in *al-Ahram*, Egyptian Mufti Sheikh Dr. `Ali Gum'ah expressed his support of the resistance in Lebanon and stated that

> the lies of the "Hebrew entity" expose the true and hideous face of the blood-sucking murderers... who prepare [Passover] matzos from human blood. All the Lebanese victims of the Israeli crimes were civilians, while those killed on the enemy's side were all soldiers. That is reality that speaks for itself.[25]

Since Israel is portrayed as a state which has no historical right to exist; created by immoral actions; that is perpetrating ethnic cleansing and its existence is a pure proof being an apartheid state, The PA TV rebroadcast hateful series showing Israelis as child murderers.[26]

One well-known anti-Semitic weapon used on a daily basis in the Arab and Muslim war-propaganda against Israel is cartoons. It is well documented and explained, inter alia, in Arieh Stav's publication;[27] in MEMRI;[28] and in the Intelligence and Terrorism Information Center.[29] No one can underestimate the impact of this propaganda tool. It is one of the few means in the Arab-Islamic political culture proven to gain support from the masses.

Walid Al-Rashudi, a Saudi Scholar, announced:

> One of the important things that we must tell people is that what is going on in Palestine today is a real holocaust. A holocaust is not the burning of 50-60 Jews in Germany or Switzerland. Nevertheless, the Jews continue to call it the Holocaust. There was indeed a holocaust, but how many died? 50-60 people? Afterwards, they used it to blackmail those two countries. So what are we supposed to say in the face of the Gaza holocaust? By Allah, we will not be satisfied even if all the Jews are killed.[30]

### The Protocols of the Elders of Zion and other *Isra'iliat*

*The Protocols of the Elders of Zion,* a fictitious book distributed worldwide for over a century, is used as an important means of spreading anti-Semitic myths both in the Arab and Muslim world and in Western countries. Many copies of *The Protocols* were published and distributed. TV Programs, films, and "research documents" claim that the State of Israel was founded on *The Protocols of the Elders of Zion,* which exposes the Jewish plot to take over the world. They depict Jews as murderers, bloodthirsty demons, and criminals. They used that book to back up false claims that the Jews symbolize the forces of evil and strive to rule the world. Zionist Jews would not settle for domination of the region between the rivers of Euphrates and Nile, but they strove to take over the entire world, and establish a global Jewish government, as discussed in the first Zionist congress in Basel, Switzerland, in 1897. Moreover, the Balfour Declaration was made after British politicians associated with the Zionists embraced the agenda of *The Protocols of the Elders of Zion.*

The Hamas spokesman, Dr. Ismail Radwan cites from the Quran: Surat al-Isra (17) verse 7. This verse was previously cited by Yasser Arafat and Hezbollah leader Hassan Nasrallah as a reference for the claim that Israel must be wiped off the map. Then he cites from the *Hadith*:

> The hour of resurrection will not take place until the Muslims fight the Jews and the Muslims kill them, and the rock and the tree will say: "Oh, Muslim, servant of Allah, there is a Jew behind me, kill him!' We must remind our Arab and Muslim nation, its leaders and people, its scholars and students, remind them that Palestine and the al-Aqsa mosque will not be liberated through summits nor by international

resolutions, but through the rifle. Since this occupation knows no language but the language of force.[31]

The Egyptian researcher, Muhammad Al-Buheiri, discussed the Protocols of the Elders of Zion and blood libel. His position was that the infamous document and the claim that Jews use non-Jewish children's blood for baking matzot on Passover was an influential and successful strategy to de-legitimize and de-humanize Israel. He claims that even an Israeli professor from Bar-Ilan University, Ariel Toaff proved scientifically that there was indeed a group of extremist Jews, who used to slaughter Christian children to collect their blood in order to make the Passover matza. It had to be a child who had not reached puberty. These are religious rituals that some sources in Jewish Halachah say that preparing a single matza on Passover this way is sufficient for all the Jews.

The Jews of the Banu Nadhir and Banu Qurayzah tribes are not the same Jews who live in Israel today. Some commentators, historians, and professors say that the Jews from the time of Muhammad are not the same Jews who live in Israel today. No Israeli researcher can claim that his lineage goes back to the ancient Jews. They are all from Romanian, Polish, Russian, or English families. Not a single one ... the Jews in Israel are not the accursed Jews, they are not the Jews mentioned in the Koran.[32]

Lies and libels have been used for many years by the Palestinian Authority to present Israel as a dangerous existential threat to the Arab and Muslim world. One of the repeating libels is that Israel is planning to conquer all Arab lands, "from the Euphrates until the Nile." The following are some of these PA fabrications:

The term is written above the gates of the Knesset and on Israeli money. The two blue stripes on the Israeli flag represent the Nile and the Euphrates and the Star of David represents the state of Israel. Israeli children in school are taught through repetition of the expression: "Land of Israel -from the Nile to the Euphrates."[33]

Children on Hamas TV call to "liberate" al-Aqsa mosque by force of Jihad and to "wipe out" the Zionists to the last one:

"al-Aqsa Mosque is crying out: "Where is the people of the frontline, the Palestinian people?" The al-Aqsa Mosque has fallen into malicious hands of those who know nothing but injustice. How can we rescue it from the shackles of the Zionist occupation? It will be returned by means of force— because the Zionist entity, your enemy, the enemy of Allah, the enemy of Islam, knows nothing but injustice. To al-Aqsa, to al-Aqsa—we shall unite our ranks. We will wipe out the Zionists, and will not leave a single one of them.[34]

While the Palestinian Authority announces in English its demand for a two-state solution, to its own people in Arabic it continues to define all of Israel as "Palestine," and to promise Israel's destruction. Video clips and programs broadcast numerous times daily on TV, passionately promises that every Israeli city, shown on the maps or in picture, will be "liberated" because its "identity is Arab" and "Palestinian." That motto is reiterated many times a day with slogans such as:

> We will liberate the Land ... Palestine is Arab in history and identity ... Palestine belongs solely to the brave and courageous Palestinian people ... From Jerusalem and Acre, from Haifa and Jericho, from Gaza and Ramallah, From Bethlehem and Jaffa and Be'er Sheva and Ramle, And from Nablus to the Galilee, and from Tiberias to Hebron.

Muhammad Nimr al-Zaghmout, head of the Islamic Palestinian Council in Lebanon:

> The only way to liberate Palestine is by Jihad. Our No. 1 enemy is Satan, embodied by the Protocols of the Elders of Zion; then comes the greatest Taghout idol ... Muhammad promised us that the Jews will gather in Palestine, and Muslims will fight them, and totally kill them. This is the core of our belief.[35]

The official Palestinian Authority newspaper *al-Hayat al-Jadidah* published a vicious anti-Semitic article, from Muhammad Khalifah, that includes many of the classic anti-Semitic libels:

> Jews start wars, including the war in Iraq, to promote Jews' power and control; Jews are the dominant force in United States policy; Jews control international finance; Jews control international media.[36]

### The Palestinian Anti-Semitic Schoolbooks

Anyone who hopes for peace should be horrified by the content of the Palestinian schoolbooks. In many respects, these books, written by Fatah-appointed Palestinian educators contain more egregious anti-Semitism than such books produced by the Nazis. They not only deny Israel's right to exist, but anticipate its destruction and define the conflict with Israel as religious, and homicide bombers as sanctified heroes. By that, there is absolutely no difference between Fatah and Hamas. What all the Palestinian children learn in school is religious and ideological. The Palestinian conflict with Israel is an eternal fight with a special Islamic destiny until its elimination.

There will be no peace but destruction. Israel's right to exist is totally denied. Palestine will be liberated by its men, its women, its young and its elderly" (*Arabic Language and the Science of Language*, grade 12,

p. 44). Palestine's war ended with a catastrophe that is unprecedented in history, when the Zionist gangs stole Palestine and expelled its people, and established the State of Israel" (*Arabic Language, Analysis, Literature and Criticism*, grade 12, pp. 104, 122). The place of Israel, all its territory, is marked as "Palestine" on all the maps, in the schools and in official institutions. "Palestine" is defined as a Dawlah, a "state." Because Israel has no right to exist, and must be fought and destroyed for Islam, violence and terror are justified and glorified as Muqawama, resistance. Israel is presented as an illegitimate enemy to be hated, fought and destroyed (*Arabic Language, Analysis, Literature and Commentary*, grade 12, p. 105).

The PA schoolbooks teach World War II without any reference to the Holocaust. There are extensive details about the history of the war, lessons about the Nazi "race theory" and even mention of "an international court to bring to trial the senior Nazi leaders as war criminals" (*The History of the Arabs and the World in the 20th Century*, grade 12, p. 46). However, the books fail to mention why the Nazis were on trial, or that their "race theory" involved elimination of Jews.[37]

The PA textbooks adopt or condone anti-Israeli stereotypes, they do not operate in a void. They conform, in fact, too much of the anti-Jewish and anti-Israeli stereotyping that has prevailed in the Arab world. When Egyptians accuse Israeli expert farmers who help develop Egyptian agriculture, of poisoning Arab land and destroying the local farming industry, no one should be surprised that the Palestinian representative in the Human Rights Commission in Geneva accuses, with impunity, Israelis of injecting the AIDS virus into hundreds of Palestinian children. When Robert Garaudy, the notorious French anti-Semite and Muslim convert who denies the Holocaust in his "scholarly research," is given a hero's welcome in the Arab world, it is no coincidence that denial of the Holocaust among Arabs/Muslims becomes a universal consensus. They overlook and deny the antiquity of Jewish presence in Israel and even attribute Israel's peace measures to dark schemes reminiscent of The Protocols of the Elders of Zion, calculated to take over the Arab world culturally and economically in the "New Middle East."

These organized and institutionalized attitudes towards Jews and Israel cannot but encourage Palestinian children to express those feelings and attitudes in public, and to restore the anti-Semite stereotypes of the Jews and Israel as the reality. While Palestinian children absorb at home and from their environment basically anti-Israeli and anti-Jewish stereotypes, and bring them as their luggage of knowledge and conviction, it is reinforced by the educational system as the total truth. The most worrying conclusions that arise from the reviewed textbooks are clear: this political indoctrination program is instilled and pushed in the growing children of today and the adults of tomorrow into ominous grounds of hostile action.

### Israel Textbooks

Only a few years after the establishment of Israel, the writer Yizhar Smilansky, author of the monumental novel *The Days of Ziklag*, claimed that teaching values in schools is an act of indoctrination. He was not the only one who entered the ranks of those who opposed Jewish Zionist education in the State of Israel. It seems that exerting influence on the education of the young is desired by almost every group with a social, political or religious ideology in every society. That includes people who work in our Ministry of Education who are expected to act in a non-political way because they serve the majority of the public except for those who attend private schools. The fact is that all education, elementary and secondary, public and private, and even university level education, is based on values of different kinds; professional-instructional, personal, national, and so forth. No educational effort could possibly be free of values. Hence, value-free education is a contradiction in terms, despite the fact that famous writers supported that position. Whoever claims to seek a value-free education—for young or old has a hidden agenda. Each nation must decide on the degree to which a person must be educated in the history and culture of his own People and country.

Sadly enough, as the Muslims increased the indoctrination of their schoolchildren against Jews and Israel, Israel systematically reduced the extent and quality of studies designed to foster Jewish-Zionist views and values. Their important place in our national curricula has been supplanted by what leftist like to call universal values (not including the Ten Commandments). Is it necessary to point out that Jewish education in Israel did not preach hatred of Arabs or of Israel at any time whatsoever, not in the past or in the present. The entire story of Muslim hatred toward Jews, Judaism and Israel presented above in this document is virtually unknown to Israel's schoolchildren and to the vast majority of Jewish adults in Israel.

We wish to emphasize that indoctrination in Education is not necessarily found in what a curriculum teaches to students. It is found, perhaps first and foremost, in what is not taught. Indoctrination can be, and is, a sin of omission not only of commission. Our ancient sages distinguished clearly between commandments that were to be performed and those acts from which we must desist. To educate our young in the ways of their fathers, in their laws and customs, in their history and identity, is a positive commandment, something we must perform (*v'Shinantem l'Vanecha*). If we do not do that we are in breach of the covenant with our conscience, with our God, with our People.

When we ask students about what they learned in school, most likely they will be unaware that when they tell what they studied they will also be telling you about what they did not learn or don't remember. That conclusion must be deduced by the listener. Ben-Gurion was a devoted student of *Tanach*, and he certainly was adamant about *Tanach* being taught in the schools. But Ben-Gurion omitted from his view the long history of rabbinic literature, including the *Mishnah* and the *Midrashim*, not only the *Gemarrah*, as well as a large part of what Jews wrote, in Hebrew as well as in other languages, in various countries.

Those Jews who attended school in Israel during the early years of the State did not learn much about rabbinic literature except for a few legends (*Aggadot*), and that because Bialik and Ravnitsky could see into the future. Our public school students' study of history jumped from the destruction of the First Temple by the Babylonians in 586 BCE to the time of Moses Mendelssohn, to the Enlightenment and the Emancipation in Europe. On the way they heard a little about the great Hebrew poets (like Yehudah Halevi and Shlomo ibn-Gabirol—well known streets in Tel Aviv) who lived in Spain or the Provence from the tenth to the fifteenth century. It was Bialik again who contributed so much to the study of Hebrew literature in the late Middle Ages by writing a six-volume commentary on the complete poetry of Shlomo ibn-Gabirol.

Of course our students also learned a little about the great Eviction of the Jews from Spain in 1492. That's about it. Incidentally, Bialik also began a project that he did not have an opportunity to work on very much, and that was the publication of the Mishnah with vowels so it could be read more easily by the Jews without a traditional Jewish education. That project, including a new commentary and complete vocalization, was completed in the 1950s by Chanoch Albeck and Chanoch Yalon. There was also a great project, actually begun at the end of the nineteenth century and continued here in Israel, to collect the great works of Hebrew literature of the Middle Ages (by the Chevrat M'kitzei Nirdamin) and to translate modern works of Jewish scholarship into Hebrew, such as the translations by Yisrael Eldad of books by Leopold Lippmann Zunz on the History of Poetry in the Synagogue and others.

Yuli Tamir one of the founders of the Peace Now movement, and her extreme leftists predecessor Shulamit Aloni who was also minister of education for a short while, invested considerable energy in limiting and devaluating the Jewish-Zionist components of Israel's education and culture. Without exaggeration Shulamit Aloni, to my mind, can be called a virulent anti-Semite when it comes to anything related to Jewish historical-religious tradition. Much effort will have to be expended on the part of Jews devoted to the Zionist vision in this country, and by Jews everywhere, to limit the negative influence that Tamir, Aloni and their cohorts exerted on Israel's education. By the term cohorts I refer to academics such as Yisrael Bartal, Moshe Zimmerman, Ayal Naveh, Dani Yakobi, Yosef Ofek, Hanna Eden, Uri Ram and others of their persuasion. These academics, along with the civil servants of the Ministry of Education, have truncated, curtailed, diminished and actively obstructed the teaching of Jewish and Zionist history and literature from being taught in Israel's schools, until, over the past two decades, those subjects became a shadow of their former selves. Amnon Rubenstein would not be able to recognize the secondary school curricula of today compared to when he was Minister of Education.

We must also realize that what is threatened by the juggernaut of educational decimation implemented by the Left eager to de-Judaize Israel, is precisely the entire progress of the re-Judaization of Jewry, gathered here from the four corners of the earth and still coming, that began in the period of the Mandate. The far-left radical socialists thought, once upon the time, that Hebrew labor in Palestine would achieve all the goals of Zionism. But, despite his years of preoccupation with his struggle against Herzl, Ahad Ha-Am was more than right when he called for a reawakening of the Jewish spirit, of Jewish culture and history, alongside the redemption of the land. Many Jews came here and saw the land. They saw the opportunity to work the land. They created a new religion of labor, not altogether different from what was preached by A. D. Gordon. But unlike Gordon, they could not see the history of all the generations that wanted to come and couldn't, ("My heart is in the East, but I am at the ends of the West" wrote Yehuda Ha-levi in twelfth-century Spain) or who did come back to their homeland starting with Abraham, Joshua, Zerubavel and so on up to our day, with Herzl, Ahad Ha-Am, Bialik, Jabotinsky, Lamdan, Hazaz, Agnon, Shlonski, Uri Zvi Greenberg, to mention only a few.

It is enlightening, and sad, to present just a few short quotations from our academics' words of wisdom when they directed the work of the

Ministry's curriculum committee. I am indebted for these quotations to the research published by Yoram Hazoni (2001; see also Hazoni, Polisar and Oren, 2000).

Disengagement from Zionist historiography is an intellectual event of decisive importance in Israel's academia.… It has a critical element of 'revisionism' … historical research is freeing itself from the Zionist story that was designed by the 'founding fathers' of Zionist historiography, a quiet revolution in whose wake the components of the picture we had of the past are being changed systematically and fundamentally (Bar-Tal, 1996).

The man referred to as the "founding father" of Israel's Zionist education is Ben-Tsion Dinur. It is not unreasonable to say that in schools today the classical Zionist story is "a narrative … that has departed from the academic world" (Bartal, 1994).

The same person who made the statement I just quoted, Yisrael Bar-Tal, chairman of the committee asked to prepare the curriculum in history for Israel's secondary schools, also said at the time:

> There is no longer any agreed upon historical truth. The old history books years ago presented students with the Zionist narrative as if it were an undisputed historical fact. [That approach] is no longer appropriate for the historical-political discussion that takes place now, after the myths have been demolished. It is no longer possible to disregard the fact that Israel is now a multicultural society (Bar-Tal, 1998).

Nor should we disregard the contribution to a Zionist vacuum in Israel's education made by the Israeli historian Moshe Zimmerman. In 1995 he was of the opinion that there were no longer any "consumers" of Zionist history. Consequently, the entire collection of assumptions that provided the foundation for the old Zionist narrative was no longer valid. To quote:

> If all the ground under the feet of the Zionism has been removed, as well as from under the entire orthodox Zionist interpretation of Jewish history, then all of Jewish history requires a new interpretation.

Indeed, Zimmerman suggested a new universal view of Jewish history without the problematic feature of any unique Jewish nationality. Each Jewish community stands in its own right, and has no necessary connection with any general identity that encompasses all of them, as was preached by traditional Jewish historiography (Zimmerman, 1996). Instead, we should understand how a series of great civilizations, such as Greece, Rome, Germany and the United States, affected the Jews who lived in the relevant countries. By so doing, we will be equipped to comprehend how the Jewish historical experience became fixated at the level of Israeli national sovereignty and its decidedly ethnocentric character as a Jewish State. Indeed, that very idea inheres in the history book written by Dani Yakobi (1999) who treats the great events of the collapse of the totalitarian regimes and the rise of the democracies, the emergence of significant innovations in technology that effectively blurs the importance of national borders that separate nations from one another.

What Yakobi minimizes or disregards completely is the Jewish perspective. Apart from the fact that Israel and the Palestinians in particular, and the Arabs in general, began a process of peace negotiations, not a single event is considered to be of sufficient importance to warrant mention in Yakobi's history book published by Israel's Ministry of Education for the edification of our youth. The Holocaust, the establishment of the State of Israel, the unification of Jerusalem, and so forth, are totally absent from Yakobi's book. It seems that its author and the Ministry of Education were located in Iraq or in Iran, or perhaps in Malaysia or Indonesia. Wherever they were, they stayed there in spirit but, unfortunately, not in body. It is to be noted that not the entire book is as extreme as the examples presented here, although throughout that work the principle of universalism prevails.

Noteworthy too is the fact that in the 1980s, authors of history books for the ninth grade devoted fully 67 percent of the material to Zionism, the Holocaust and to the State of Israel, whereas in the new book those topics occupy less than 30 percent of the material. The difference (i.e. between the 67 percent in the old book versus 30 percent or less in the new book) is made up by discussing "the process of de-colonization and the establishment of Algeria," "new trends in the arts," "the welfare state and the European community" and "the scientific revolution." Chaim Weitzman, David Ben-Gurion, Menachem Begin are given short shrift, and most of their careers of leadership are never mentioned. Nor do their pictures appear in the book, while photos of Franklin Roosevelt, Winston Churchill, Adolf Hitler, Gamal Nasser, Sigmund Freud, Salvador Dali, and the Beatles do appear. But not all of Israel's history is ignored.

The "peace process" receives much more attention from the Ministry of Education. In connection with that subject, despite the fact that Ben-Gurion is not mentioned, there are eight pictures of Menachem Begin, Yitzchak Rabin, and Shimon Peres meeting with Arab representatives and shaking their hands. The ins and outs of the peace process since 1990 are described in 15 out of a total of 38 pages of the book. That is the total number of pages in the new history textbooks that deal with Israel after 1948. An entire page is devoted to the text of the unofficial "draft of agreement" formulated in 1995 by Yossi Beilin and the representative of the PLO Mahmoud Abbas known as Abu Mazen, who currently holds the title of president of the Palestinian Authority (but not for long). From the history book one could erroneously conclude that Chaim Weitzman, David Ben-Gurion, Golda Meir, Moshe Dayan, Shimon Peres (who, as we know, is the only one of that group who is still alive and still plotting his future moves) Yitzchak Rabin, Ezer Weitzman, and Menachem Begin, who devoted most of their lives to the existence of a Jewish State, are of little or no interest to Israel's high school students. Moreover, our political leaders of the past are important only when they affix their signature to a peace agreement with the Arabs. Only then does universal history direct sustained attention to their behavior. Bartal, in his 1998 text went even further and he had previously:

> The success of Zionism in Israel was a disaster for the local Arab population. One must learn—and show that national movements by their very nature redeem the people of one group and destroy hose of another (Bartal, 1998, p. 60).

Viewing these pronouncements by the anti-Zionist historians in a broad context, one could observe that their main attack on Jewish and Zionist history and education is through their devaluation of Jewish national existence. Jewish national life, in their view, is replaced by a so-called cosmopolitan-universalist perspective: Jews, Jewish history, Zionism and the State of Israel, are to be viewed as occupying an inconsequential sideshow whose actors are either puppets or hired hands on the stage of history. Not only has the Arab League portrayed the map of the Middle East without Israel on it. Our Jewish-born historians in Israel have done much the same.

A. B. Yehoshua made his entrance into modern Hebrew literature with his story ("Mul Yaarot") about the Karen Kayemet forest which the forest ranger discovered was built on the ruins of an Arab village. The ranger's conscience led him to burn down the forest. In addition to our historical-cultural heritage, there are, of course, strictly professional aspects of public education which, alas, have also seen a long period of neglect in favor of negative indoctrination. For the Jews, the last few years have been a Naqba: The committee charged with the preparation of curricula for secondary education in subjects such as history, citizenship and their related disciplines, has been staffed by post-Zionist professors from Israel's universities They are intent on tearing down the remnants of Jewish historical-political-cultural reconstruction in Israel. "Out. out damned spot," says Lady Macbeth. Our historians are echoing that Shakespearean line in multiple ways and employing it as a simile for Israel.

The Zionist literary critic, Yosef Oren, has spelled out the views of the post- and anti-Zionist authors of Israeli literature, and I must refer you to his publications (Oren, 2003). In reaction, many Jews in Israel are poised to apply Lady Macbeth's outcry to a host of spots presently disfiguring our political landscape. The spots related to in this short discussion cover our academic and educational landscape. Not only a huge quantity of spot remover is needed to clean up our educational efforts, but a relatively large group of dedicated educators and politicians is absolutely required. Their task must be performed systematically while avoiding the impulse to exceed sound Jewish-Zionist and professional judgment. To do so would be to fall into the pattern set by our anti-Zionist predecessors.

A new era of Jewish education in Israel will be ushered in when the long awaited change in government occurs that, we hope, will place a Jewish-Zionist agenda at the center of Israel's public educational system. Once again, each and every nation seeks to transmit its historical heritage to the next generation. That is not indoctrination. That is trying to guarantee our nation's survival over time, and that is the moral responsibility of every nation's educational efforts.

## Notes

1.    <http://www.wponline.org/vil/Books/Q_LP/index.htm>. <http://www.islam-online.net> (English); <http://www.qaradawi.net> (Arabic); <http://www.islamonline.com> (concerning fatawat).
2.    al-Ahram al-Arabi (Egypt), February 3, 2001. See also his interview on August 19, 2005, al-Arabiyah: MEMRI Special Dispatch Series, No. 961, August 19, 2005.
3.    <http://www.islam-online.net/English/News/2001-09/13/article25.html.<
4.    <http://dehai.org/archives/AW_news_archive/1125.html>.
5.    <http://news.bbc.co.uk/2/hi/uk_news/3874893.stm>.
6.    <http://www.islamonline.net/fatwa/arabic/FatwaDisplay.asp?hFatwaID=2042>; on his weekly religious program on Al-Jazeerah, he reiterated on January 24, 1999, <http://www.aljazeera.net/programs/shareea/articles/2001/7/7-6-2.htm>, and on November 30, 2000; <http://www.aljazeera.net/programs/shareea/articles/2000/11/11-30-3.htm>, MEMRI Special Dispatch Series, No. 447, <http://memri.org>, December 6, 2002.
7.    <http://memritv.org/archives.asp?ACT=S9&P1=45>. See also: MEMRI Special Dispatch Series, No. 971, <http://memri.org>, August 26, 2005. MEMRI Special Dispatch Series, No.1045, <http://memri.org>, December 9, 2005.
8.    MEMRI Special Dispatch Series, No. 1051, <http://memri.org>, December 18, 2005.
9.    Qatar TV, August 26, 2006, Clip # 1249: http://www.memritv.org/search.asp?ACT=S9&P1=1249
10.   Qatar TV, February 25, 2006. http://www.memritv.org/search.asp?ACT=S9&P1=1052 .

11.  In an interview, on al-Aqsa TV, July 13, 2008: MEMRI, October 28 2008.
12.  **Wail Al-Zarrad**, *al-Aqsa TV, February 28, 2008: MEMRI*, No. 1722 February 28, 2008. *http://www.memritv.org/clip/en/1722.htm*
13.  *al-Aqsa TV, May 2, 2008*. No. 1761, May 2, 2008: <http://www.memritv.org/clip/en/1761.htm>
14.  *al-Aqsa TV, April 11, 2008*. No. 1739 | April 11, 2008: http://www.memritv.org/clip/en/1739.htm
15.  <http://www.kalemat.org/sections.php?so=va&aid=93>.
16.  MEMRI Special Dispatch Series, No. 858, <http://memri.org>, February 4, 2005.
17.  al-Aqsa TV, August 21, 2007: MEMRI, No. 1553, August 21, 2007.
18.  MEMRI Clip 1471, Sudan TV, May 25, 2007. <http://www.memritv.org/search.asp?ACT=S9&P1=1471>
19.  al-Aqsa TV, August 21, 2007: <http://www.memritv.org/subject/en/364.htm>; <http://www.memritv.org/clip/en/1553.htm>
20.  al-Aqsa TV, April 18 2008. *Aqsa TV, April 22, 2008.* MEMRI, No. 1756, April 22, 2008
21.  al-Jazeera TV, August 23, 2005: MEMRI, No. 824, August 23, 2005. <http://www.memritv.org/clip/en/824.htm>.
22.  See the analysis of Yigal Carmon: <http://www.memri.org/bin/opener_latest.cgi?ID=IA30706>
23.  Jihad Al-Khazin, "From One Intifada to Another," al-Hayat, July 6, 2006: MEMRI, July 7, 2006, No. 1200: http://www.memri.org/bin/opener_latest.cgi?ID=SD120006 .
24.  al-Hayat (London), July 24, 2006: MEMRI, July 28, 2006, No. 1219: http://www.memri.org/bin/opener_latest.cgi?ID=SD121906 .
25.  al-Ahram (Cairo), August 7, 2006: MEMRI, August 18, 2006, No. 1255. http://www.memri.org/bin/opener_latest.cgi?ID=SD125506 .
26.  Palestinian Authority TV, June 2005 and July 2006. From: Palestinian Media Watch Bulletin, December 18, 2006.
27.  Arieh Stav, The Peace – Arab Caricature: A Study in Anti-Semitic Image, Tel-Aviv: Schoken, 1996.
28.  A sample of cartoons from June-July 2007: http://memri.org/bin/latestnews.cgi?ID=IA36807. http://memri.org/bin/latestnews.cgi?ID=IA36807 http://memri.org/bin/latestnews.cgi?ID=IA36807 http://memri.org/bin/latestnews.cgi?ID=IA36807. Cartoons depicting Jews as Nazis: http://memri.org/bin/latest-news.cgi?ID=IA36807
29.  http://www.terrorism-info.org.il
30.  al-Aqsa TV, February 29, 2008: MEMRI, No. 1711 | February 29, 2008
31.  PA TV, March 30, 2007: Palestinian Media Watch Bulletin - April 12, 2007
32.  MEMRI, March 2, 2007, No. 1485: <http://www.memri.org/bin/opener_latest.cgi?ID=SD148507>
33.  PA TV, January 31, 2001; May 4, 2001; July 22, 2002; June 18, 2004; August 5, 2005; January 1, 2006; July 7, 2006; al-Hayat al-Jadidah, October 28, 2001; al-Hayat al-Jadidah, February 11, 2002; al-Hayat al Jadidah, August 10, 2003; al-Hayat al-Jadidah, September 22, 2003; al-Hayat al-Jadidah, March 20, 2006; al-Risalah, December 7, 2006; al-Ayyam, February 12, 2000; al-Ayyam, June 4, 2007: Palestinian Media Watch Bulletin - June 12, 2007.
34.  al-Aqsa TV, December 3, 2007: No. 1625 | December 3, 2007.
35.  al-Kawthar TV, May 15, 2007: MEMRI, May 30, 2007, No. 1601: <http://www.memri.org/bin/opener_latest.cgi?ID=SD160107> <http://www.memritv.org/search.asp?ACT=S9&P1=1463>.

36.  al-Hayat al-Jadidah, October 23, 2006: Palestinian Media Watch Bulletin - Nov. 1, 2006.
37.  See in details: *Palestinian Media Watch Bulletin*, February 25, 2007

# 6

# The Arabs and Islam: Their View of Israel

*"Jews don't issue killing fatwas. Nowadays, you have to be careful if you depict Muslim or Arab leaders."*
*—Tim Benson (Head of the caricaturist union in Britain)*

*"Only a People who knows how to cry about its past after such a long time can survive the terrible future that lies ahead."*
*—Napoleon Bonaparte (on what the Jews are crying about on the ninth day of the month of Av)*

## Jerusalem and Islam's View of Israel

The accepted view of Israel by Islam and particularly by the Palestinian Arabs is that Jerusalem is sacred to Islam and that Muhammad visited Jerusalem at the site of the al-Aqsa mosque. That event laid the foundation for the centrality of Jerusalem in Islam and for the Arabs. Moreover, as typical of Islamic-Arab culture, no other religion has any significance in Jerusalem because everything there belongs to Islam. That view is accompanied by all-encompassing practical implications, namely the claim to total control of the entire area and utter rejection of all other people's claims to, or connection with, Jerusalem. Everything found in that area is the possession of Islam and the Arabs, for which no "scientific" confirmation is required and no other political-religious entity need acquiesce to that claim. The claim is supported by power and violence. It belongs to them because they said so. What is mine is mine, and what is yours is mine too. It's all mine and you have nothing. That typically "totalistic" view is singularly applicable in the case of Jerusalem.

In sharp contrast to Islam, Jerusalem holds the central spiritual and physical place in the history of the Jews as a people. Their thoughts and prayers were directed toward Jerusalem. Jewish ritual practice, holiday celebration, and lifecycle events include recognition of Jerusalem as a core element of the Jewish experience. It is fair enough to declare that

Jewish life without Jerusalem is defective. It is indeed "If I forget thee, O Jerusalem, let my right hand forget her cunning." The Hebrew Bible mentions Jerusalem directly 349 times. Including her many other indirect name names, Jerusalem is mentioned 669 times. Zion, another name for "Jerusalem," is mentioned 108 times (Pipes, 1997, 2001).

Three major periods can be distinguished in the Koran's treatment of Jerusalem: The Umayyad, Ayubi and the Jewish-Zionist periods. The basic fact that must guide any analysis of the place of Jerusalem in Islam, and specifically in the sacred trilogy of Islamic texts, the Koran, *Hadith* and *Sirah* on which the *Shari'ah* is based, is that Jerusalem is not mentioned at all. To Islam and the Arabs, the holy places are Mecca and Medina. The al-Aqsa mosque is the third place of worship (called *Qiblah*) that lasted a total of only seventeen months without ever mentioning its name. A famous passage in the *Hadith* refers to the fact that one prayer at the site of the Ka'bah in Mecca is worth 500 prayers in Medina and a thousand prayers in the al-Aqsa mosque.

The Land of Israel was conquered by the Muslims in 634 CE by 'Umar bin-Khattab, but the Muslims did not bother to conquer Jerusalem until four years later. That is certainly an indication of the importance of Jerusalem as far as Islam is concerned. Had Jerusalem been of any real significance for Islam and the Muslims, it certainly would have been conquered earlier. There was no military opposition to the immediate conquest of Jerusalem, but neither was there any compelling reason to do so.

In addition to the absence of any real significance of Jerusalem in the eyes of Islam, immediately after it was conquered, the Muslims reached an agreement of surrender with the Christian leadership and thereupon proceeded to leave Jerusalem and ignore it, preserving its Christian character, as testified by the works of Tabari, Baladuri, Ibn-Habbal and Ibn-Sa'd. Once again, had Jerusalem occupied an important religious role in Islam, the Muslims would not have abandoned it to the Christians immediately following its conquest and would not have granted the Christians such far-reaching autonomy. That is precisely how the situation is described by a Muslim historian who lived in that period:

When 'Umar bin al-Khattab, the conqueror of Jerusalem, arrived in the city, he turned with his soldiers to the Temple Mount and ordered them to bring Ka'ab al-Akhbar (a Jew who had converted to Islam). In the meantime, the morning rose and 'Umar prayed in front of all the people with his face turned to Mecca. Ka'ab arrived and Omar asked him: Where do you think should be set the *Mutslah* (i.e., the indication of the direction in which people should bow down, a place not covered by a roof). He [Kaab] pointed to *al-Sakhra* [the rock, namely the site where the Holy Temple had been located]. Then `Umar said: by Allah, Ka`ab, you are behaving in accordance with the tradition of Judaism. I saw you take off your shoes [in deference to the holiness of the place]. Ka`ab replied: I wished to touch the rock with my feet. `Umar said: I understand [your true intention]. But I will determine the direction of prayer at the tip of the rock. We have not been instructed about the rock, only about the Ka'bah.

This document confirms that `Umar did not recognize any special significance of Jerusalem, did not accept the idea of the rock [Temple Mount] having any sanctity in the eyes of Islam, turned his back on it, and decided that the direction of prayer was toward the Ka'bah in Mecca. `Umar even suspected, and rebuked, Ka`ab who clung to his Jewish traditions. If the al-Aqsa mosque indeed was located on the Temple Mount, could we imagine that he would belittle it and, by so doing, deny the validity of its source in the Qur'an? Obviously not. The fact is that there is no reference in the Koran to al-Aqsa or to any particular sanctity of the Temple Mount. Moreover, when Omar completed the conquest of the Land of Israel he decided to make Caesaria the capital of the region. Later, the town of al-Ramleh became the capital, which was the first, and perhaps the only city in the Land of Israel to be erected by the Arabs. It is worth noting again that had al-Aqsa been located in Jerusalem, could any Muslim blatantly disregard it?

Clearly, Jerusalem is not mentioned and received no attention despite the fact that Muhammad, throughout the Koran (*Surat al-Ma'idah*, 5: 21; 7; 137; 37: 104) refers to the Children of Israel, to their history and development, and he recognizes the Land of Israel and its unique sanctity for the People of the Book. The absence of Jerusalem is doubly surprising in light of the fact that the Koran frequently refers to stories from the Bible and to the prophets who functioned in Jerusalem, to Kings David and Solomon who resided in Jerusalem, the city of the Holy Temple. Nevertheless, Jerusalem is not mentioned.

To comprehend how utterly strange is this phenomenon we must recall that the cities holy to Islam, Mecca and Medina, are described frequently, and these descriptions are accompanied by mention of historical events. Moreover, before Muhammad began to prophecy he engaged in commerce and once visited Damascus. Jerusalem was well known. Commercial caravans to Syria passed near Jerusalem. Equally amazing is the fact that Muslims did not construct buildings in Jerusalem or in other parts of the Land of Israel (with the exception of al-Ramleh), although they built many cities in the territories they conquered.

Muhammad refers frequently to the Land of Israel. In keeping with Jewish tradition, he calls it *al-Ard al Muqadassah*, the Holy Land; *al-Ard al-Mubarakah*, the Blessed Land; *Ard Bani Isra'il* , the Land of the Children of Israel. The territory of Israel is called *al-Ard al-Adna*, the "Nearby Land." Therefore, the Land of Israel is not called "al-Aqsa" which means The Far-Away Land, but rather the "Nearby Land," because geographically it is the land closest to Mecca and Medina. One is hard pressed to believe that Mohammad attributed great importance to Jerusalem and yet failed to mention it. Consequently, no conclusion from this evidence is possible except that Jerusalem had no religious—or any other kind—of significance for Islam.

The only reference in the Qur'an regularly employed by Muslims, by means of their egregiously distorted political interpretations in our time, in respect to the sanctity of Jerusalem for Islam, is the first verse in Surah 17, *Bani Isra'il*, accompanied by contemporary Muslims' identification of Al-Aqsa as located in Jerusalem:

> Glory to (Allah) who took his servant for a journey by night from the sacred Mosque to the farthest Mosque, whose precincts we did bless—in order that we might show him some of our signs: for He is the One who heareth and seeth."

This verse, *Isra'*, is connected to *Mi`ragh* (*Surat al-Najm*, 53, 1-18; 81, 19-25). These verses describe how Muhammad had visions at night in which he hovers with the angel Gabriel through the seven worlds while riding on the horse al-Buraq (in Aramaic, *Susa Barqayah* or white horse) and returns to Mecca the same night. On the way he meets the prophets: Adam, St. John and Jesus, Joseph, Idris, Aaron, Moses and Abraham.

Flying horses, flying dragons and gods able to fly, were common myths centuries before Muhammad. These myths were often grafted onto new religions. The whole story may have been influenced by the story of the prophet Elijah who flew into heaven in a burning chariot pulled by horses (2 Kings, Chapter 2, verses 11-12). Of course, long before the Elijah story, Moses ascended Mount Sinai and received the two tablets of the Ten Commandments. In other words, the story of Muhammad has its source in the Hebrew Bible.

The only source from which Muslims derive the belief in the sanctity of Jerusalem in Islam rests on their interpretation of this event in the life of Muhammad, that is, his night journey on the white horse. The assertion that the Mosque that stands today on the north edge of the Temple

Mount in Jerusalem is the same mosque called al-Aqsa in the Qur'an, and that the holy mosque is the one in the center of the Temple Mount called The Mound of the Rock—that assertion is completely modern that lacks any historical foundation. Muhammad intended to reach heaven in order to behold Allah. Moses is one of Muhammad's heroes, along with Abraham. Moses beheld God face-to-face so to speak. Hence, it is reasonable to deduce that Muhammad, who, in his opinion, ended the line of prophets, had to believe that he was in a similar situation because he was more important than his predecessors.

The problem is that the Jews never claimed that Moses functioned in, or ever visited, Jerusalem. Nor did Abraham, who lived a large part of his life, and died in, Hebron, ever visit Jerusalem, which most probably was a very small Jebusite village during Abraham's day (see the *Biblical Encyclopedia*, volume 3, column 792). There are no Jewish sources from antiquity that can be cited as the source of the story by Muhammad. Nor can it be said that there was some misunderstanding or inaccurate interpretation on Muhammad's part. In order to explain this conundrum, Muslim clerics assert that the text in the Koran adopted by Islam is a form of "Isra'iliat," namely Jewish traditions that filtered into the Koran and Islam and which the Muslims tried hard to eradicate because they constituted some foreign influence from other religions.

### Theories about the Name Al-Aqsa

There are six theories about the name al-Aqsa, all from Arab-Muslim sources.

a)   The name designates a place of prayer located approximately twenty kilometers north-east of Mecca. The well-known investigator of the *Hadith*, al-Waqidi, founded this suggestion on the chain of testimony of authentic witnesses (called *Isnad*) who said that the al-Aqsa mosque, in the time of Muhammad, was relatively near Mecca. Other scholars locate the mosque sixteen kilometers from Mecca in the direction of Medina, at a place called Ji`aranah.

b)   Ibn Hisham stated that there are additional testimonies of Muhammad's nocturnal journeys that were carried out while he was sleeping and were not included in the Qur'an. These journeys did not include visits to other places (such as Damascus, for example) apart from Mecca. Ibn Ishaq cites the testimony of Muhammad's beloved wife, `Aisha, who related stories about how Muhammad's body would be lying next to her the entire night but Allah took his spirit to heaven during that time.

c)   Ibn-Sa`d was of the opinion that the event that appears in Sura 17, verse 1 occurred eighteen months before the *Hijrah* (when Muhammad fled to Medina from Mecca) at a place called Maqam Ibrahim near the well of Zamzam in Mecca. The same report was given by al-Bukhari and al-Nisa'i.

d)   The Biblical source is, as noted, the ascent to heaven of the prophet Elijah in a chariot of fire. That text hints at Muhammad's aspiration to ascend to heaven to view Allah who resides in the most distant firmament. That is the primary finding of al-Tabari who collated all of the Islamic sources in volume 15 of his work. He claims that Muhammad's goal was to reach Allah's house located in the uppermost heaven. The interpretation that Muhammad rode to heaven on the heavenly White Horse is the correct version. Moreover, al-Tabari indicates that Muhammad did not get off the horse and did not pray at in any mosque. Rather, he pursued his journey to heaven to see Allah and from there he returned to Mecca. Had Muhammad prayed in the al-Aqsa mosque, his followers would have been constrained to pray there, but that is not the case (Ibn Hanbal). Nevertheless, the al-Aqsa mosque grew in importance in wake of the Muslim penchant to protect their status through the construction of mosques on the site of buildings sacred to the Jews, such as the Temple Mount in Jerusalem and the Cave of the *Machpelah* in Hebron where the patriarchs are buried (Gen. 23, 9), now located inside the large mosque in Hebron.

e)   In an interpretation of the Qur'an that relates to the direction in which a Muslim must pray. Al-Tabari states that Muhammad initially chose the direction toward Jerusalem toward which Muslims should turn when praying, after the Jewish example. However, after realizing that he will not succeed in persuading the Jews to join him as the final prophet, he decided that the direction of prayer should be toward the Ka'bah in Mecca. In this context we can appreciate the significance of al-Aqsa as representing not Jerusalem but the edge of the world, the farthermost point in the world, reflecting Muhammad's aspiration to encompass the entire world.

f)   The Egyptian investigator Ahmad Muhammad 'Arafa (2003) through the medium of the Egyptian Ministry of Cultural Publications, expressed his view in great detail. He wrote that Muhammad's night journey related in Sura 17 verse 1 refers to the *Hijrah* of the prophet from Mecca to Medina. The journey was not to Jerusalem but to Medina. The word *Isra'* in Arabic that appears in the Qur'an means "to move secretly from a dangerous location to a safe place." In that way the prophet obeyed the instructions of Allah to the effect that Mecca was dangerous, his enemies were plotting to kill him, and he was to escape secretly at night to Medina. Muhammad's praise for Allah in the *Surah* referred to above, demonstrates the importance of the event for Mohammad.

The first name attributed to Jerusalem by Muslims was given by 'Umar in 638 after the city was conquered. That name was: Iliya, Madinat *Bayt al-Maqdis*. Iliya was the Roman name for Jerusalem (Iliya Capitolina, a name chosen by Emperor Hadrian whose first name was Ilius. See: Yevin, 1952). *Bayt al-Maqdis* in Arabic is from the Hebrew *Beit ha-Mikdash* which means the Holy Temple (Literally, the House of the Sanctuary)—of the Jews, of course. Somewhat later the Muslims used a shortened version of that title— *Bayt al-Maqdis*. The name al-Quds (the Holy City), popular today among Arabic speakers, was unknown to the famous Muslim clerics and exegetes of the ninth century, among them the famous Ibn Sa`d, al-Baladhuri and al-Tabari. The theologian al-Muqaddasi was the first one to use that term in 985. The name al-Haram al-Sharif, commonly used today by Muslims to refer to the Temple Mount as a means of distinguishing it from the Jewish Holy Temple, came into use only during the Ottoman Empire.

## The Historical Setting

The Umayyad Dynasty established in Syria had little influence in Mecca or Medina due to a conflict with the ruling tribes who were in-imical to the House of Umayyad. As a means for securing his religious sovereignty in his realm, the caliph `Abd al-Malik (685-705) selected Jerusalem, most probably because it was geographically close to Mecca and Medina and to Damascus, in order to make Jerusalem attractive to Muslims from all over the Islamic world with equal status to Mecca and Medina. `Abd al-Malik was a truly important figure for Muslim history in Jerusalem. In 691 he built the mosque called the Dome of the Rock on the Temple Mount, as related by the ninth century historian al-Ya`qubi:

> At that time [874 CE] `Abd al-Malik forbade the people of Syria to make a pilgrimage to Mecca because Ibn Zubeir forced the pilgrims the swear allegiance to him. He built a dome over the Rock and hung drapes there. The masses walked around the Rock, a ritual that persisted during the entire Umayyad dynasty.

According to al-Muqaddasi (985), an historian in Jerusalem (as his name testifies), the Dome of the Rock sought to elevate and sanctify Jerusalem, thus serving as a counterweight to the Christian churches that dominated the city, such as the Church of the Sepulcher. Ibn Malik's son, al-Walid, was the first to construct a mosque on the Temple Mount in 715 that he called al-Aqsa. Jerusalem still remained insignificant as far as Islam is concerned. The region's capital was determined by Sulei-man, al-Walid's son, who chose al-Ramlah for that purpose. A number of factors contributed to this situation:

> First, the rebel forces of `Abdallah ibn al-Zubayr controlled the Hijaz (Arabia) and prevented members of the Umayyad tribe from participating in the Haj (pilgrimage

to Mecca). Furthermore, the Umayyad Dynasty sought to legitimize their control of Syria: They had competitors in Arabia as well as in Iraq for the control of Mecca. Finally, in the absence of a spiritual center, the Umayyad needed a location like Jerusalem. That is why there sprung up an entire literature about the "praise of Jerusalem" (*Fada'il al-Quds*). But the latter appeared only in the eleventh century with the struggle against the Crusaders.

The House of Umayyad fell in 750, slaughtered by the Abbasids. As a result, the feint glimmer Jerusalem enjoyed for a time as a religious center was dimmed. For 350 years, up to the conquest of Jerusalem by the Crusaders, no Islamic entity displayed any interest in the city. The "Praise of Jerusalem" literature, that emerged for political reasons during the Umayyad dynasty, disappeared, and a new contradictory literature appeared that belittled the importance of Jerusalem. In fact the new literature considered Jerusalem a source of heresy and rejection of Islamic sacred writings. In 1016 the Dome of the Rock, most symbolically, collapsed and no one bothered to restore it as a holy site of worship.

The conquest of Jerusalem by the Crusaders in July 1099, failed to arouse any sense of shock or cultural-religious humiliation in the Islamic world. Isn't the silence about the fall of Jerusalem just a bit strange in light of the alleged status of the city as the third most important site of worship in the Muslim world? The Christians provided their move to conquer Jerusalem with a distinctive Crusader character. They destroyed mosques and synagogues, and built churches on those sites. Most of all, they pointed to Jerusalem as the pinnacle of their religious campaign. On the other hand, the Muslims do not refer to the conquest of Jerusalem as a goal. Only a few voices mention the city, such as that of `Ali the son of Tahir al-Sulami—a cleric who resided in Damascus—who preached the need for a holy war, Jihad, against the Crusaders. Another few sources can be cited in the reports of travelers of that period who barely mention Jerusalem in a religious context and certainly not as an important site for tourists.

A change can be discerned in the middle of the twelfth century when Nur al-Din, the ruler of Aleppo and Mosul pressed hard for a jihad against the Crusaders. He employed religious motifs such as the notion of "liberating al-Aqsa"—the site from which Muhammad leapt into heaven. But, a genuine change in the attitude toward Jerusalem emerged only when Salah al-Din al-Ayubi was dubbed the "liberator of Jerusalem" (al-Quds) in 1187, a cornerstone event founded in religious belief. A booklet called "the Praises of Jerusalem" mentions that. The main motifs of the booklet were defined on the basis of the city's sanctity deriving from the mosques found on the Temple Mount, the fact that Jerusalem was the third most important place in the world for worship, and its role at "the end of days"—as the bridge over which souls will travel between Mount Olives and the Temple Mount (*al-Sirat*) (Livni-Kafri; El'ad; Sharon).

Yet, Salah al-Din al-Ayubi's (known in English as Saladin) effort to make Jerusalem a religious center was, despite his relative success, short lived, and in retrospect, of limited influence. No significant religious institutions were built in Jerusalem during his reign. His success was more political than religious: He invested great effort in a struggle against "infidels" attempting to gain sovereignty over Islamic territory. Religion frequently served as a mask to conceal the desire to obtain legitimacy for political demands. Upon termination of the Crusader era, Jerusalem again sank into relative oblivion. It rose again into the limelight beginning with the 1930s when it became the focus of conflict with Christians, and today, with Israel. In the past, once the city's religious importance dimmed- namely, there was an absence of struggle with "infidels,"— even its minor significance was eclipsed.

The rise of puritanical trends within Islam also contributed to the neglect of Jerusalem. The Hanbali exegete, Ibn Taymiyah (1263-1328), who lived in Syria, is identified with this trend more than anyone else. He was active in abolishing Jerusalem's elevated status. He strenuously asserted that Jerusalem occupied no important religious role whatsoever in Islam, and that the city's prominence derived exclusively from Judaism and Christianity. Furthermore, to bow down to Jerusalem was nothing less than heresy (*Bid`ah*). Ibn Taymiyah's position professed a literalist doctrine to the effect that Muslims should direct their lives according to the literal meaning of what appeared in the Qur'an and in the *Hadith*, and he objected to any additions and to the sanctification of places not mentioned in the Qur'an. That opposition included all of the "graves of the righteous," thereby totally rejecting the importance of Jerusalem. In his Great Compilation of Letters dating from 1323 he stated that directing prayer toward *Bayt al-Maqdis* (the Holy Temple) was nullified, and whoever does so is a heretic who has changed his mind about Islam, an apostate (*Murtad*). If he doesn't retract, he is to be executed.

In fact, beginning with the eleventh century, Islam became increasingly rigid and ceased absorbing new ideas. Clerics viewed themselves as appointed to the task of safeguarding the purity of the faith. They opposed anything that smelled of innovation, first and foremost the notion that Jerusalem was sacred in any way. They feared that the sanctity of Jerusalem will outweigh that of Medina. Innovations, they asserted, were derived from Judaism. A verse in the *Hadith* was quoted to prove that the construction of the Holy Temple in Jerusalem was tantamount to the destruction of Medina (Yath'rib). Consequently, the anti-Jerusalem struggle was won by the formal and learned Islam of the clerics, against the trends of the populist Sufis who lacked influence.

These trends became apparent during the reign of the Mamluks who came from Egypt and secured their control over the Land of Israel and Syria after their victory over the Mongols in 1260. Jerusalem once more fell into awe full neglect and poverty with no economic or political support. It was subject to the whims of the bureaucrats who resided there. Safed and Gaza were granted status as independent provinces but not Jerusalem, and Cairo, Damascus, Constantinople and many other urban centers were considered to be of religious significance.

Jerusalem certainly did not occupy the same status as Mecca and Medina, nor was it considered to enjoy the status of the other cities mentioned above. The only exception to this rule was the architecture that characterized a few buildings still standing to this day.

Four hundred years passed during the Ottoman conquest, 1517-1917, and Jerusalem remained in its inferior and impoverished status under the regional rule of Damascus (*Villayet*-province). Suleiman the Magnificent rebuilt the walls of Jerusalem, and reinforced public structures, soon after its conquest. But these steps were taken merely because Jerusalem serviced pilgrims on their way to Mecca, and many public buildings constructed during the reign of the Mamluks fell into disrepair or were closed. But the city flourished when Christians and Jewish pilgrims flocked there and when Jews began to settle in the Land of Israel (Harel).

In sum it may be concluded that no real relationship existed was ever established between al-Aqsa and Jerusalem. Muhammad's style was consistent, clear and direct. He was always careful to mention names, places and events. The al-Aqsa is referred to only in reference to Muhammad's ascent to heaven. The name al-Aqsa appears as an identifiable geographical location eighty-five years after Muhammad's death, and then exclusively for the purpose of obtaining political goals, not for religious reasons. The city received attention after Christians functioned there during the period of the Crusades and in contemporary Israel, never due to Islam.

Had it not been for the struggle between the Umayyads and Abdallah Ibn al-Zubayr who rebelled against them, no mosque would have been built in Jerusalem with the name of al-Aqsa, and no claims would have been made by Muslims about the sanctity for them of Jerusalem. Had it not been for the Christian Crusaders and their aspiration to establish the "Kingdom of Jerusalem," and had it not been for Zionism's activity and establishment of the Jewish State of Israel, Jerusalem would have remained on the margin of the Islamic world. No national-political struggle over the city would have ever arisen, and certainly not a struggle accompanied by the invention of an entire set of myths lacking any historical–religious-political foundation.

## Under the Eretz-Israel Arabs

Jerusalem was forgotten, until the twentieth century. The Grand Mufti of Jerusalem, Haj Amin al-Husseini, with his political-religious ambitions, identified (in 1920) immediately the potential of Jerusalem to attract the support of the Arab and the Muslim states to his cause in his struggle against the Jews. Husseini was a close follower of Hitler during World War II, hoping that the Nazis, after winning the war, would annihilate all the Jews in Palestine. Nobody had a greater influence on the Jerusalem issue than al-Husseini, who as president of the Supreme Muslim Council was not only the supreme religious authority but also the central figure in Palestinian nationalism (Porath, 1977, p. 76).

Al-Husseini referred to the parallels between Muslim and German ideals: the unity of leadership; obedience and discipline; the struggle and the honor of falling in battle; education of family and offspring; and the attitude toward the Jews. He saw Jerusalem as the crystallization point for the "rebirth of Islam" with Palestine in its center.

Under the Mufti's encouragement, the Islamic movement, `Izz al-Din al-Qassam Black Hand," whose name is borne by Hamas's homicide bombers, was the first to unite the ideology of a devout return to the original Islam of the seventh century with terrorist jihad against the infidels. The "Arab revolt," which began in April 1936 as a wave of strikes against Jewish immigration and British rule was sparked and led by the Mufti. The character of the violence was determined by the Mufti and al-Qassam supporters (Ibid, p. 250). The Mufti succeeded in rallying religious movements in the Arab world, mainly the Egyptian Muslim Brotherhood. The "Jewish threat" and "saving Jerusalem" was a central theme in the Muslim Brotherhood propaganda. In September 1938, they called for a jihad to defend the Al-Aqsa Mosque in Jerusalem (Ibid, p. 199).

Yasser Arafat was a nephew of Haj Amin al-Husseini. Arafat chose the same road of anti-Semitism, and of Jerusalem at the center of the struggle against Israel. Arafat was born in Cairo named Rahman Abd al-Rauf al-Qidwa al-Husseini. However, only in 1967, after Israel liberated

Jerusalem, did he "discover" Jerusalem. Arafat cleverly cultivated the Palestinians' claim that Jerusalem is their third holiest city in order to give credence to another Arab myth that the non-People called Palestinians was a nation with a history. Never did Muslim conquerors of the Land of Israel ever establish a capital in Jerusalem. The crowds of praying Muslims weren't there until the leaders began claiming that Jerusalem is their third holiest city.

Before Arafat, Abdullah, King of Jordan, decided to conquer Jerusalem at all costs in 1948. His intention was to make Jerusalem the capital of Jordan. He thought that by doing so he would be able to achieve some religious importance for his kingdom following the loss by the Hash-emite family of Mecca and Medina to the dynasty of Ibn Saud. He also sought to enhance his political significance, his prestige and status, and his legitimacy in the eyes of the Arab nations.

However, Arafat systematically pursued his goal of having the Arabs support the notion of Jerusalem's critical importance for them as the Palestinian's capital and its ties to Islam. In that capacity Jerusalem could serve as a point of Identification and national pride in order to create a Palestinian people and nation, which, as noted, never existed at any time in the past. Arafat strove to have the West recognize Jerusalem as the Muslim capital of the world and to recognize him as Islam's international political leader.

Israeli leaders should have comprehended Arafat's strategy, but their treatment of the subject of Jerusalem testifies to their consummate failure in this matter. Israel should have repeated incessantly that Jerusalem was never the capital of any People or nation at any time in history ex-cept for the Jewish People. Nor are there any capital cities in the world whose territory is divided between two different nations, with the one new exception of Cyprus in the wake of the Turkish invasion. Jerusalem has no relevance whatsoever to the Arab Palestinians. Israel should have raised an objection each and every time that Arafat mentioned Jerusalem, it should have removed the city's name from any attempt to discuss Jerusalem by some official body (such as the U.N.), and it should have abandoned the site of the meeting.

Unfortunately, any form of planned strategic thinking never character-ized Israel's policies. In the realm of diplomacy, Israel has consistently operated almost solely in the form of ex post facto fire fighting that sends out the fire trucks after a fire has flared up somewhere without warning. Israel was seen to be stuck in square one, while Arafat was already in square ten at least, when it came to carrying out an appropriate policy.

On October 6, 2002, the Palestinian Governing Council passed a law signed by Arafat called The Jerusalem Law that crowned Jerusalem as the capital of the Palestinian state, and emphasized its absolute sovereignty over Jerusalem, including all of the sites holy to the three monotheistic religions. The same law asserted that any agreement or law to the contrary that might be accepted by any entity whatsoever is null and void. The law itself can be amended or changed only by a two-thirds majority of the Palestinian governing council (*al-Hayah al-Jadidah*).

According to the statement made by Sheikh Dr. Yusuf al-Qaradawi, whoever abandons the al-Aqsa mosque will also abandon the al-Haram mosque in Mecca, as well as all of the places holy to the Islamic nation. The al-Aqsa mosque is a symbol -- said Dr. al-Qaradawi -- of the city of Jerusalem, and Jerusalem symbolizes the entire issue of Palestine (*al-Manar*). On October 27, 2001, Arafat stressed the following message, as he began the terror of the Intifada:

The Palestinian caravan is on its way toward the first prayer to be offered at the third most sacred site where Muhammad leapt into heaven and where Jesus was born. Oh noble Jerusalem, the capital of Palestine: we stand at the crossroads of the world-wide struggle of Islam against Zionism.

If anyone thinks that Abu Mazen is less radical or wishes to be more moderate, let them note that he has displayed an uncompromising position on Jerusalem. Just like Arafat, he declared that the Palestinian People was appointed by the entire Islamic Nation to be the guardian of Islam's sacred property on the Temple Mount in Jerusalem. Israel should cease entertaining its expectations for compromises about Jerusalem. There will be no compromises of that kind. Abbas expressed the absolutist and uncompromising demand of the Palestinians to the effect that Jerusalem is entirely their property (Hirsch and Hauson; Reiter; Shragai. See Qattan re the legal aspects of the one-sided Palestinian position).

Arafat exceeded the extremism of Haj Amin Al-Huesseini. But Israel's Arab citizens have become more extreme than Arafat. The Islamic movement is the main agent driving this process, particularly the group led by Ra'id Salah. That group recognizes the Haram al-Sharif as exclusive of any other title. It constitutes the main theme of the group's activities, the essence of their political-ideological power needed to achieve legitimization. Its identifying slogan is "al-Aqsa is in danger." That group or movement over the past few years has been determining the nature of the extremist Islamic atmosphere on the Temple Mount expressed through construction and archaeological excavations carried out since 1996. This activity is concentrated on the southern underground portion of the site close to the Hulda Gate, known also as Solomon's Stables.

The Islamic Movement in Israel published an article on its website in January 2004 by `Abd al-Rahim Barkat, who does research on Jewish history, with the following statement: "The imaginary tale regarding the Temple of Jerusalem is a lie, a crime, and the most enormous forgery in history." What is the proof for this remarkable statement? His rationale is:

> King Solomon built the Temple in order to safeguard the Ark of the Covenant.... If we can prove that the Ark of the Covenant did not exist in the time of Solomon there would have been no reason to construct the Temple.

Barkat then cites a variety of hypothetical explanations as to why the Ark of the Covenant did not exist in the time of Solomon, mainly because it had been lost during some military campaign. In any case the Jews did not observe the commandments and there was no need altogether for the Ark. The existence of the Holy Temple is not based on any historical or archeological testimony and simply does not exist except in the minds of the Jews. Furthermore, the al-Aqsa mosque encompasses the entire city of Jerusalem similar to the mosque known as the Haram al-Sharif whose name refers to the entire city of Mecca. Therefore, Jerusalem in its entirety belongs to the Muslims and Jews have no relationship whatsoever to that city.[1]

The negation of the existence of the Jewish State of Israel is the cornerstone of Ra'id Salah's position. He will not admit the legitimacy of Judaism as a religion. Islam must be the world's only religion. Jerusalem was the seat of the Islamic Caliphate. On September 16, 2006, he announced that Jerusalem will be the capital of the Islamic Caliphate when the Israeli occupation will be eradicated. A year later, on September 4, 2007, he accused Israel of having a plan to damage the al-Aqsa mosque (on the Temple Mount in Jerusalem). Part of the alleged plan was to destroy the dilapidated Mughrabi gate: "That (plan) requires that we alert the entire Muslim and Arab world to prevent this crime." According to Sheikh `Akramah Sabri, the Mughrabi road is Waqf—Islamic territory and an integral part of the al-Aqsa mosque. A few months later (August 18, 2007) Salah announced that Israel sought to impose its rule over the Al-Aksa mosque and to Judaize Jerusalem. He insisted that the Muslims must strengthen the al-Aqsa mosque,

> "Our finest moments … said Salah … will be when we meet Allah as Shuhadaa' in the al-Aqsa mosque."

The quintessential expression of these trends in Muslim thinking and proclamations is the statement by Kamal Rieyan:

> The al-Aqsa mosque is sacred because it is mentioned in the Qur'an. It is more holy that the mosque in Medina. It is the closest place between heaven and earth. The direct connection between heaven and earth goes through the al-Aqsa mosque. The door to heaven is located about the Dome of the Rock. In Mecca the Qur'an came down to Muhammad, but he ascended to heaven from al-Aqsa. (Islamic web site, October 2002)

The message repeatedly emphasized by the Palestinian Authority in all of its institutional settings including its media, educational system and in daily political activity is the denial of Israel's right to exist, and, of course, the denial of Jerusalem's Jewishness. Dr. Hassan Khadir, founder of the *al-Quds Encyclopedia*, recently aired a program on PA TV in which he repeated the Arab position that Jews have no historical connection to Jerusalem. He remarked, *inter alia*, that:

> The Jewish connection to this site is a recent one, began in the 16th century. It is not ancient like the roots of the Islamic connection. The Jewish connection to this site is a fabricated one, a coincidental one. The true name of the Western Wall is the al-Buraq, named after Muhammad's horse which was tied to the wall. Who would have believed that the Israelis would arrive 1,400 years later, conquer Jerusalem, and make this wall into their special place of worship. (PA TV, October 13, 2006)

The person who heads the delegation to engage in negotiations with Israel is the Arab-Palestinian Ahmed Qure'i, considered by the U.S. and Israeli policy makers to be a moderate. He recently stated that

> The Israeli occupation authorities are trying to find a so-called Jewish historical connection between Jerusalem and the Temple Mount, but all these attempts will fail. The Temple Mount is 100 percent Muslim. The world must be mobilized against all these Israeli attempts to change the symbols and signs of Jerusalem. There is nothing Jewish about the Al-Aqsa mosque. There was no so-called Jewish Temple. It is imaginary. Jerusalem is 100 percent Muslim. The Arab world is called upon to interfere and stop the Israeli plans for Jerusalem, and stop Israeli attempts to create a Jewish character for Jerusalem (*al-Ayyam*).

The media in Israel ignored these comments in order not to tarnish Qure'i's image as a moderate Palestinian who is pursuing peace like all other Palestinian Arabs, including the Israeli Arabs. Arafat's approach was actually more radical than that of Haj Amin al-Husseini. However, the Arabs who are citizens of Israel are more radical than Arafat. The Islamic movement is the major driving force behind this phenomenon, particularly, as noted, the wing of that movement led by Ra'id Salah. For this group the Temple Mount (and it seems all of Jerusalem) has only one name, Haram al-Sharif. That name points to the movement's plan-of-action directed at achieving power and legitimacy under the slogan of "al-Aqsa is in danger." The movement's main manifestation is the excavation and construction going on since September 1996, in the southern underground section of the area, close to the Hulda gate (Solomon's stables) in the walls of Jerusalem.

The holiest site of Judaism, and the cradle of its homeland, is being systematically robbed and eradicated by the Islamic authorities in Israel, the Waqf, and carried out by the Islamic movement in Israel. The Israeli Arabs have a convenient explanation to cover up the real nature of their activities in Jerusalem, to wit—Israel is seeking to undermine the foundations of the Temple Mount by means of controlled demolitions and the weakening of its substructures. The Arabs employ their well-known tactic of "he hit me and then cried, he caught up with me and then complained." They are also excavating wildly, destroying the Jewish substructures and erasing all evidence of them. Of course they have an alibi intended to silence any criticism by Israel and buy time, namely that Israel is trying to destroy all the places sacred to Islam.

When a relatively small earth quake occurred on February 16, 2008, several pits were exposed on the Temple Mount. Immediately the charity association called "the al-Aqsa Institute" of the Islamic movement proclaimed that Israel was guilty (*Ma'ariv*, February 17, 2008). The occasion of the earthquake was exploited to stir up the Islamic world to undertake a jihad war to eliminate Israel. An Israel parliamentary committee (the Or committee) had been told much earlier by Ra'id Salah that "The First and Second Temples were never constructed on the Temple Mount. The Jews have no rights in Jerusalem. No stone there belongs to it" (Zinger, 2001).

Even prior to that, the Arab member of the Knesset Abd al-Malik Dehamshe announced that he would happily be the first Shahid to guard the Holy of Holies of Islam on the Temple Mount (Bender, 2000).

The Arab rejection of Jewry's connection to Jerusalem is absolute. The Arabs have no need for science or objective knowledge. It is theirs because it is theirs, period. Despite the fact that Jerusalem is not mentioned even once in the Qur'an or *Hadith*, that Islam had no sacred locations in Jerusalem other than the mosques erected in 691 and in 715 CE, and that they had no historical significance for Islam before the twentieth century, their assertions are absolute and unqualified. That is exactly how the Arab-Islamic political culture operates. The first Muslim to recognize the importance of Jerusalem was Haj Amin Al-Husseini. The second was Abdullah I, King of Jordan. But it was Arafat who raised that claim to the heights of an art, when he said that the Holy Temple was originally built in Nablus (Shchem) and the Israel Arabs are its continuity. Nor does Jerusalem belong to the Palestinians only, but to all Muslims. When archaeologists uncovered artifacts and structures from the period of the First Temple built by Solomon (destroyed 586 BCE by the Babylonians) —an event that aroused great excitement—the Arab member of Knesset Ibrahim Srasur said:

The time has come to stop all the lies that connect the Jews with the ground on which al-Aqsa is built. Israel did everything it could and excavated in every place it could and did not succeed in proving that there exists some connection between the Jews and that Muslim location. (*Ma'ariv*, October 22, 2007)

These proclamations suffice for the Muslims in place of evidence. No one has rebutted their claims or tried to silence them. Goebbels' statement—that the biggest lie becomes truth if you don't refute it—continues to be the dominant characteristic of Muslim communications about Israel, Jerusalem and the Temple Mount. As long as Israel fails to respond to these mendacious and absurd proclamations by the Israeli Arabs and the Palestinians, the unfounded assertions will become more and more frequent and more extreme. The same goes for their demand to take possession for themselves of all of Israel's territory that they dub Palestine, since they claim to be the Palestinians.

The Palestinians at large know quite well that there was nothing similar to what they claim in all of history up to the middle of the twentieth century. But they continue in the same measure to deny all of the rights of the Jews to the Land of Israel, including the Jews who reside in Israel and in the world today, who are the descendents of the Jews who lived in Israel two thousand years ago. The Arabs have no truck with compromise. It all belongs to them and that's it. There is no need for evidence or proof.

Summarizing the issue, Jerusalem never occupied any place of importance in Islam. It was never considered to be a holy city and no religious institutions were established there as were in other urban centers. Jerusalem was left in a condition of neglect, socially and economically. It never became a regional capital in the Muslim empires, not to speak of a national capital. The Muslims woke up about Jerusalem only when the Christians tried to conquer the city in the time of the Crusades, and today, due to the "threat" of the Jews/Israelis. Once the crusader threat passed, Jerusalem returned to its miserable condition that prevailed earlier. Remarkably enough, the reasons for that were religious: To prevent the sanctity of Jerusalem for overshadowing that of Medina. The awakening of the contemporary Palestinians in regard to Jerusalem is purely political, a reaction against the States of Israel and the desire to achieve prestige and legitimacy in the Muslim world.

## Nationalism is a Universal Phenomenon.

The fundamental character of nationalism is national particularism, to wit: each ethnic-nation group exerts sovereignty over its own territory. Western national identity is based on culture—each group's historical tradition that it shares in part with the other Western nations—and on political theory—on the principles of freedom, democracy and equality before the law. Both the political and cultural dimensions of Western society are under attack from a variety of "intellectual" sources, one of which preaches an ideology of multiculturalism, relativism, and post-nationalism. The latter is one variety of post-modernism that preaches a secular proto-Messianic vision of universal redemption which, in real terms, translates into the deconstruction of the national State. The attempt to transform the national State into a multi-cultural society is not merely naïve. It actually harbors a deep and destructive animosity toward national sovereignty. Obviously, the supporters of the anti-nationalist ideology fail to recognize the potential consequences of their quest which would lead to the creation of relatively small nation states that suffer from chronic instability who would be embroiled in perpetual conflict with one another. There would be an entire collection of nations torn by political strife and characterized by a multicultural civilization to which no one feels allegiance.

Multiculturalism seeks to exchange individual rights for group rights defined by ethnicity that will eventually result in the collapse of Western liberal democracy. Everything that now characterizes the liberal democratic state in the West will collapse and vanish. The multi-cultural state, like the former Soviet Union or like Yugoslavia, disintegrated amidst great confusion and violence. In our day, there are some Westerners devoted to demolishing the West in the name of some bizarre intellectualism motivated by sheer ignorance.

However, the problem is very grave. Just as the issue of multi-culturalism is expiring in Europe—with, quite remarkably, Holland and Belgium leading this process while England is still far off—it is being reinforced in Israel. Angela Merkel, the Chancellor of Germany, said recently that the concept of multiculturalism disintegrated. Whoever comes to live here—that is, to Germany—must respect our Constitution and our cultural, Christian, and Western roots. Holland once preached an absolute multiculturalism. Today she has awakened from her dream world after the assassination in February 2002, of a descendent of the famous artist Vincent van Gogh, namely Theo van Gogh, who was also an artist as well as the head of the National Movement party.

Holland recently enacted a new immigration law, similar to the one adopted by Denmark, that unequivocally states the country's national values (although it also brought a legal suit against Geert Wilders, the head of a nationalist political party, for alleged incitement against Islam). Israel, on the other hand, manifests a trend to change over from a "melting pot" policy toward its immigrant population, to an approach known as "a nation for all its citizens." That latter phrase is a code that conveys the total annihilation of Israel as a Zionist State, and its ultimate result in the formation of a Arab-Palestinian state in Judea, Samaria and ultimately in Jordan as well.

Multiculturalism thrives in Israel. Professor Amnon Rubenstein expressed it quite accurately when he identified Israel's condition as a nation suffering from a malignant disease that negates its own existence as the Jewish People, the Jewish nation, and the Jewish State. Zionism and the Jews' right to self-determination will vanish (Rubenstein, 2005).

The latter attitude is expressed by the anti-Semitic, anti-Zionist Jews who wish to see the Jews disappear as a collective entity with its own national homeland. The journalist Hagai Segal (2008) observed that the radical Left in Israel organizes itself around the Supreme Court that seeks to eliminate any definition in Israel of "Who is a Jew?" and substitute for it a definition of "Who is an Israeli?" That is tantamount to establishing a State for All its Citizens, the code term for an Arab-Muslim nation in place of the Jewish State of Israel. The Law of Return will amalgamate with the the Right of Return demanded by the Muslims for the so-called Arab refugees from Israel, so that 'Israel' (as an Arab-Muslim nation) can extend from the Nile to the Euphrates, and even all the way to Afghanistan.

The Europeans too are beginning to acknowledge the fact that there is an essential connection between anti-Zionism and anti-Israelism. To deny the right of the Jewish People to self-determination and self-definition and to deny the right of Israel to exist, is a racist undertaking par excellence. Ironically, it is in Israel itself that the anti-Zionist Left, that favors self-immolation and national suicide, proposes the formula of "a nation of all its citizens" as a variation on the theme of multiculturalism. Europe has begun to acknowledge the need to close its doors to further

Muslim immigration. Yet, Israel, which stands on the brink of annihilation by virtue of its friendly neighbors, is being pressured by some of its own citizens to open its doors to the unlimited immigration of Muslims. They call themselves refugees, although genuine refugees are grateful to be received into a new country, whereas the Muslims do not abandon their original goal of murdering Jews.

Israel's liberals avidly follow those preachers with their universal message of killing infidels (i.e., Jews and Christians). The anti-Zionist Jews in Israel accuse their country of causing most if not all of the world's problems. They want to de-legitimize their country by calling it a re-enactment of South African apartheid. That effort duplicates the strategy of the communications media by constantly repeating the mendacious statements that Israel carries out ethnic cleansing of the miserable Palestinians and constitutes an evil force that commits crimes against humanity. It follows that the world should eliminate Israel as a political entity. There is considerable evidence to support the assertion that, however radical it may seem, the Jewish anti-Zionist Left in Israel taught the Palestinian Arabs to employ those accusations: The Left persuaded the Arabs that their best strategy was to de-legitimize Israel in the eyes of the world.

A central role in this task was carried out by the media. The media today enjoy an unprecedented degree of power and influence over the public, a virtual empire with its own emperors, and the true super-power of today's world. For most of the population the media is the only source of information, given that professional or scientific journals and books have relatively limited circulation. Consequently, the media frames the public's perceptions and values. The manner in which the media are managed and conducted is a prescription for catastrophe. The media today consider themselves obligated to whip the government and to serve as the watchdog of democracy. But then, why do the media support the Arab autocracy and forces of terror and darkness? They provide free advertising to Israel's enemies that threaten to obliterate us. Journalism deals with Man and Society. It should be aware of its responsibilities toward those encompassing features of human survival, instead of its current hyper-sensitivity to ratings and scoops. Its critical prowess should be directed, in part, to the ravages of propaganda which it can too easily service and to the contents of declarations, polls and other quasi-research enterprises that it implements and disseminates. Unfortunately, that is not the case at this time. Every line appearing in newspapers exudes unilateralism and prejudiced intentions.

When England was engaged in the struggle with the IRA underground, we were not exposed to their pictures shown on television of rebel leaders, only to some shadowy features of the head. Nor were their voices heard, only the voice of some person whose sounds were artificially made to be coming out of their mouths. We should recall that the IRA never intended to threaten to destroy Great Britain, nor could it. Conditions are, of course, very different in Israel.

France has singularly rigid laws safeguarding the privacy of individuals. Those laws prevent en face photographs of people who might be vulnerable to attack to be shown by the media. Even in the United States, the media have undergone enormous change since the 9/11 attacks. They would not dare interview terrorist leaders, transmit their messages, or to photograph up close the victims of terrorism. Sadly, Israel's media, both printed and electronic, have not learned their lesson in this regard. The media in Israel are not "yellow" journalism but "red." We alone can boast of irresponsible media.

There is an unholy alliance between academia and the media, as well as with the cultural bohemia. The alliance in Israel is similar to the one that exists in Britain ever since the Munich agreement with Hitler in the days of Chamberlain and his defeatist policies. Faculty members at Oxford and Cambridge, along with well-known journalists, were among the most vociferous supporters of the Munich agreement. They condemned Churchill and his policies in no uncertain terms, going so far as to demand his execution. In Israel, academics screamed out their complete support for the Oslo agreement, which was the most blatant tragedy in Israel since the State was founded in 1948. Despite Arik Sharon's fairly obvious and extensive corruption that was far greater than anything revealed thus far about Ehud Olmert, Sharon was transformed into some lily white symbol impervious to any criticism—except perhaps, for the Disengagement that he executed that even those who supported it at the time admit that it was a national tragedy.

During the Second Lebanese War, academics blatantly and actively assisted Hezbollah. They grossly undermined national morale by means of reports to the media, namely: short surveys submitted to television programs about current events and other news, topics brought up during interviews on the radio, long and frequent articles about anti-Semitic Jews, and Arabs. The media dedicated many prime time broadcasts to the speeches delivered by Hassan Nasrallah and others who are declared enemies of Israel. Particularly repugnant was the readings of wills left by Muslim suicide bombers whose survivors sat in booths intended for mourners and had spokesmen speak for them. The media quoted Jewish anti-Zionist-anti-Semitic organizations on a daily basis, providing assistance to the Arab population in Judea and Samaria. There was a clear and symbiotic relationship between many academic personnel in Israel and the media.

For example, *Ha'aretz* newspaper pioneered in the use of the term Israelism instead of Zionism or Judaism. That terms harps back to the early days of the State when there was a small group of Jews who called themselves Canaanites and rejected any tie with Jewry outside Israel, with 2000 years of Jewish history in the *Galut*, etc. It turned out, however, that some of the original members of that group became well known figures in Israel in literary circles, translators into Hebrew from other languages, and members of what today is called right-wing groups. But the intention of the *Ha'aretz* newspaper today is the establishment of a multicultural-multi-religious State. That message has appeared in the *Ha'aretz* newspaper for the past few decades, alongside the use of any and all means at its disposal to undermine the legitimacy of the Jewish-Zionist State.

The general Jewish population of Israel seems largely unaware of the nature of our country's anti-Zionist academics, and of any connection between them and the media. Certainly a great deal of confusion reigns in the country regarding Israel's political positions regarding the Arabs, the government's treatment of topics related to Jewish religious tradition, its anti-Jewish treatment of education in the nation's public schools, etc. In effect the academics and media have chosen a path that leads straight to Hell. If and when they get the opportunity, the Arab Palestinians will joyfully implement Dante's depiction of Purgatory for its Jewish "clients" including the academic collaborators of the Arabs who, like the Holocaust in Europe, will not derive personal benefits from their treason. Arab victory over Israel will result in a far more bloody Purgatory for the Jews than Dante ever imagined. For that prediction we can rely on the precedent of Islam's historical record to date: We will be doomed to relive the past, not because we forgot it but because, in this case, it predicts the future with frightening accuracy. Those who disagree can have no recourse to any experiment to test their hypothesis because all outcomes of the experiment will be final with no equivocation, no variability from which to draw some statistically defensible conclusion. It will be all or nothing.

So our media go along their merry way, broadcasting massive justification for the Arab Palestinians against Israel, holding Israel responsible for Arab violence and terrorism. Ben Dror Yemini (2008) said exactly that about Muslim terrorism in Mumbai (November, 2008). The perpetrators of the Mumbai torture, death and murder, that included the young Holzberg couple, were not called terrorists but gunmen. A visitor from outer space who read the media's reports of the Mumbai tragedy would think that it was the result of social activists who search for justice and who are struggling to counteract the terrible effects of exploitation. The media and the so-called intellectuals serve the purposes of the evil doers.

Quite a few authors have written about the symbiotic relationship between the media and international terrorism. That observation was made by Ted Koppel, a well-known American news anchor (quoted by Netanyahu, 1987).

If the terrorists or the consequences of their horrible acts do not appear on television, it's as if nothing happened at all. They are out to strike terror in the heart of society not just kill a few people who happened to get in the way of their bombs. Terror without television is like a tree that fell in the forest when no one was looking. The television is terrorism's life blood. Look at what the media gain from terrorism: Violent sensations all the time that catch people's attention. That spins out into investments from sponsors of the news programs or talk shows that discuss the latest blood curdling events perpetrated by our local terrorist group as if it were a morality play. The television has been the single most effective tool for disseminating the horrors of terrorism, far more than the terrorists themselves (Gerbner, 1992). Whenever Bin Laden or one of his henchmen, from their multi-million dollar cave palace in the mountains of Afghanistan, want to make an announcement, they send a video to the media and the message is broadcast to the four corners of the earth. That's a lot better than setting up a television station out there in the sticks.

The Israel television has evolved into a powerful spokesman for the anti-Zionist Left. It emphasizes the Palestinian view of events. It is one of the primary instruments for getting Israel to kneel before anti-Semitic sentiment going around the Western and Middle Eastern world, and to exert pressure on Israel's Jewish population to cling to a defeatist position. Ben Dror Yemini defined the situation accurately:

> One has to take the microphones out of the hands of the small gang that have monopolized them and transfer them to others because the domination of the majority by the minority is the heart of the problem. That is domination by virtue of the "law of the market place." (Yemini, 2008)

The motifs publicized by the Israel Left are all set out on the same continuum to the effect that Israel is guilty for the fact that the Arabs hate us and are conducting a war to annihilate us. The occupation is the fountainhead of all our sins, the source of all our problems, without which peace would reign in the Land and, for that matter, in the entire world. That is the logical conclusion that follows from the premise that Israel is responsible for the world's misfortunes (*Die Juden sint unser umgluck*).

However, the Left prefers to ignore the fact that the conflict between Israel and the Palestinians never had anything to do with territory. The occupation always refers to the establishment of the State of Israel in 1948, so that Israel's elimination is the only solution to the Israel-Palestinian conflict. That truth is explicit and unequivocal, and not in need of research to be discovered or made public. Despite that fact, the territorial "question" is constantly regurgitated and chewed over. Undoubtedly, the Arab Palestinians have put the term occupation to good use. After all, the world "knows" that territorial disputes can be solved, whereas religious-historical conflicts are irresolvable and present an impasse that causes embarrassment and confusion to the world's nations and leaders. The ideology of annihilation that guides the Palestinians and other Muslim countries vis-à-vis their policy about Israel cannot be recognized as legitimate by the international community so that explicit pronouncements to that effect must be avoided by the Arabs. Our anti-Zionist Jews in Israel have supplied the term most appropriate for Arab propaganda, namely – occupation.

The Palestinians persistently publicize their accusations of Israel and their unequivocal intention to annihilate Israel by means of suicide bombers, by terrorist organizations such as the Hezbollah in Lebanon and the Hamas in Gaza, by the widespread use of propaganda, incitement and efforts to de-legitimize Israel as if it practices apartheid, by demanding the return to Israel of Arab "refugees" whose obvious purpose is to destroy Israel by demographic inundation. By all of these methods and many more like them, the Arabs strive to transform Israel into a part of the Palestinian State. Two mechanisms are employed simultaneously: Jihad of terror and violence, and the one of disinformation, propaganda, incitement, lies and deceit. The very same danger is presented by the anti-Semitic Jews.

Shlomo Sand's book entitled *The Invention of the Jewish People* (2008) twists the truth and makes a joke out of history. According to this pseudo-history written by a professor of History, the Jews were "invented" in Germany in the nineteenth century by two historians: Greatz and Dubnov. It must come as news to the Ethiopian Jews or to Rabbi Ovadiah Yosef, that they were all "invented" in Germany in the nineteenth century (Frantzman, 2008). These are but two examples of people who will be quite shocked to read these vicious stupidities. Sand's book is the logical outgrowth of other attempts by Israeli intellectuals and academics to write "controversial" works about the Jews and Jewishness.

Sand's point of departure, like his critical predecessors, is that the Jewish national movement is not only morally wrong but that it must be based on a myth, on the Benedict Anderson idea of an "imagined community." Again, like his predecessors, Sand had to uncover "sources" to prove his thesis and ignore any source which contradicts it. This grossly un-scientific method also characterized the works of Ilan Pappe. It picks and chooses sources that fit one's views, an approach Sand calls historiography.

Historiography is the analysis of how history is written. For example, historiography would not be concerned with the history of the Holocaust but rather with the history of how and why people have written about the Holocaust. A historiography of the Jewish people is not a history of the Jewish people so much as a history of how people have written about them. Paul Kriwaczek's *Yiddish Civilization* and Tudor Parfitt's *The Lost Tribes of Israel*, have shown to some extent that Jews themselves were not always interested in writing their own history. This supposedly adds to the Sand thesis because it allows him to claim that in the absence of Jews writing their own history, their history was created by Europeans and then invented in the nineteenth century. Obviously, Sand never realized that the Jews did not need to write history books about themselves because they had the Torah, the Siddur, the Machzor, the Talmud and other living histories that they studied in the Yeshiva.

Sand describes his own venture into historic revisionism as an exploration in historiography, and notes,

> My initial intention was to take certain kinds of modern historiographic materials and examine how they invented the 'figment' of the Jewish people. But when I began to confront the historiographic sources, I suddenly found contradictions. And then that urged me on: I started to work, without knowing where I would end up. I took primary sources and I tried to examine authors' references in the ancient period—what they wrote about conversion.

Sand takes historiography one step further and rather then analyzing simply how Jews wrote about themselves in the nineteenth century he goes one step further and creates a new history of the Jewish people. So the Sand ideology was not just to write about how people wrote about Jews. Sand, who was once active in the Israeli splinter Maoist group Matzpen, also wanted to learn about stories of conversions to Judaism and then to connect those strands into a theory that claimed that all Jews everywhere are the descendants of converts. That being the case, Jewish Peoplehood must itself be a fabrication invented in nineteenth century Germany, contemporaneous with the antecedents of Nazism. For Sand this is not a coincidence, because then Zionism can be shown to be similar to Nazism. Consequently, Zionism is illegitimate and so Israel should not exist at all.

Sand was preceded by Arthur Koestler who argued in his book *The Thirteenth Tribe* (1976) that all Eastern European Ashkenazi Jews were descendants of the Khazars, a kingdom that converted to Judaism. Koestler, who was a Zionist, wanted to convince the world that Jews are indeed an interesting, exotic, group of people, who deserve respect and interest. The anti-Zionist Sand's goals are the opposite.

Koestler's book has been distorted and misused by neo-Nazis and Islamic extremists to "prove" that today's Jews are Khazar interlopers, with no legitimate claims to the land of Israel. Sand's book seems to be popular among the same crowd. Large numbers of people who buy Koestler's book these days also buy Holocaust Denial and Neo-Nazi books. A book that is described as

> The Synagogue of Satan is the first book ever to document the secret history of the evil conspirators responsible for wars, revolutions, and financial debacles around the world. It is a virtual encyclopedia of fresh new information unmasking the Jewish elite and their sinister goals and hidden influence.

So Sand belongs to the same crowd of book writers who claim that Zionism is Nazism, that Zionism is ethnic-cleansing, and that the Holocaust is an 'industry' exploited by the Jews for money. Ofri Ilani published an interview with Sand in the Israel press (*Ha'aretz*). He explained Sand's thesis: "the exile of the Jewish people is originally a Christian myth that depicted that event as divine punishment imposed on the Jews for having rejected the Christian gospel."

Sand's "proof" is thus based on a simplistic deconstruction of history. Sand claims that

> no one exiled the [Jewish] People [i.e., from Palestine]. The Romans did not exile Peoples and they could not have done so even if they had wanted to. They did not have trains and trucks to deport entire populations. That kind of logistics did not exist until the 20th century.... (Hence) Judaic society was not dispersed and was not exiled.

If indeed that was the case, one may ask how the Mongols, with no trains or trucks, managed to get to Eastern Europe, and how the Arabs ended up in Morocco. For Sand "the chances that the Palestinians are descendants of the ancient Judaic people are much greater than the chances that you or I are its descendents." If so, why doesn't Sand call the Palestinians 'Jews'? Sand's 'evidence' for this is: "Yitzhak Ben-Zvi, the second president of the State of Israel, wrote in 1929 that, 'the vast majority of the peasant farmers do not have their origins in the Arab conquerors, but rather, before then, in the Jewish farmers who were numerous and a majority in the building of the land." Can a single citation taken out of context serve as proof for that theory?

That is the typical manner of Sand's misuse of history and of selective quotations intended to "prove" things. For instance, when someone objects to the term "indigenous" being used for the Arab Muslim Palestinians, one is always told to 'read Jabotinsky' because he referred to them as the "indigenous" inhabitants. Similarly Sand ignores the origins of the Ben-Zvi citations. Ben-Zvi was not alone in believing that the rural peasantry of Palestine was descended from the Jewish people. The British general, Charles Gordon, was in the Holy Land in 1883. Like Ben-Zvi and Sand, he was a self taught expert on the history of the Land of Israel. He claimed that one could clearly see the Jewish people's original facial structure in the faces of the Fellahin.

Gordon also believed he had found the "true" tomb of Christ outside the Damascus Gate at a place called the Garden Tomb. He believed rumors circulated at the time that some of the Bedouin tribes practiced Judaism. There are even some Rabbis today who claim that they have found Jews among several Palestinian families in the Hebron hills. The source of the 'Palestinian Fellahin as Jews' idea is not original to Sand, and it's also not true that every Zionist believed that story. What is true is that leading Zionists from the late nineteenth and early twentieth century did see among the Fellahin a people that were descendants of the Jews, just as they themselves were, and they felt that if the Fellahin could be freed from their Muslim and nationalist leaders that they would return to Judaism, just like, years later, some Ethiopian Jews who had converted to Christianity (referred to as Falash-Mura) were encouraged to return to Judaism along with the Marranos. But the existence of some Ethiopian Jews-turned Christians or Marranos does not make the rest of the Ethiopian Jews or Sephardim not Jewish. They were simply some people who had been disconnected and should be brought back to Judaism.

Sand argues that the Palestinians are the real Jews, a fact that might be surprising to some of the Jerusalemite families such as the Dajanis who believe they are descendants from great Muslim Arabs of the seventh century. It might be a surprise to some of the light skinned Hebronite Arabs who are reputed descendants of the Crusaders. Or maybe the Jews are descendants of the Crusaders who borrowed their ideology from the Nazis? In Sand's reading of history, new myths are used to replace what he sees as old myths. Not unlike General Gordon's creation of a new 'tomb of Jesus' to replace what he saw as the mythical tomb of Jesus in the Holy Sepulcher.

For Sand, the Sephardim are actually descendents from Berber tribes.

> I asked myself how such large Jewish communities appeared in Spain. And then I saw that Tariq ibn Ziyad, the supreme commander of the Muslims who conquered Spain, was a Berber, and most of his soldiers were Berbers. Dahia al-Kahina's Jewish Berber kingdom had been defeated only 15 years earlier. And the truth is there are a number of Christian sources that say many of the conquerors of Spain were Jewish converts. The deep-rooted source of the large Jewish community in Spain was those Berber soldiers who converted to Judaism.

Sand does not even suggest how he connects the Berbers with Judaism. As noted, Sand also asserted that Zionism has no claim to land in the Arab world because the Jews were invented in Europe and thus belong in Europe. But if some of the Jews are Berbers, then don't they deserve a state somewhere in North Africa? Aren't they the 'indigenous' people of North Africa? Sand might dismiss that idea as imperialist colonialism. Sand tries to revive the long-disproved Koestler myth about the Khazars being the fathers of East European Jewry.

The Zionist historiography claims that their origins are in the earlier Jewish community in Germany, but they do not succeed in explaining how a small number of Jews who came from Mainz and Worms could have founded the Yiddish people of Eastern Europe. The Jews of Eastern Europe are a mixture of Khazars and Slavs who were pushed eastward.

Sand also dabbles in demography of which he understands next to nothing. He ignores the problem posed by the remarkable claim that a half million Palestinian refugees now number nine million people. The Khazars were dispersed and disappeared between the tenth and thirteenth centuries. Sand claims that it is demographically probable that they were the fathers of the three million Polish Jews who existed in the twentieth century. Never mind that Polish Jewry had no Khazar family names, spoke Yiddish, and contained numerous Cohens and Levis who could not possibly be of Khazar ancestry. Being a Cohen or a Levi is passed to offspring through the patrilinear line and cannot be obtained via conversion. Demography actually tells us that it is far more likely that German Jewish immigrants became the millions of Jews of Eastern Europe through migration and natural growth.

Sand's theories are all predicated on his basic view that Jews have no right to be in Israel at all. It is clear that the fear is of an undermining of the historic right to the land. The revelation that the Jews are not from Judea would ostensibly undermine any legitimacy for our being here out from under us.

Sand does not believe the Jewish People exists, except perhaps as Arab Palestinians. He does believe that there is a "Yiddish" people, the descendants of Khazars, and also an 'Israeli' people that have nothing to do with Jewishness. Sand's "Israelis" are connected to the old ideology of Canaanism, which was once an ideological fad among some Israeli intellectuals who believed the creation of Israel would lead to the creation of a new people of Hebrew-speaking Canaanites, the new Israelis.

According to Ron Kuzar, himself a radical leftist, The Canaanites re-defined the forming nation as a new Hebrew (rather than Jewish) nation which had its roots in the glorious days of the Biblical era. They claimed that large parts of the Middle East, which they named the Land of Kedem (kedem "East/antiquity"), constituted in antiquity a Hebrew-speaking civilization. Hence the Hebrew renaissance should aspire to rebuild a nation based on the same geographical area, which should embrace the whole local population, liberating them from Islam and from pan-Islamic and pan-Arab tendencies.

Canaanism was a small splinter movement made up of poets and intellectuals, some of whom became members of the revisionist underground groups, the Etzel and Lehi, and some later became extreme anti-Israel leftists. One-time adherents to Canaanism or fellow travelers include Uri Avnery, author of Israel without Zionists: a Plea for Peace, Meron Ben-venisti, and Boaz Evron, author of Jewish State or Israeli. Sand identifies with those he sees as the "actual Jews," the Palestinians, noting, "If I were a Palestinian I would rebel." Meaning become a terrorist? For Sand, Israel is based upon "an ethnocentric, biological, genetic discourse." Of course Palestinian nationalism is not. In Sand's upside-down world, the Palestinians, who by and large never considered themselves to be a People at all before 1967, are an unchallengeable ethnic-nation, while the oldest ethnic-nation on earth, the Jews, are a bunch of interloping converts not entitled to self-determination.

Sand's prescriptions for a non-Jewish Israeliness appear mild:

It is necessary to add, for example, pan-Israeli holidays. To decrease the number of memorial days a bit and to add days that are dedicated to the future. But also, for example, to add an hour in memory of the Nakba [literally, the 'catastrophe'—the Palestinian term for what happened when Israel was established], between Memorial Day and Independence Day.

In short, the Palestinians, who are the real Jews, need more memorials inside Israel, but the other Jews, the "Yiddish" and "Israeli" nations, do not. Sand is modest in his description of himself: "As a historian it is my duty to write history and examine texts. This is what I have done." But Sand also has a radical alternative:

Since the beginning of the period of decolonization, settlers have no longer been able to say simply: 'We came, we won and now we are here' the way the Americans, the whites in South Africa and the Australians said. There is a very deep fear that doubt will be cast on our right to exist.

Sand's theory is also part of his re-definition of himself: "I don't think that the historical myth of the exile and the wanderings is the source of the legitimization for me being here, and therefore I don't mind believing that I am Khazar in my origins." So Sand is a self-defined Khazar who identifies with the real Jews, the Palestinians, and would join them if only he were a real Jew like they are; but he is not, he is a Khazar. It is hard to debate the Sand discourse because it is so convoluted, based on so many dubious assumptions, so out-of-step with the history he claims to understand, including demography, technology, and the movements of people. Nevertheless, it is necessary to point out several key flaws with it.

The Sand belief that Jewish nationalism is connected to other European nationalism is not unique. His belief that Zionism must be subjected to the same critique of nationalism as other nationalisms is also neither unique nor problematic. Sand claims that the search for a "mythical" Jewish past is connected to the interest of Greek nationalism in Classical Greece or German nationalism's interest in the Teutonic tribes. So for Sand

at a certain stage in the 19th century, intellectuals of Jewish origin in Germany, influenced by the folk character of German nationalism took upon themselves the task of inventing a people 'retrospectively,' out of a thirst to create a modern Jewish people.

But what is strange is that no one denies that the German People may live in Germany or that Greek people may live in Greece. Even though modern German nationalism may be illegitimate and the Greeks are in large part descendants from Slavic migrants rather than Pericles and

Homer, no one says that Greece should be given to Turkey or Germany given to Russia. Germans and Greeks get to keep Germany and Greece, even if their old nationalist myths are false. But the Jews, alone among the world's peoples, are said to have a national myth which makes them illegitimate as owners of a State. Books such as *Japan's Modern Myth* by Roy Andrew Miller critique Japanese national myths, but don't suggest the Japanese should be expelled back to Korea, whence some claim they came, nor that Japan should be given to China. But for people like Sand, that is the implication: the Jews must go, so that the 'real Jews', the Palestinians, can have their ethnic-nationalist state.

Herein lies the second problem with the Sand thesis. He holds the Jews to a very "high standard," claiming that because some people converted to Judaism over the last two thousand years, therefore all modern Jews are descendants from converts. But he does not hold the Muslim Arab Palestinians to a similarly high standard. For him, their nationalism is legitimate, and he sees in them the ancient Jewish tribes and perhaps Canaanites. Hence they necessarily predate and have more legitimacy than the modern Jews.

However, any critique of nationalism should be the same for all peoples, including Jews and Arabs. The Arabs cannot be depicted as a homogenous people who are allowed a mythical national narrative, while the Jews are said to be no more than a myth. For Sand this is precisely what happened. In fact he helps create a mythical Palestinian history in order to tear down Jewish history. This is de facto anti-Semitism: holding the Jews to a different standard than other peoples, singling them out for special hatred and contempt, while raising up other peoples.

Furthermore Sand's argument that Jews are either Berbers, ancient Yemenite "remnants of the Himyar Kingdom in the Arab Peninsula, who converted to Judaism in the fourth century," or Khazars should actually mean that Jews have a right to three new states; Yemen, Algeria and perhaps Azerbaijan. Instead, for Sand the Jews deserve no state, which means once again they are alone among the world's Peoples in not being allowed self-determination, even if they are descendents of Yemenites, Berbers and Khazars.

Another problem with the Sand thesis is that it is Eurocentric: only the Europeans "invented" the Jews. Since those Jews were then said, by anti-Semites, to control Europe, as per the Elders of Zion, the same Europeans decided to exterminate the Jews they had created, according to Sand's thesis. According to that 'logic,' Jewish existence depends on what Europeans decide, for better or worse. Europeans create the Jews, then hate them, then accuse them of controlling the world, then exterminate them, and now claim that all Jews are really Europeans.

But who are Europeans? What is their pedigree? Why are their states legitimate? This is a problem that returns us to the old ghosts of the colonialist past, where Europeans practiced pseudo-scientific anthropology wherever they went, creating 'martial tribes' and describing others as "naturally slaves." That is a classic example of circular reasoning. European civilization into the 1950s was based on Christianity and anti-Semitism was inspired by Christianity. Yet now we hear that Europeans invented the Jews, the very people to which Jesus belonged.

Sand's thesis is profoundly racist. He is welcome to think that the Ashkenazi elite of Israel is based on a mythical history, but by what right does he claim that the Sephardim were 'invented' in Europe? When European civilization consisted of people clubbing each other to death, the Jews of Babylon were a rich community of intellectuals and scholars. Today's European wants to believe he created the Jews, but Christian European civilization and Islamic civilization could not have arisen without the Jews and Judaism that existed and developed long before them. Both Christianity and Islam were built upon the foundation of Jews and Judaism.

It is quite alarming to have a professor at a leading Israeli university point to the Sephardim, the Ethiopians, and the Yemenite *Mizrachim*, all who happen to be darker skinned Jews, and say 'we created you; you are a myth; you are based in Europe; your heritage is a lie.' Their heritage is actually older than that of the Ashkenazi Jews. Is it just a coincidence that Sand's condemnation of the Sephardic, *Mizrachi* and Ethiopian heritages targets those Jews who happen to be of darker skin? These are also people who came as refugees from the Islamic world (except for Ethiopian Jews who came from Orthodox Christian Ethiopia), their rich heritage destroyed and crushed and their lives broken, only to try to succeed in Israeli society. They are now being told by an Austrian-born Israeli academic that they are a myth. They are being told they should be deported "back" to Europe, their "origin," a continent that sought to exterminate all the Jews when they lived in Europe in relatively large numbers.

Sand's thesis has one other simple problem: history. Sand picks and chooses sources, Christian or anti-Semitic, that agree with him, just as Dr. Ariel Toaff "proved" that the Blood Libel was true in Bloody Passovers: The Jews of Europe and Ritual Murder (he used Jewish confessions extracted under torture to "prove" that the Jews "might" have drank the blood of Christian children). But he misses the real history.

Apion, who lived from 20 BC to 45 AD, wrote anti-Jewish works and encouraged communal riots against Jews. In 70 AD the Jews of Judea revolted against Rome and their polity was destroyed. In 118 the Jews of Cyprus and North Africa revolted against their Roman and Greek administrators and massacres resulted. In 415 AD Theodosius II of Byzantium forbade Jews from holding public office. In the seventh century Mohammed complained that the Jews refused to recognize him and he exterminated one of the Jewish tribes of Arabia. In 1096 Crusader knights massacred Jews in the Rhine valley on their way to the Holy Land. In 1148 the Almohades conquered Cordoba and ordered the Jews to convert, die or leave. Many fled, including the family of Maimonides. In 1290 Edward I of England expelled the Jews from his country. In 1306 Philip IV of France expelled the Jews from his France. In 1492 the Jews were expelled from Spain. In 1543 Martin Luther published his anti-Semitic Jewish text, On the Jews and Their Lies. In 1573 Jews were expelled from Berlin. In the Chemielnicki massacre of 1648 some 300 Jewish communities were destroyed in the Ukraine by Cossacks. In 1821 the first recorded Pogrom took place in Odessa.

Who were these Jews, who appear so often in history, in official edicts of expulsion, and tractates of anti-Semitism? Sand would have us believe that they were all imaginary and mythical characters. So then why did so many of them have to die over the years? Why were 6 million of them exterminated? Why were Jews depicted as sucking at the breasts of sows in Germany, while they were ordered to wear special clothes, enter through special gates and live in segregated ghettos, locked at night?

The ultimate question is: If the Jews never really existed, why did Islam the Nazis and Christianity spend so much time suppressing them? David Ben-Gurion at the Zionist Congress in Basel, 1937, explained the issue:

No Jew has the right to relinquish the Jewish People's right to the Land of Israel. That is not within the authority of any Jew. It is not within the authority of any Jewish group. It is not even within the authority of the entire Jewish People alive today to relinquish any part of this land. That is the exclusive right of the Jewish nation throughout history, a right that cannot be abrogated under any conditions. Even if some Jews at any time were to announce that they were discarding that right, they have no authority to abrogate that right on behalf of future generations. No act of surrender of that kind obligates the Jewish People. Our right to the Land, to the entire Land, remains for an eternity. We will not relinquish our right until our complete and total redemption takes place.

# Note

1.    www.islamic-aqsa.com/ar.

# Conclusion

The typical distortion of history and values by Arab and so-called Palestinian spokesmen and society was, unfortunately, assisted by anti-Zionist Jews. They conducted a propaganda campaign of their own suffused with their hatred for Israel. Our Jewish anti-Zionists assert that Israel belongs to the Arab Palestinians, unequivocally and totally, and they deny any need for evidence or proof of any kind. Whoever asserts that there was a Palestinian entity at some time in the past should ask him or herself: What was the religion of that entity, what language was spoken there, where were its borders, where were its capital city and its other main urban centers? Did the period of the Palestinian state overlap with known historical periods and with known nations or empires? Are there any archaeological findings from the Palestinian state? Who were its leaders? In regard to the claim that the Palestinian nation was settled and prosperous, and lived with a sense of pride—how did it happen that no one in the Middle East knew about it or related it? The so-called Palestinian state is a virtual reality created *ex nihilo* by the Arab nations as part of their plans for destroying Israel. That fictional nation was identified only after Israel's victories of 1948 and 1967.

What is unique about the social groups that arrived in the territory of the Land of Israel from neighboring countries? Their common denominator is their hatred for Israel. Does anyone think that the various groups who call themselves Palestinians will live in peace with one another? Won't they disintegrate into sub-groups composed of extended families that will display considerable violence toward one another and ultimately set out to annihilate their foes—if and when Israel would disappear? That is not just a prediction but a conclusion based on the contemporary state of affairs prevailing among Arab nations, between extended families, and in their inability to find a common denominator apart from their hatred for Israel. Nor will the Arab nations stand bye and allow little Arab satrapies to war with each other and serve as an ideological and political focus for violence. The surrounding Arab nations will simply annex portions of the Land of Israel (those that were controlled by Arabs) as they did before Israel was established in 1948. Hence the notion of a "Palestinian State" will most probably remain alive and breathing as long as Israel continues to exist. That is the great tragedy of the Jewish People that the Palestinians are a surrogate sister of Zionism that they wish to destroy.

Arafat succeeded in identifying the "genetic code" of Western politics in the post-modern world. Those politics are infested with the disease of political correctness, with mirror-like images and with the guilt complex of imperialism. The Western world is bathed in the petro-dollars from Saudi Arabia. Those cultural values have been crystallized by academia's formulations of post modernism and post-imperialism. The primary principles of this approach are: (1) the right to self-determination is reserved for those Peoples who were subject of Western colonialism. (2) There is no justification whatsoever for territorial conquests and for one nation to rule over another. (3) The "developing countries" may not be criticized because everything is relative. Their behavior must be understood against the background of the Western nations' guilt over imperialism.

The victory of the postmodern discourse in the academic world and in the media deepened the guilt feelings of Europe. The Third World nations reacted quite understandably, albeit violently, to the imperialist yoke. The Christian mea culpa added to their burden. However, blaming imperialism runs up against some facts that are not consistent with that claim. The countries that manifested violent reactions to Western colonialism were, almost exclusively, Muslim nations, whereas non-Muslim nations that also sustained imperialist domination did not do so. According to the "imperialism as culprit" theory, Africa too should have caused widespread revolution and terror, since it suffered an overwhelming portion of misery and poverty under colonial rule. But, the violence of fanatics and terrorists is not related to the rebellion against imperialism. The latter express a religious-cultural demand to conquer the free world. It is not a reaction to Islam's history of frustration at imperialist domination. Rather, its chief motive is to regain its former glory, to restore Islam to its 'rightful and natural" status. It stems from an ideology of perpetual expansion.

Arafat cleverly exploited the West's burden of guilt over its colonial past by arguing that the West should seek absolution for its sins. The West should despise itself for the crimes it committed against the Islamic nations, and should be willing to forgive the Muslim's justified acts of terror. Arafat reaped an amazing degree of success in his campaign to identify Zionism with colonialism. By so doing he was able to cause Israel to be de-legitimized to no small degree. He brought about a radical change in public opinion on the emotional level without the need to examine evidence and without an attempt to comprehend social-political reality. Arafat understood that Europe still harbored guilt feelings over the extermination of European Jewry, so he waged his campaign to convince the West that Israel is the last vestige of imperialism in the Middle East.

Arafat's campaign increased sympathy for the Palestinian cause in three ways: (1) Israel was accused of conquering the Palestinians' territory, despite the fact that, following World War II, there is no justification for invading any country and changing its borders; (2) Israel is destroying the Palestinian's tradition and culture. The latter have a right to self determination on the territory known as Palestine; (3) Israel employs racist Nazi methods of apartheid and ethnic cleansing. Hence, Europe should feel relieved of any sense of guilt toward the Jews. Israel is the same apartheid state as South Africa was and, consequently, should be eliminated.

That is how the Palestinians externalize their guilt and project it onto the Europeans. The Palestinians then conclude that Europe should change its policies and perceptions and wipe out the terrible distortion called Israel that Europe is responsible for establishing. Anti-Semitic Europe killed the Jews and in the wake of its guilt established Israel. Now the Jews of Israel are executing the very same acts committed against them by the Nazis. Therefore, the Europeans are responsible for the present problem and are duty bound to solve it.

Arafat played his game on the international stage in a completely different way than the one known by the West. He was able to realize his greatest achievements by playing the Middle-Eastern game of shes-besh (a board game using dice and checkers) according to the rules of chess known to the West. He always presented himself as a poor old man, totally impoverished, who is seeking a tiny little homeland for his People. His would roll his eyes around and hold on tight to his hosts' hands, pleading for his patrons' mercy. That is how he made himself immune to the severe punishment that was inflicted on other leaders who were summarily dismissed from office due to their continued failures.

Simultaneously with the above charade, Arafat displayed considerable political sophistication in his behavior toward Israel. He cancelled the policy called Abadan (in Arabic), namely- "never for an eternity," as well as the claim that all of Palestine/Israel belongs to the Arab Palestinians.

Those policies had been a staple of the Arabs in Palestine since the 1930s of the twentieth century. This change came about in June 1974 when "voted" on by the Twelfth Palestinian National Council. Since that time, the Arab Palestinians embraced the policy called "the strategy of phases," to wit: Any territory from which Israel will withdraw will be taken over by the Fatah, but it will never relinquish its goal of "liberating" all of Palestine. That position became Arafat's official policy even when it was known by different names appropriate for prevailing conditions. Fatah's ambassador to Lebanon, Abbas Zaki defined their policy thus:

We speak in political terms but our principles are clear. We are proceeding in stages. Our strategy has not changed. When we take Jerusalem, Israel will collapse and we will evict them from all of Palestine.

Arafat was consistently deceitful, going one step forward and two backward, disseminating a flow of lies and distortions. He systematically drove down two parallel propaganda avenues: He sweet-mouthed the international community and simultaneously became an excited nationalist who was uncompromising when he addressed the Arabs. The very same approach was employed when he signed the Oslo agreement: "A peace for brave people," which is how he addressed Israel, and Khudaybiyah code word (Muhammad's treaty in 628) and Jihad when he spoke to the Arab Palestinians. Those two slogans were amplified by a third: "Millions of *Shuhadaa'* are marching on Jerusalem." Arafat's "peace for the brave" meant the elimination of Israel as a nation and a People. That was Arafat's method of deception: to say something and its opposite and to mislead Israel and the West. The Oslo agreement was defined by Arafat and by Feisal al-Husseini as a Trojan horse used as a trick to assist in the conquest of Palestine. The war of terror that he initiated in September 2000 was the phase when the soldiers descended from the Trojan horse at night after they had entered Palestine, under the auspices of the "wise men of Oslo" who had delusions of a long-term peace very similar to those entertained by Neville Chamberlain.

Arafat had three flags that he waved, one at a time, according to the prevailing winds:

1. The rocks thrown by the masses (*Shabab*) that riot on command and appear to the TV cameras to be sheep brought to the slaughter.
2. The rifles carried by the "policemen," i.e., terrorists who took their orders exclusively from Arafat and who operated against Israel as ordered.
3. Negotiations carried out as ordered by his messengers who conversed in English with broad smiles about peace and harmony. Arafat pursued

his own agenda without informing any of his minions. He continued to play his theatrical role with consummate skill, faithful to his chosen profession as an actor. It seems almost certain that he identified with his adopted persona as the "politician of misery and suffering," the tired grandpa whose lips quivered (only in English), but who appeared to remain steadfast in his quest for a Palestinian state. Sometime later it became evident that Arafat possessed two additional flags that he waved—the womb of the Palestinian mother—namely the demographic dimension, and "peace activists" who roamed around Europe proclaiming that the Palestinians were moderates and Israel was performing horrendous crimes against humanity. Their functioning was well planned: First and foremost, Europe is responsible for the Palestinian tragedy, so it must do something—i.e., eliminate Israel—to rectify the injustice done.

Arafat invested considerable energy in trying to rob the Jews of their historical-cultural heritage in regard to the Land of Israel and transfer it to the Arabs while delegitimizing Israel as a nation. That is the *Dhimmi* syndrome that deletes the history, culture and political existence of the *Dhimmi* nation (see Bat Ye'or, 2003) and hijacks them all for the Muslims, the sole heir of the (Western and Middle Eastern) world. (They would like to inherit China too but they would encounter five thousand years of resistance.) Arafat wanted to change the history and geography of the Jews and give them to the Palestinians, and exchange Israel for a Palestinian state. That was to be accomplished by a systematic distortion of history by Arafat, who had a genius for those kinds of assertions based on wish fulfillment, the interpretation of which even Freud would have trouble analyzing. According to Arafat and his heirs, including the President of the Palestinian Authority, Mahmoud Abbas, the Jews have no historical roots; they invented everything and particularly their historical rights to their territory which, the Palestinians say belongs to them. In fact, the Jews falsified so much that they no longer know that they are not Jews at all. Regarding the latter view neither Sigmund nor Anna Freud would have any difficulty in identifying it as the product of the psychological mechanism known as projection.

For their part, the Arab Palestinians created something ex nihilo, as is written about God in the Book of Genesis regarding the creation of the universe. Arafat enlisted God and the universe to make the case for the Palestinian. They owe their history, culture, their very existence, and whatever else they needed to the God of Israel, They did not inherit any of the things they needed because they were born recently quite nude, and their forefathers had already exchanged the God of Israel for Allah and

Mohammad who wanted Mecca and Medina, not Israel or Jerusalem. The entire myth of the Arabs owning Israel, Jerusalem, Jewish history, Jewish identity and what have you was fabricated by the Muslims, translated, expanded and improved by Arafat. His example deserves to be recorded in the history books for its sheer inventiveness and for the 4,000 year breadth of his invention, including Israel's present persecution of the Palestinians just like the ancient Israelites' slaughtered' the Canaanites in the second millennium BCE. Obviously, nothing has changed, said Arafat, because "everyone knows"—he thought—that today's Arab Palestinians are the descendents of the ancient Canaanites.

The Arab Palestinians were twice blessed with luck: Israel's 1948 victory over the Arab nation that attacked her—that prevented Israel from annihilating the absurd claims of Palestinianism. There is a consensus to the effect that had Israel been defeated by the Arab nations, they would have annexed portions of the Land of Israel, each one annexing the territory contiguous to it, such as the Negev to Egypt, the Galilee and Golan to Syria, and the central section to Jordan. That process most likely would have been accompanied by severe conflicts between those Muslim countries, each of which would have wanted to rule all of Palestine. No Palestinian consciousness or independent nationalism would have existed. "Palestinians" who would demand a state of their own, like Professor Edward Said, would have been summarily relegated to the underworld. The catalyst for Palestinian survival, duplicity, and terror was Israel's 1948 victory over the Arab nations that attacked her.

The very same situation obtained in the wake of Israel's 1967 victory. Until that time the territory referred to in UN General Assembly decision number 181 of November 29, 1947, called the Partition Plan, had been transferred to the various Arab nations with two goals in mind: the Jordanian goal—annexation of the central part of Palestine and the Jordanizing of its population; the Egyptian goal—establishing military rule in the southern part of the Land of Israel (that included Gaza) while observing the "civil liberties" of the laws of the Mandate. Both the Jordanian and the Egyptian interests were profoundly inimical to Palestinian aspirations of any kind that would even suggest the independence of any Arab-Muslim group in proximity to their countries. There were Arab refugees but no Palestinian refugees who might think they are part of some Palestinian People. "Arab refugees" is the name that appears as late as the UN decision 242 of November 22, 1967. As noted, it was Israel's victory in the 1967 war that resulted in the use of the term "Palestinian People" as referring to a separate entity, to a Palestinian national movement. That is when the Palestinians became the murderous step-sister of Zionism and effortlessly reaped the benefits of Israel's victories.

The study presented here examined a rather unique phenomenon, namely how two groups from different national-ethnic entities with very different motives, adopted and continue to strive to implement the same goal. That goal is to transform the State of Israel from a Jewish-Zionist nation to a bi-national one. Some of the Jewish anti-Zionist might be satisfied with that goal as a final one and have no further ambitions in that arena. However, as was shown here, the Palestinians have far broader goals. They seek to establish one large country on the entire territory of Palestine, and that, in the long run, includes the Hashemite Kingdom of Jordan. The present work also demonstrated that the so-called "occupation" was not, and is not, a central issue in the conflict between Israel and the Arabs. The conquest or occupation to which the Arabs refer is not the consequences of the 1967 war, but of the 1948 war, what Israel calls the War of Independence, which means the destruction of Israel.

The dimensions of the refugee problem, of the Arabs who fled in anticipation of the Jewish State, were also examined here, including facts about their living conditions and the enormous financial assistance they have and continue to receive. In fact, this work points out that employing the term refugees in regard to the Arabs who left Palestine-Israel is really an egregious error because there are no refugees today, considering their real economic and social situation. The people who call themselves by that term are definitely not members of a category of that kind and should not be the recipients of massive financial assistance given to them by the United Nations and the international community. The reasons for that are not humanitarian but mere political interests. In Asia and Africa there are tens of millions of refugees who are presently living in far worse conditions who receive little or no attention from international institutions. All in all in the world there are almost one billion people whose conditions and fate are much worse.

Another point made in this book is that Palestinian terror does not stem from poverty, deprivation or lack of education. Rather, it emanates from nationalist ideology and profound religious influences. Terrorist organizations—and not only Islamic and Palestinian ones—have proven beyond a shadow of a doubt that their leaders and members are well educated, graduates of institutions of higher learning, and do not come from the lower classes. The goals of the terrorist groups are not economic ones, nor are they in search of education, democracy, improving the social conditions of the people, or anything of the sort. In point of fact their goal is quite the opposite: A return to Islamic fundamentalism. Their ideal is the first Caliphate of the middle of the seventh century. Anti-Semitic Palestinians have their roots deep in the cultural and religious conceptions of Islam. As far as the anti-Zionist Jews are concerned, the sources of their beliefs are from Communist ideology, particularly from the Trotskyite version, as well as from the "Galut (Diaspora) mentality" to which they still belong. We also dealt here with the branch of anti-Zionists who are anarchists who have fascist roots and whose heritage stems from ideologies once common in Europe.

# References

Aharonson, Shlomo, "Zionism and post-Zionism: The Historical-Ideological Context."
In Y. Weitz (Ed.) *From Vision to Revision: A Hundred Years of Historiography of Zionism*, Jerusalem: The Zalman Shazar Center, 1997, 291-309.

Alexander, Edward (Ed.), With Friends Like These: The Jewish Critics of Israel, New York: Shapolsky Publishers, 1993.

Allport, Gordon, *The Nature of Prejudice*. New York: Doubleday, 1958.

*Al-Ayyam*, November 4, 2008.

*Al-Hayah*, London, November 23-24, 2000.

Al-Hayah al-Jadidah, October 7, 2002.

*Al-Manar*, Beirut, December 5, 2005.

al-Tabari, Tarikh al-Muluk wal-Ruasa',

Ali, Tariq, *The Clash of Fundamentalism*. London, 2003,

Aloni, Shulamit, *Democracy in Chains*. Tel-Aviv: Am Oved, 2008     (Hebrew).

Aloni, Udi, *Yediot Aharonot*, Literary Supplement 7 Nights, May, 2003.

Almog, Oz, *The Sabra—A Profile*. Tel-Aviv: Am Oved, 1997 (Hebrew).

'Arafa, Ahmad Muhammad, "Was the Prophet Muhammad's night journey to Palestine or Medina?" *Al-Qahirah*, August 5, 2003.

Arfa, Milton, "Toward the study of Hebrew culture in the Golah." *Nativ*, September 2005, 56-63, originally written in 1947.

Atzmon, Gilad, "Beyond comparison." *Al-Jazeerah*, August 12, 2006. See: http://www.al-jazeerah.info/Opinion%20editorials/2006%20Opinion% 20Editorials/August/12%

Avneri, Arieh, *The Claim of Dispossession*. New York: Herzl Press, 1980

Balduri, *Futuh al-Baldan*, vol. 1.

Balint, Benjamin, Writing in the Dark by David Grossman, translated by Jessica
Cohen, New York: Farrar. Strauss and Giroux, 2008.

Baron, Salo W. *A Social and Religious History of the Jews*, Columbia University, The Jewish Publications Society of America, 18 volumes, 1952-1983.

Baron, Salo W. *Modern Nationalism and Religion*. New York: Harper & Row, 1947.
Revised 2nd edition: Philadelphia: The Jewish Publication Society, 1960.

Bar-Tal, Daniel, *Living With the Conflict*. Tel-Aviv: Carmel, 2007     (Hebrew).

Bar-Tal, Daniel and Teichman, Yona, Stereotypes and prejudice in Conflict: Representation of Arabs in Israeli Jewish Society. New York: Cambridge University Press, 2005.

Bartal, Israel, "Post-Mapai" *Ha'aretz*, October 5, 1994.

Bartal, Israel, *Ha'aretz*, March 29, 1998.

Bartal, Israel, "The Quiet Revolution: Myth, Science and In-between." *Cathedra*, 81, September, 1996 (Hebrew).

Bat Ye'or, Islam and Dhimmitude: Where Civilizations Collide. Teaneck, New Jersey: Fairleigh Dickenson University Press, 2002.

Bat Ye'or, *Eurabia: The Euro-Arab Axis. Teaneck*, New Jersey: Fairleigh Dickenson University Press, 2004

Ben-Amos, Avner and Bar-Tal, Daniel, *Patriotism*. Tel-Aviv: Tel-Aviv University Dunon, 2004.

Bender, Arieh, *Ma'ariv*, July 12, 2000 (Hebrew).

Ben Dor, Oren, "Hamas Victory: A New Hope? The Palestine Chronicle," February 1, 2006: http://www.cpcml.ca/Tmld2006/D36012.htm#9.

Ben Dor, Oren, "Who Are the Real Terrorists in the Middle East? *Independent*, July 26, 2006.

Ben-Gurion, David, *From Class to Peoplehood*. Tel-Aviv: Am Oved, 1974 (Hebrew)

Beres, Louis Rene, "Israel Occupies no Arab Territories." *The Jerusalem Post*, Nov. 18, 2008.

Biblical Encyclopedia, *Jerusalem, Jerusalem*: Mossad Bialik. 1958, vol. 3 (Hebrew).

Benvenisti, Meron, *The Morning After*. Jerusalem: Carmel Publishers, 2002 (Hebrew).

Bogdanor, Paul, "Anti-Israel Hate fest at the Van Leer Institute." http://www.paulbogdanor.com/vanleer.html, 2006

Bruegel, Irene, JFJP , letter to the Guardian, January 24, 2004.

Bukay, David, From Muhammad to Bin Laden: the Religious and Ideological Sources of the Homicide bombers Phenomenon, New Brunswick: Transaction, 2007.

Bukay, David, Facts and Fables in the Mythology of Islamic and Palestinian *Terrorism*, Policy Paper no. 162. Shaarei Tiqva: Ariel Center for Policy Papers, 2006.

Bukay, David, "The Leftist Media and the Al-Aqsa Uprising." In S. Sharan (editor) *Israel and the Post-Zionists*. Brighton: Sussex Academic Press, 2003, pp. 87-113.

Bukay, David, "Jewry's Galut Mentality: The True Danger of Israel's Collapse." (unpublished paper, 2004).

Carlebach, Nathan Azriel *Ma'ariv*, February 19, 1993 (reprinted from 1955).

Cassirer, Ernst, *The Myth of the State*. New Haven: Yale University Press, 1946.

Chason, Yisrael (Ed.), *Fada'il Bayt al-Maqdis*, Jerusalem, 1979.

Denkner, Amnon, *Ma'ariv*, January 19, 2001. See also *Ma'ariv*, June 13, 2001.

Dor Shav, Netta, *The Self-Destructiveness of the Jews*, Shaarei Tikvah: The Ariel Center for Policy Research, Policy Paper 24, 1998.

Dothan, Shmuel, *Reds in Palestine*, Kfar Sava: Shevna Ha-Sofer, 1996.

Doward, Jamie and Hines, Nico, "Boycott Threat to Israeli Colleges." *Observer*, April 17, 2005.

El-ad, Amikam, "The Temple Mount in the Ancient Moslem Period." In Isaac Ritter (Ed.), The Sovereignty of God and Man–Holiness and Political Centrality on *the Temple Mount*. Jerusalem: The Jerusalem Institute for the Study of Israel, 2001.

Epstein, Raya, "Post Zionism and Democracy," In S. Sharan (Ed.), *Israel and the Post-Zionists: A Nation at Risk*. Brighton: Sussex Academic Press, 2003.

Ezrachi, Yaron, "Enough of the Evil Axis," *Ha'aretz*, August 22, 2007.

Ezrachi, Yaron, www.defeatist-diary.com/index.asp?p=article_Ezrahi.

Farber, Seth, *Radicals, Rabbis and Peacemakers*. Common Press: Monroe, 2005.

Fonte, John, "The Future of the Ideological Civil war Within the West," In S. Sharan (Ed.), Israel and the Post-Zionists: A Nation at Risk, pp. 136-154.

Frantzman, Seth, "Shlomo Sand's Revisionist pseudo-History of the Jewish People." December 5, 2008.

Freud, Anna, *The Ego and the Mechanisms of Defense*. New York: International Universities Press, 1936.

Fromkin, David, *A Peace to End All Peace*, New York: Henry Holt, 1986.

Gabriel, Brigitte, *Because They Hate*. New York: St. Martin's Press, 2006.

Gerbner, G, "Violence and Terror in and by the Media," in M. Raboy and B. Dagenais (eds), *Media, Crisis and Democracy*. London: Sage, 1992, 94-107.

Gerstenfeld, Manfred, *Academics against Israel and the Jews*. Jerusalem: Jerusalem Center for Public Affairs, 2007

Gerstenfeld, Manfred, "Anti-Israelism and Anti-Semitism: Common Characteristics and Motifs," Jewish Political Studies Review, vol. 19, 2007.

Gerstenfeld, Manfred, Jews against Israel: Post-Holocaust anti-Semitism. *Jerusalem* Center for Public Affairs, No. 30, March 1, 2005.

Glatzer, Nahum, *Franz Rosenzweig: His Life and Thought*. Philadelphia: The Jewish Publications Society of America-Schocken Books, 1953.

Glick, Caroline, "The Olmert Government's Assault on Zionism." *The Jerusalem Post*, July 24, 2007.

Gold, Dore, Hatred's Kingdom: How Saudi Arabia Supports the New Global *Terrorism*, Washington, D.C.: Regnery Publishing Co., 2003.

Greenberg, Hayim, *The Inner Eye*. New York: Jewish Frontier Association, 1953.

Greenstein, Tony, "The Seamy Side of Solidarity." *Guardian*, February 17, 2007

Harel, Menasheh, "The Contribution of the Three Monotheistic Religions to Jerusalem and Israel," *Nativ*, September, 2005, pages 65-73.

Hazaz, Chaim, *The Bronze Doors*. Tel-Aviv: Am Oved, 1956/1968 (Hebrew).

Herzl, Theodore, *Altneuland*, 1902 (The Old-New Land). New York, 1960).

Hodgson, Martin, "British Jews Break Away from Pro-Israeli Board of Deputies," *Independent*, February 5, 2007.

Hornik, David P. "Ha'aretz: Israel's Self-hating Newspaper." *FrontPageMagazine.com*, February 2, 2004.

Hornik, David P. "Hypocrisy of the Israel Left." *Isracampus.org*, October 27, 2008. FrontPageMagazine.com, October 3, 2008.

Hirsch, Moshe and Hauson, D'vorah, "Where to Jerusalem? Suggestions regarding the future of Jerusalem." The Jerusalem Institute for the Study of Israel, 1944.

Hazoni, Yoram, "The Quiet Revolution in the Educational System," *T'chalet*, No. 10, 2001, 41-64.

Hazoni, Yoram; Polisar, Daniel and Oren, Michael, *The Quiet Revolution in the Teaching of Zionism: A Comparative Study of Textbooks*, the Ministry of Education Regarding the Twentieth Century. Jerusalem Shalem Center, 2000.

Horowitz, David, *Ha'aretz*, June 26, 2001.

Horowitz, David, The Professors: The 101 Most Dangerous Academics in America. Washington, DC: Regnery Publishing Co., 2006.

Horowitz, David, Indoctrination U.: The Left's War against Academic Freedom. New York: Encounter Books, 2007.

Huntington, Samuel, The Clash of Civilizations and the Remaking of World Order, New York: Touchstone. 1996.

Ibn Hanbal, *al-Musnad*, vol. 5.

Ibn Sa'd, Kitab al-Tabaqat al-Kubrah, vol. 3.

Ibn Warraq, Debunking Edward Sa'id: Edward Sa'id and the Saidists, or Third World Intellectual Terrorism, ,http://www.secularism.org'articles/debunking.htm.

Isaac, Rael and Erich, "Israelis against Themselves," In E. Alexander (Ed.), *With Friends like These*, New York: Shapolsky, 1993.

Israel Academia Monitor, http://israel-academia-monitor.com.

Israeli, Raphael, *Arabs in Israel: Friends or Foes?* Jerusalem: Ariel Center for Policy Research, 2008. Originally published in Hebrew, 2002.

Israeli, Raphael, *Islamikaze: Manifestations of Islamic Martyrology*, London: Frank Cass, 2003.

Israeli, Raphael, *Living with Islam*. Netanya: Achiasaf, 2006 (Hebrew).

Jamal, Amal, "Homeland, People and Nation: Patriotism among the Palestinian Minority," In Kramer, Martin, *Ivory Tower on Sand*. Washington, D.C.: Institute for Near East Policy, 2001.

Judt, Tony, *Israel: The Alternative*. The New York Review of Books, October 23, 2003.

Judt, Tony, From a speech at the University of Chicago, October, 2007. The text is available at: http://mrzine.monthlyreview.org/dfreedom161007.html

Julius, Anthony, "Jewish Anti-Zionism Unraveled." Parts I and II. Israel Academia *Monitor*, (Internet) April-May, 2008.

Kaplan, Lee, "Rivka Carmi, President, Hails Anti-Israel Activity on Her Campus." *www. isracampusorg.il.* 2008.

Katz, Gary, "Extremist-Leftist Lies and Lethal Legacies." gk68@myway.com

Karsh, Efraim, *Fabricating Israeli History*. London: Frank Cass. 1997.

Kattan, Henri, *Jerusalem*. New York: St. Martin's Press, 1981.

Katznelson, Berl, *Davar* (newspaper), May 1, 1936

Kaufmann, Yehezkel, *Exile and Alienation*, Tel-Aviv: Dvir, 1930 (Hebrew).

Kaufmann, Yehezkel, *In the Throes of Time*. Tel-Aviv: Dvir, 1936 (Hebrew)

Kitchen, Knneth, *On the Reliability of the Old Testament*. Grand Rapids, Michigan: Eerdmans Publishing Co., 2003.

Kuhn, Thomas, *The Structure of Scientific Revolutions*. Chicago: University of Chicago Press, 1962.

Laor, Yitzchak, Poem entitled "Hymn for the Gush".

Leibowitz, Yeshayahu, *Ha'aretz*, September 27, 1985.

Leshem, Micah, "Israel's Right to be Racist." *Israel Academia Monitor*, March 22, 2007.

Lessing, Theodore, "Jewish Self-Hatred." *Nativ*, 96, January, 2004, pp. 49-54.

Levin, Kenneth, *The Oslo Syndrome: Delusions of a People Under Siege*. Hanover, New Hampshire: Smith and Kraus, 2005.

Levin, Kenneth, Diaspora Jews Embracing the Indictments of their Enemies: Post-Holocaust and Anti-Semitism, Jerusalem Center for Public Affairs, 2007.

Lewis, Bernard, "Roots of Muslim Rage." *The Atlantic Monthly*, September, 1990, pp. 47-55.

Lewis, Bernard, *The Jews of Islam*. Princeton, Princeton University Press, 1984.

Lewis, Bernard, *Islam and the West*. New York: Oxford University Press,       1993.

Livni-Kafri, Offer, "The Hub of the Earth in Muslim Tradition." *Kathedra*, 69, September, 1993.

Lord, Amnon, *We Lost Everything Dear to Us*, Tel-Aviv: Tamuz. 2000 (Hebrew).

Mack, R. W. and Snyder, R.C, "The Analysis of Social Conflict," *Journal of Conflict Resolution*, June 1957, pp 212-248.

Makiya, Kan'an, *Cruelty and Silence*. New York: Norton and Company, 1993.

Matalon, Ronit, *Yediot Aharonot*, April 27, 2001.

Megged, Aharon, "The Israeli Suicide Drive." *The Jerusalem Post*, International edition, July 2, 1994.

Minahan, John, *Nations Without States*. Westport: Greenwood Press, 1996.

Netanyahu, Benjamin (Ed.), *Terror: How Can the West Win?* Tel-Aviv: Ma'ariv, 1987

Neuwirth, Rachel, "The Noam Chomsky File: Portrait of a Jewish Anti-Semite." *Nativ*, 107, 2005.

Neuwirth, Rachel, "The Expulsion Libel: 1948 Arab Exodus Reconsidered." *American Thinker*, April 3, 2008.

O'Brian, Connor Cruise, *The Siege: The Saga of Israel and Zionism*. New York: Simon and Schuster, 1986.

Oppenheimer, Yochai, *Ma'ariv*, December 23, 2003.

Oren, Michael, "Is the Creation of Palestinian State Essential or Deadly?" *The Journal of International Security Affairs*. October 3, 2008.

Oren, Yosef, "Post Zionism and anti-Zionism in Israeli Literature." In S. Sharan (Ed.), *Israel and the Post-Zionists: A Nation at Risk*, pp. 188-203.

Oz, Amos, *Yediot Aharonot*, August 6, 1989.

Oz, Amos, *The New York Times*, September 14, 2001.

Palestinian Authority Television, October 13, 2006. From Palestinian Media Watch Bulletin, October 19, 2006.

Pappe, Ilan, *The Ethnic Cleansing of Palestine*. Oxford University Press, 2006.

Peters, Joan, *From Time Immemorial*. New York: Harper and Row, 1984.

Plaut, Stephen, Israel's Academic Fifth Column, personal communication, 2007.

Peres, Shimon, *Ha'aretz*, June, 13, 2002.

Pipes, Daniel, "If I Forget Thee: Does Jerusalem Really Matter to Islam? *New Republic*, April 28, 1997.

Perlmutter, Amos, *Jerusalem Post International Edition*, October 28, 1995.

Pipes, Daniel, "The Muslim Claim to Jerusalem," *The Middle East Quarterly*, September, 2001,

Porath, Yehoshua, The Palestinian Arab National Movement: From Riots to Rebellion, Vol. 2, 1929-1939 (London, 1977)

Reinhart, Tanya, *Yediot Aharonot*, March 9, 2003.

Reiter, Yitzchak, *The Temple Mount, Haram Al-Sharif: Points of Agreement and Disagreement*. Jerusalem, The Jerusalem Institute for the Study of Israel, 1997.

Rose, Jacqueline, Response to Edward Said, in Edward W. Said, Freud and the Non-European : The Letters of Martin Buber, New York, 1991.

Rose, Jacqueline, *States of Fantasy*, Oxford, Oxford University Press, 1996.

Rose, Jacqueline, *The Question of Zion*. Princeton, New Jersey, 2005.

Sachar, Howard, A History of Israel: From the Rise of Zionism to     Our Time. New York: Alfred Knopf, 1979.

Said, Edward, quoted in *Ha'aretz*, August 18, 2000.

Sand Shlomo, *Matai Ve'ech Humtza ha'Am haYehudi*? (When and How the Jewish People Was Invented? Tel-Aviv: Resling, 2008.

Sarason, Seymour, *School Change: The Personal Development of a Point of View*. New York: Teachers College Press, 1995.

Selektar, Ofira, "Tenured Radicals in Israel: From New Zionism to Political Activism." *Israel Affairs*, vol. 11, No. 4, 2006.

Schoenfeld, Gabriel, *The Return of Anti-Semitism*. Encounter Books: San Francisco, 2004.

Scholem, Gershom G, *Major Trends in Jewish Mysticism*. New York: Schocken Books, 1941.

Scholem, Gershom, *Sabbetai Zevi*. Tel-Aviv: Am Oved, 1957 (Hebrew).

Schweid, Eliezer, *Zionism after Zionism*. Jerusalem: The Zionist Library, 1996.

Schweid, Eliezer, "A Nation that Abandons its Social Memories Will Lose Its Physical Existence." *The Jerusalem Post International Edition*, April 15, 1995.

Schweid, Eliezer, *Toward a Modern Jewish Culture*. Tel-Aviv: Am Oved, 1995.

Segal, Hagai, *Ma'ariv*, December 19, 2008

Sharan, Shlomo, "Jewish anti-Semitism in Israel." *Nativ*, 46, 1995, pp. 43-49.

Sharan, Shlomo, "Israel and the Jews in the Schoolbooks of the Palestinian Authority." *Nativ*, 66, 1999, pp. 70-78. Also in A. Stav (Ed.), *Israel and a Palestinian State: Zero Sum Game?* Tel-Aviv: Zmora-Bitan, 2001, pp. 170-181.

Sharan, Shlomo, "Zionism, the Post-Zionists and Myth," in S. Sharan (Ed.), *Israel and the Post-Zionists*.

Sharan, Shlomo, and Bukay, David, "Israel and the Palestinians: What is the Refugee Problem?" *Nativ*, Internet, November 2008).

Sharansky, Natan, "Foreward" *Jewish Political Studies review*, 16, 2004, 34.

Sharansky, Natan *Defending Identity*. New York: Public Affairs, 2008.

Sharon, Moshe, *Problems in the History of the Land of Israel Under Muslim Rule*. Jerusalem: The Ben Zvi Memorial Foundation, 1976, pp. 62-64.

Shavit, Ari, "Why do they remain silent." *Ha'aretz*, June 26, 2001.

Shiloah, Zvi, *Leftism in Israel*. Beit-El: Yaron Golan, 1991 (Hebrew).

Shirer, William, *The Rise and Fall of the Third Reich*. New York: Simon and Schuster, 1960.

Sivan, Emmanuel, *Interpretations of Islam: Past and Present*. Princeton: The Darwin Press, 1985.

Shragai, Nadav, The Mountain of Conflict: The Struggle over the Temple Mount, Jerusalem: Keter Publishing Co., 1996.

Stav, Arieh, *Peace: The Arabian Caricature: A Study of Anti-Semitic Imagery*, Jerusalem-New York: Gefen Publishing House, 1995.

Stav, Arieh, *The Israeli Death Wish*. Tel-Aviv: Modan Publishers, 1998. (Hebrew).

Sternhell, Ze'ev, *The Founding Myths of Israel*. Princeton: Princeton University Press, 1998.

Sternhell, Ze'ev, *Davar*, April 15, 1988.

Sternhell, Ze'ev, *Ha'aretz*, May, 2001. See also Jerusalem Post, December 1, 1990.

Talmon, Jacob, *The Beginning of Democratic Totalitarianism*. Tel-Aviv: Dvir Publishing Co. 1956 (Hebrew).

Tamir, Yuli, *Ha'aretz*, August 13, 1999.

Vaihinger, Hans, Philosophy of "As If," translated into English (from German) by C.K. Ogden in 1924, published in 1911 (written in 1893, approximately).

Viereck, Paul, *Metapolitics: The Roots of the Nazi Mind*. New York: Capricorn, 1965.

Vital, David, A People Apart: A Political History of the Jews in Europe, 1789-1939. New York: Oxford University Press, 1999.

Vital, David, "On the Unspoken Principles of Herzlian Diplomacy." *Israel Affairs*, 2008, 14, 325-354.

Volkov, Shulamit, *The Magic Circle: Germans, Jews and Anti-Semites*. Tel-Aviv: Am Oved, 2002 (Hebrew).

Wheeler-Bennet, John and Nicholls, Anthony, The Semblance of Peace: The Political Settlement after the Second World War. New York: Norton, 1974.

Wilson, Scott, "A Shared History, a Different Conclusion." *Washington Post Foreign Service*, Sunday, March 11, 2007. (washingtonpost.com)

Windschuttle, Keith, "Edward Sa'id's Orientalism Revisited." *The New Criterion*, 16, No. 5, January, 1999.

Wistrich, Robert S. The Jews of Vienna in the Age of Franz Joseph. Oxford, 1990.

Wurmser, Meyrav, "Can Israel Survive Post-Zionism?" *Middle East Quarterly*, vol. 6, 1999.

Yakobi, Dani, *A World of Changes*, Jerusalem: The Ministry of Education, Culture and Sport. Ma'alot Publishing Co., 1999.

Yemini, Ben Dror, *Ma'ariv*, December 19, 2008.

Yemini, Ben Dror, *Ma'ariv*. December 26, 2008

Yariv, Saba shel (Pen name of David Ben-Gurion), *The Communism and Zionism of Hashomer Hartzair*. Tel-Aviv: Mapai Political Party, 1934.

Yevin, Shmuel, *The Bar-Kochba War*. Jerusalem: The Byalik Institute, 1952.

Zach, Natan, *Ha'aretz*, November 15, 1990.

Zachi, Abbas, NBN TV station in Lebanon, April 9, 2008.

Zertal, Idith and Eldar, Akiva, *Lords of the Land*. New York, 2007, pp. 74-75, 215-98.

Zimmerman, Moshe, "The Polemics of Historians: The German Experience and the Israeli Experience," *Theory and Criticism*, vol. 8, summer 1996, 91-92.

Zinger, Zvi, *Yediot Aharonot*, January 29, 2001.

# Index

www.ingramcontent.com/pod-product-compliance
Ingram Content Group UK Ltd.
Pitfield, Milton Keynes, MK11 3LW, UK
UKHW020431010325
455677UK00029B/1096

9 781138 508736